# BEFORE WRIGLEY BECAME
# WRIGLEY

## THE INSIDE STORY OF THE FIRST YEARS
## OF THE CUBS' HOME FIELD

### SEAN DEVENEY

Sports Publishing books may be purchased in bulk at special discounts for sales promotion, corporate gifts, fund-raising, or educational purposes. Special editions can also be created to specifications. For details, contact the Special Sales Department, Sports Publishing, 307 West 36th Street, 11th Floor, New York, NY 10018 or sportspubbooks@skyhorsepublishing.com.

Sports Publishing® is a registered trademark of Skyhorse Publishing, Inc.®, a Delaware corporation.

Visit our website at www.sportspubbooks.com.

10 9 8 7 6 5 4 3 2 1

Library of Congress Cataloging-in-Publication Data is available on file.

ISBN: 978-1-61321-648-4

Printed in the United States of America

# Contents

# CHAPTER ONE

# The Cubs and the
# North Side, Day One

For the Cubs and the team's sitting president, Charley Weeghman, it was the strangest of weeks. It was as though every actor in the drama that had unfolded over the previous two years made some sort of cameo appearance around the team—enemies, rivals, friends, well-wishers, and even peripheral players who had popped up only in tangential roles. The 1916 season was getting underway, but there was no avoiding his confrontations with the recent past. It could all be met with a smile and a wave, now that circumstances had shoved Weeghman into the spot he'd long coveted, the leading role as a baseball magnate with the Cubs. But that didn't change the bizarreness. The season opened on the road on April 12 in Cincinnati. It was there, just over sixteen months before, that Weeghman's first run at purchasing the Cubs, aided by Reds owner Garry Herrmann, had fallen apart, because of the obstinance of owner Charles Taft and the negative influence of former Cubs president Charles Murphy. And just four months before in that city, at a happier moment, a deal was hammered out with Taft which ultimately delivered the Cubs to Weeghman.

On the day before the opener, Weeghman and the Cubs arrived in Cincinnati with a group of fans, and were met at the train depot by a marching band. The team, the fans, and the band proceeded to romp around the streets of Cincinnati, celebrating and blocking city traffic in the process. As the *Chicago Daily News* described the surreal scene which would have been so difficult to imagine the previous year: "Traffic cops, street cars, autos and other vehicles were swallowed up in the mob, which first stormed Herrmann's headquarters in the Wiggins building. From there the fat, perspiring but noisy drum major led the cavalcade to the offices of Mr. Taft. The former owner of the Cubs passed the season's compliments to Mr. Weeghman, at the head of the procession, from a third-story window, while the musicians sputtered and blew down below. There was another face at the window which gave the scene a touch of the melodramatic. None other than C.W. Murphy popped out as Mr. Taft was making his third bow. . . . The Chicago mob recognized him and swung into the strain of, 'How Dry I am.'"[1]

The Cubs would win their Opening Day game, with George "Slats" McConnell—who had once been a source of tension between Weeghman and the very Cubs he now ran—on the pitcher's mound. They would, however, lose their next four and by the time they were ready to return to Chicago for their own home opener eight days after their first game against the Reds, they were just 2–4 and struggling. But their record didn't much matter, because for the Cubs, April 20, 1916, was destined to go down as a red-letter day in team history. It would be their first game at Weeghman's concrete-and-steel park at Addison and Sheffield on the North Side, the Cubs having deserted their longtime home on the West Side after Weeghman bought the team. Many in Chicago felt that the Cubs belonged to the West Side, that there was some sacrilege in the team playing anywhere but the section of town that had supported them through the wildly successful years just after the turn of the century when the team was the most dominant in all of baseball. But Weeghman aimed to silence doubters quickly. He knew how to hold a celebration, and he did not skimp on this one. Plans were laid for a motorcade to leave from Grant Park, through Chicago's busy downtown Loop district, back up Michigan

Avenue to Sheridan Road, and over to the park on Sheffield. Mayor William Hale Thompson and Governor Edward Fitzsimmons Dunne were slated for spots in the motorcade. Speeches, marching bands, the unfurling of the largest American flag in Chicago history—Weeghman had big plans. As the Chicago Tribune reported, "It looks as if Chicago's Cubs are to experience the greatest opening they ever had in Chicago."[2]

Meanwhile, Weeghman's manager, former Cubs great Joe Tinker, was more concerned about the club's poor start and the fact that many of his players had never performed for so much as an inning at the North Side park. On April 19, while Weeghman was prepping the park with a new section of seating that would fit 3,000 fans along the first- and third-base lines—more than 100 carpenters were hurriedly working to finish the job—Tinker called for his players to report for hitting practice at 10:30, allowing his men the afternoon off to find apartments in the city. When rain scotched those plans, Tinker held a strategy session in the team clubhouse until it was dry enough to take some swings, after noon. The fences down the left and right field lines in the park were notoriously short, and, when batting practice started, players "'sized up' the length of the fields. Immediately an effort was started to drive the ball over the barricades." The apartment-hunting, apparently, had to wait.[3]

By Opening Day, all was prepared. The park was sold out, the seats were finished, the Cubs players had at least gotten a look at their new home. The parade, which got underway at 1 PM, proved to be a bad idea—though it was unseasonably warm, even reaching the low seventies, it was rainy, and neither Mayor Thompson nor Governor Dunne showed up. Still, when the group reached the park, an array of fireworks went off, and the procession of players and dignitaries was greeted by thousands of waiting fans. "The rooters went wild with enthusiasm," the Daily News reported, "for it was the first appearance of Manager Tinker and the Cubs on the local grounds. . . . Cubs rooters with all sorts of noise making implements cheered and greeted the Cubs as if they were world champions."[4] As game time neared, the crowd filled in, with about 18,000–20,000 in attendance, many standing on the field itself. Among them was Weeghman's friend-turned-enemy, Charles Comiskey, owner of the South Side's White Sox and now back on friendlier terms. Garry Herrmann, too, was in attendance, as was another friend of Weeghman's, former baseball magnate James Gilmore. The arrival of the players was followed by a long list of ceremonies, including the somewhat strange tradition of local groups presenting flowers to the team's stars, who were obviously unaccustomed to floral gifts. As one writer noted, "The sight of a ball player standing awkwardly in full view of 18,000 people, with his arms full of American Beauty roses is a beautiful sight. . . . They always give him roses instead of chewing tobacco or something appropriate. No one would ever think of sending a soubrette a box of cigars. Then why give a ball player flowers?"[5]

Maybe a more apt gift was presented to Weeghman by the 25th Ward Democrats—a donkey. Weeghman, ever popular around the North Side, was once considered as a Democratic candidate for alderman of the ward. Another four-legged gift came courtesy of one of Weeghman's fellow Cubs investors, meatpacking millionaire J. Ogden Armour, who offered a live black bear cub. The bear would become the team's mascot and would be nicknamed JOA in Armour's honor. The donkey wisely "galloped under the friendly shelter of the stand on the appearance of the Armour bear."[6] By the time Judge Thomas Scully was ready to give the speech dedicating the Cubs' debut in the North Side park, the crowd was getting restless. Speeches at ballparks were difficult enough in those days—there were no microphones, and standing at home plate, only a few in surrounding seats could hear—but the boisterousness of the bands made things tougher for Scully. "Nobody paid any attention to him," one account noted. "Even the players, clustered around him, were looking at the crowd. A band struck up. He grew red in the face and evidently lifted his voice to compete. It couldn't be done." Eventually, other bands struck up, too, and the result was a miserable cacophony. "It reminded one of the time one had typhoid fever," the account said.[7]

Well after the appointed time of 3 PM, umpire Hank O'Day—who had been the Cubs' manager for a season in 1914—got the game started. It would be a long one. Cubs starter Claude Hendrix struggled with his control from the beginning, yielding two runs in the first, but the Cubs were able to tie the score in the bottom of the inning by plating two runs off of

Pete Schneider—who, two years earlier, had actually been signed by Tinker but was scooped up by the Reds before reaching Chicago. Schneider settled down and the Reds built a 6–3 lead going into the eighth. But the Cubs tied the game with two runs in the eighth inning and one in the ninth, and it wasn't until after 6 PM that the North Siders finally won in the eleventh inning when first baseman Vic Saier knocked in center fielder Cy Williams with a hard-hit ball over second base and into center field. It was a memorable victory, and Weeghman capped it off by heading a block north to the popular local tavern and music venue, the Bismarck Gardens, for dinner and a cabaret show with Garry Herrmann and the visiting Reds contingent. It was a fitting way to wind up "the biggest and noisiest Opening Day in Cub history."[8]

‡

For the West Side of Chicago, 1916 marked the first year without professional baseball since 1884. The Cubs were gone and, with them, the major leagues left that huge swath of the city forever. Now, the Cubs would belong to the North Side, which was simply unnatural to most Chicago sports fans. In the *Chicago Tribune*, just before Opening Day, humorist Ring Lardner offered "The North Side Standard Guide," a column he hoped would help introduce West Side fans to the Cubs' new home. Lardner poked fun at the array of upscale homes and hotels that had been built along the shore of Lake Michigan on the North Side, as well as the insularity of West Siders:

> The North Side is that part of Chicago situate north of the river, west of the lake, south of Evanston and east of Kedzie Avenue. Its accessibility, natural beauties, and mild climate are responsible for its popularity with people who previously have passed their summers in Europe. . . .
> The North Side is a well-equipped, modern city. It has asphalt and brick pavements, gas and electric lights, artesian water, fire department, well-stocked markets and stores, elegant churches and an increasing number of palatial apartment buildings. It is the fashionable summer resort of Chicago. Visitors find every convenience and luxury. The North Side is

renowned for its healthfulness: the climate is equable and has given new
lease of life to thousands who have come hither from the south and west.[9]

‡

Indeed, the area had developed considerably over the previous decade, but,
at the time, the move of the Cubs into what is now known as Wrigley Field
represented the most significant event in the history of the North Side, a
move that brought the neighborhood to full integration and significance
within the city. After 1916, the West Side would never quite be the same.
And neither would the North Side, with its shimmering ballpark just blocks
from Lake Michigan now occupied by a much-beloved team that was a
Chicago institution. Though it was bizarre for Chicagoans in 1916, it didn't
take long for the North Side to become synonymous with the Cubs, as has
been the case since.

But that wasn't the case when Weeghman first opened the park. No, the
first professional baseball team to occupy the North Side park actually was
Weeghman's club in the Federal League, a short-lived outlaw circuit that
boldly (and dubiously) claimed major-league status and, in doing so, chal-
lenged the dominance of the American and National leagues. They came
incredibly and frustratingly close to putting on a successful challenge too.
So, while April 20, 1916, was rightly celebrated as an epochal day for the
Cubs, the fact is, the first professional baseball game on the North Side took
place on April 23, 1914, just months after Weeghman bought the site of the
park and weeks after ground was broken.

There might not be a Wrigley Field had there not been a Federal League,
and though the Fed circuit stretched from Newark to Baltimore to Kansas
City, one of the most obvious features of the league was its utter Chicago-
ness. The league office was located in the city and its president, Jim Gilmore,
was a Chicagoan. Weeghman's franchise and ballpark were the two gems
that kept the Feds afloat, and the first two big-name players to sign up were
ex-Cubs Joe Tinker and Mordecai Brown. But the story of what happened
in the years leading up to the first Weeghman Park Opening Day in 1914
and into the first Cubs Opening Day on the North Side in 1916 remains

a crucial one for the city. It is fascinating, in retrospect, to trace the winding path that led the Cubs to that piece of land—previously the site of a Lutheran seminary—in that particular section of Chicago, because the whole thing was hardly a predetermined proposition. Modern Chicagoans couldn't imagine the North Side without a ballpark. But at so many turns, the story could have gone drastically different and there would be no big league baseball on the North Side. Weeghman could have bought a major league team in another city, the Cubs could have been owned or sold to someone who invested in a new park on the West Side, or the big leagues could have welcomed a minor league team to the North Side, keeping the Cubs from moving in.

In any of those instances, it is possible that the Cubs would still be on the West Side, or even that they'd have bolted to some Chicago suburb. So many things had to align in order for the Cubs to wind up anchoring the North Side the way they do. It is a worthy testament, then, to both the Federal League and to Weeghman that one of the only remaining landmarks of their tenure in the spotlight is the park now known as Wrigley Field, universally loved by local fans and visitors alike. As former Braves manager Bobby Cox once said, "It's always been my favorite place to go. Always. Forever. It's the head of the class for some reason. I can't put my finger on it. It just seems like it should never be touched. It's too much of a treasure."[10]

But before it was a treasure, before it was Wrigley Field, home of the lovable Cubs, it was Weeghman Park, home of Chicago's Federal League club. And the story of how that came to be has deep roots in the history of Chicago and baseball.

# CHAPTER TWO

# The Chicago Theological Lutheran Seminary Lot

The story of the early days of Wrigley Field doesn't begin with the Cubs or with Charley Weeghman or with big league baseball at all. It begins with a church and some minor league magnates with a big idea. Start with Charles Havenor, the owner of the Milwaukee Brewers of the eight-team American Association which, with the International League, was one of the top two minor leagues in baseball. Havenor was wealthy, one of Milwaukee's best-known citizens and was a powerful alderman in the city. That changed somewhat in 1905, when he was among the first to be caught up in a massive graft scandal that would topple much of the city's municipal government and would lead to more than fifty arrests of public figures. But his position as a minor league magnate remained unchanged.

In 1906, Mike Cantillon—along with his brother, Joe, who had been Havenor's manager with the Brewers before moving to the big leagues with Washington—also bought into the A.A., taking the Minneapolis Millers from short-term owner Gus Koch. Cantillon and Havenor were kindred spirits. They appreciated the benefits of owning a team, but they had bigger aspirations, too. They wanted to raise the level of the

American Association, and since the league was already as high as any
minor league circuit could get, that meant turning it into a third major
league alongside the American and National leagues. The key to making
that happen, they felt, was Chicago's North Side. The lure of Chicago
was strong and the financial benefit to American Association owners
was obvious. It was the U.S.'s second-biggest city, and the explosion of
industry there in the late 1800s ensured that a third team in the city
would draw plenty of financial backers. There would be no shortage of
fans on the North Side, either—that section of the city was smaller than
the South and West sides but still had a population of about 500,000
more people than the biggest city in the A.A.—Milwaukee.[1] As a bonus,
the team that would likely move to Chicago would be St. Paul, whose
proximity to the Cantillons' Minneapolis club put a dent in their profits.

By late 1907, rumors of the designs on Chicago had been circulating
"continuously for over a year, and spasmodically for a longer time than that."[2]
A story emerged that a faction of the A.A. had made an offer of a Chicago
franchise to former White Sox pitcher and outfielder Jimmy Callahan. This
was significant because Callahan was a baseball outcast, blacklisted in '06
for having started a semipro team on Chicago's North Side—in forming his
'Logan Squares,' as they were called, Callahan had signed players who were
technically under contract with other teams. That was a serious offense to the
rulers of the sport and earned Callahan the label "The Baseball Anarchist."
Though there was no question that Callahan was an excellent manager (his
Logan Squares beat both the 1906 Cubs and the White Sox, respective
pennant winners in their leagues), any effort to bring Callahan into the fold
would not only draw the ire of the powers that governed baseball, it could
be enough to strip the A.A. of its status as an official minor league altogether.
Because of the sensitivity of the issue, any discussions about moving into
the North Side were to be kept secret. Callahan, however, spilled the beans,
telling the press about the offer he had received after meeting with Havenor
in December of '07. Havenor quickly tried to squelch the story, denying
having spoken to Callahan and saying that the whole thing merely "was
a good advertisement for Callahan." Callahan, though, showed a signed
document saying he was to have an A.A. club in town.[3]

THE CHICAGO THEOLOGICAL LUTHERAN SEMINARY LOT

Callahan's involvement was not the only problem for the Chicago plan. Both the White Sox on the South Side and the Cubs on the West Side were vehemently opposed to a third team in the city, even if it was a minor league team. The move would not be sanctioned by the major leagues and, in fact, the American League, anticipating the A.A.'s Chicago request, had a preemptive vote on the issue of an American Association team in Chicago, and shot it down.[4] If the A.A. were to move into Chicago anyway, it would become an outlaw organization, losing its support from the rest of baseball. The Cantillons were willing to take that chance, and they thought they had the support of another owner, Kansas City's George Tebeau, who also had an interest in the Louisville club. Havenor and George Lennon of the St. Paul Saints were said to be willing to go along with the plan too—Lennon wanted to sell his team, and if it was moving to Chicago, he would get a hefty price.[5] There was the potential, then, that five of the eight clubs in the A.A. would support the Chicago invasion, and in doing so, would declare open war on baseball's structure. The rebellious owners thought that if they carried out the plan, the eventual settlement would leave the league in a stronger position. But the other members of the league—Indianapolis, Toledo, and Columbus—opposed the risk. "Never have heard a thing about such a plan," Toledo president Bill Armour said. "The American Association doesn't want any war, and that is what an invasion of Chicago would mean."[6]

The pacifists won out in '07. The possibility of a war led by the minor leagues resurfaced the next year, and again, the American Association was assuaged and peace reigned. But Havenor and the Cantillons were not giving up, so they sought to find a solution to the other lingering problem of a North Side invasion—location of a park. There were some promising semipro grounds available in Chicago, but for the most part, the North Side was cluttered with residential neighborhoods that couldn't accommodate a major-league-sized stadium. Those areas with enough space for a park were not easily accessible by streetcar or the elevated train. But in 1909, finally, the would-be invaders had a stroke of good fortune.

‡

Since 1891, the city block bounded by Waveland Avenue on the north, Evanston (later Seminary) on the west, Addison on the south, and Sheffield on the east, with Clark Street cutting diagonally through the southwest section, was the home to the Chicago Theological Lutheran Seminary. It was a quaint and quiet part of town, with green lawns and tree-lined paths connecting a handful of buildings, including the president's house on the corner of Sheffield and Waveland, and the spiritual center of the seminary, St. Mark's Church. It was also more than four miles north of the downtown Loop district, which, in 1891, put it in a fairly sparse part of the city. But transportation advances changed the neighborhood over the course of two decades. The expensive row of houses along North Sheridan Road, fronting Lake Michigan, was still there, but the North Side was becoming more populous—the South Side, with the stockyards and vice houses, had become dirty, unpleasant, and dangerous, and the West Side was overcrowded. Increasingly, the North Side, which had been mostly home to small industry and rows of warehouses, was becoming residential.

Now, the Lutherans wanted out. They were sitting on a very valuable plot of land, more than 330,000 square feet, and would be better served with their seminary in a quieter spot. When Havenor and the Cantillons found out, they acted quickly. By June of '09, the Rev. Frank Jensen, representing the Board of Trustees of the seminary, met with Havenor's lawyer, with both sides eager to complete a deal. Havenor was able to negotiate a price of $175,000 for the land, and he did so very quietly—if word had gotten out that he was buying a large swath of mostly open land on the North Side, suspicions about his intentions would be raised all over baseball. Havenor had hoped to slip the transaction past the press altogether, and might have been successful, except that when some members of the seminary board got word of the selling price, they complained that Reverend Jensen should have gotten $200,000.[7]

Havenor, predictably, was indignant when confronted with the suggestion that the purchase of the seminary land had anything to do with the American Association's designs on placing a team in Chicago. "The purchase by me of property in Chicago is a private investment, and I fail to see what the American baseball association has to do with it," he said.

"Have I considered what I shall do with it? Well, there might be dozens of uses I could put it to. There is this that I can say: Everything that has been printed about the placing of a new baseball organization in the field is just dope. That's all just dope. There are some people who want to know what is going to be done, and that is why they are trying to find out from me what I am to do with my property."[8]

Havenor's denials rang hollow. Immediately, a rumor made the rounds that the Cantillons' team would be moved from Minneapolis to Chicago and that the American Association would also move franchises to Cincinnati and Pittsburgh. This wasn't a scheme to merely make more money by tapping the Chicago market, this was a full-scale onslaught. "The property is considered the best vacant location in Chicago for a baseball park, and the purchase on its face appears to portend the entrance of an American Association club into this city, with a big baseball war as a result," the *Tribune* reported. "Those close to the American Association leaders think the accession of the local tract of ground is the entering wedge and that before long announcement will be made of locations secured in Cincinnati and Pittsburgh, the only two large major cities now without a second club. With this nucleus the association magnates think they would be fitted with territory to form another major league circuit."[9]

Of course, in the landscape of modern baseball, the ascension of a minor league to major league status is ludicrous. But at the time Havenor was buying the seminary lot, baseball as we know it was in its infancy and the notion of a third league declaring war was almost common. It might not have been a fruitless venture, either. Just eight years earlier, the Western League, under the guidance of Ban Johnson and with the financial backing of Cleveland coal baron Charles Somers, put forth an assault on the only established major league at the time, the National League. The N. L. was an easy target—its owners were a fractured and dysfunctional lot; they underpaid players (sticking to an individual salary cap of $2,400), and they had decided to contract their league from twelve teams to just eight after the 1899 season, leaving plenty of available territory and players. Changing the name to the American League, Johnson declared his circuit a major league, and had a strong group of managers who were able to lure players away from the Nationals, giving the league credibility quickly. Of course, to accomplish that, the Americans had to offer players generous salaries and utterly ignore the contract rules that were in place under the National League. The A. L. had teams in three cities—Chicago, Boston, and Philadelphia—that were in direct competition with N. L. teams. After 1901, the Milwaukee team was transferred to compete with the Cardinals in St. Louis and, after 1902, the Baltimore team was moved to New York, eventually becoming the Yankees.

After that war was settled in 1903, the American League was on equal footing with the National League. To govern and coordinate the two leagues, a National Commission was formed, which would consist of an elected head of each league and a chairman of the commission, to be chosen among league owners. The rest of baseball was made up of a group of about 300 minor leagues divided into classes (A through D) and subject to the contract and drafting rules of what was called Organized Baseball. Only by signing the National Agreement and following its rules could a league be part of Organized Baseball and the Commission made the ultimate decisions. Johnson was the unquestioned head of the A. L. and thus a fixture on the commission. Reds owner Garry Herrmann served as the commission chairman, because he was acceptable both to his personal friend Johnson and to the National League because he was one of their own. The president of the N. L., however, was a post that frequently changed hands.

With a recent history showing that a baseball war could, indeed, be won by a minor league seeking major status, Havenor and the Cantillons' plan wasn't so outlandish. By the summer of '09, they had a well-suited piece of land on the North Side of Chicago to bolster their ambitions.

‡

Surely, for Joe Cantillon, the possibility of participating in a war against Organized Baseball was conflicting. He was, after all, the manager of the Senators and a baseball lifer with a wealth of friends in the game. He had made the leap to the American League with Ban Johnson as an umpire, and Cantillon was one of the best arbiters in the game—in fact, when

Johnson sought ways to speed up A. L. games to give them an advantage over N. L. games, it was Cantillon who came up with the idea of counting fouled-off pitches as strikes. In his managerial career, Cantillon was known as a great judge and developer of talent, credited for starting Walter Johnson and Gavvy Cravath on their careers.

He was also one of the most personable and well-liked men in the game, an unlikely crusader against the structure of baseball. As a player, when he was a new arrival with San Francisco back in 1892, the writer and humorist Charles Dryden was asked by fans about Cantillon's background. Dryden wrote a mock column for his paper claiming that Cantillon's actual name was Pongo Pelipe Cantillono, the son of an Italian nobleman who left his life of luxury behind to find his fortune in America. The next day, the park was packed with fans who were eager to see the Italian expatriate, and they shouted phrases in Italian to him. Cantillon, playing along despite knowing not a word of Italian, "answered them back in guttural phrases which were so natural that he had even his fellow players guessing as to whether Dryden's story was on the level or just a pipe." From that point, his nickname was Pongo Joe.[10]

One of Cantillon's best friends in the game was White Sox owner Charles Comiskey, his frequent hunting partner—sometimes they would hunt in the woods near Cantillon's property in Hickman, Kentucky or Comiskey's famed hunting grounds in Wisconsin, but they were also known to travel together to places as diverse as the Dakotas and Arkansas. That made Cantillon's involvement in the Chicago plan all the more remarkable. If Cantillon moved his team or helped any other team of the A.A. move into Chicago, he would be taking a direct shot at Comiskey's territory. More than that, he would be setting up a war of the A. L. and the N. L. against the A.A. "This tangle would be no more complex than that presented by the two Cantillons," the *Tribune* noted. "Joe, as manager of the Washington club, would be connected with a league which was fighting the organization in which he is directly connected as half owner of the Minneapolis club."[11]

By the time Havenor bought the North Side property in 1909, it was obvious Cantillon might not be long for the American League, anyway. Washington started the year 9–24, on their way to a horrible 42–110 finish and there were rumors throughout the season that Cantillon would be replaced. After Cantillon accused New York manager George Stallings of setting up a system of sign-stealing, Stallings turned around and accused Cantillon of disloyalty to the A. L. That wasn't a new accusation and it stemmed from Cantillon's involvement with his brother and Havenor in the American Association. The Senators, surprisingly, decided to bring Cantillon back to manage in 1910, but three teams (New York, Philadelphia, and Cleveland) protested and Washington finally acquiesced, letting Cantillon go.

Cantillon, naturally, landed on his feet—he became manager of Minneapolis, and in doing so, the potential conflict that would arise were he to be part of an A.A. insurrection disappeared. In the winter of '10, the possibility of an A.A. invasion into the Addison and Sheffield site cropped up again after Havenor brought on two partners in the property. One, E.T. Harmon, was a very wealthy retired Milwaukee businessman who was a neighbor of Havenor's, and the other was Edward Archambault, a wealthy Milwaukee investor, brother-in-law of the Cantillons and part owner of the Minneapolis club too. Again, the question of why these minor league magnates were holding this piece of property kept leading to the expectation of a baseball war. Havenor suggested the spot could become a railroad depot because the Cantillons had a brother who was an executive with the North Western Railroad company. When the railway denied that it had any intent to use the land, the *Tribune* reported, "On the face of the proposition as it now stands, in the opinion of local baseball men, the purchase of the property was not for investment but as a holding to insure a home for a third league whether it comes into Chicago via the peace or war route."[12]

But, despite five years of rumors, there would be no American Association war. Havenor and the Cantillons just could not get their fellow A.A. owners to stomach a shot at becoming a big league. In late 1909, the league elected a new president, Louisville's Thomas Chivington, to replace Joe O'Brien. The vote probably could have been read as a referendum on the Chicago move, which O'Brien was willing to consider and Chivington was not—only Milwaukee, St. Paul, and Minneapolis voted for O'Brien. A move to Chicago's North Side wasn't coming peacefully, either, as the White Sox and Cubs remained in opposition. Havenor and the Cantillons might have held out hope for the seminary lot, might have been able to look at it and easily picture a bustling ballpark anchoring the North Side neighborhood. But Havenor gradually gave up on the idea and sold out on the property to the Cantillons and Archambault before he died unexpectedly in April 1912, at age forty-seven. For nearly two years after that, what was once his North Side property continued to sit idle, the site of an abandoned Lutheran seminary.

# CHAPTER THREE

# Lucky Charley Weeghman

For all the accomplishments in his relatively young life, what Charley Weeghman wanted most of all was to be a baseball magnate. But, sitting on a train from St. Louis to Chicago on April 7, 1911, it seemed he had missed his chance. It had been fourteen days since the sudden death of Stanley Robison, felled by heart failure at the age of fifty-six at the home of his late brother in Cleveland, and in the immediate aftermath, word spread that Robison's best-known remaining enterprise—the St. Louis Cardinals—was to be sold. That was only logical, after all. In his will, Robison left a three-quarters stake in the Cardinals to his niece, Helene Britton, and another quarter interest to his sister-in-law, Sarah Hathaway Robison, Helene's mother. It was an odd act by Stanley Robison who was, fittingly, somewhat odd for a baseball magnate. He was a bachelor, shy and reserved, not one of the bombastic chatterers who commonly populated the ranks of baseball's power brokers. That role had been played by Stanley's brother, Frank, with whom he owned the Cardinals until his death in 1908. Frank enjoyed the limelight. Stanley didn't.

Of all Stanley's friends and family, Helene knew her uncle best, referred to him as more of a brother than an uncle, and upon his death, she may have been the only baseball fan in Missouri who was not surprised that

Stanley Robison left her in charge of the Cardinals. Though it was 1911 and progressives were having success pushing women's suffrage in the U.S., Helene Britton was only thirty-two and the mother of two children. Society had a place for her and it was not in the cut-throat, foul-mouthed, cigar-and-whiskey world of the men who ran baseball teams. Still, the will left by her uncle was clear: He wanted Helene Britton to become the first female owner of a professional baseball team. Other National League powers, underestimating the bond between Helene Britton and her uncle, assumed a sale of the team was coming. Word got out that the Cardinals could be had, at a cost of $350,000, including the stadium and grounds. Weeghman sprang into action, arranging a meeting with representatives of Britton that was to take place in Cleveland, just six days after the death of Uncle Stanley. Weeghman had worked out a plan by which he and some fellow investors would purchase the franchise and lease the Cardinals' home at Robison Field at a price below $350,000, but if he had to come up with enough money for the entire works, he had the backers to make it happen and felt confident that he would wind up with his team.[1]

Charley was only thirty-seven himself, but already he was established as a businessman in Chicago, operating a string of successful lunchrooms in downtown Chicago's Loop (that was the city's business capital, so named for the pattern formed by the elevated train whose tracks still bound the area) as well interests in movie theaters and a pool hall. He wanted a baseball team, though, and the chances of such an opportunity opening in Chicago were slim, with Charles Comiskey firmly in control of the American League's White Sox, and with the National League's Cubs in the clutch of president Charles Murphy, who had overseen a remarkable stretch of success for the West Side team. In fact, Murphy and Cubs backer Charles Taft, who also owned an interest in the Philadelphia Phillies, were rumored to have made an offer for the Cardinals, too.[2] St. Louis, just a short train ride from Chicago, was a worthwhile situation for Weeghman. After arranging for a meeting in Cleveland on March 30, he received word from Ohio telling him that Mrs. Britton would not be able to receive him and that he should plan to meet in St. Louis instead. On Friday the thirty-first, the meeting was delayed again, but Weeghman was undeterred and was already doing a victory lap. The *Tribune* reported, "Alive to the possibilities of being a baseball magnate, Mr. Weeghman [on Friday] was the busiest man in town. He continued his conferences with other magnates on the circuit by telephone and telegraph and has found that he will be welcome in the National League if he can make the deal."[3]

Still, as the weekend passed, there were more indications that Britton might not sell her team after all. Weeghman finally went to St. Louis on Monday and met with different representatives of the team over two days, but never with Mrs. Britton, who was still grieving the loss of her uncle. Finally, on April 5, Helene Britton's husband, Schuyler, appeared at the Hotel Jefferson in St. Louis and announced, with his wife nodding approvingly behind him, "The Cardinal ball club is not for sale. Mrs. Britton has decided to retain the ball club. She has received numerous offers for the property from Cleveland parties and other people in various parts of the country, but all offers were turned down. The baseball property is not for sale, at least for the time being."[4]

Weeghman was discouraged. That Friday, he boarded a train at Union Station in St. Louis, accompanied by Charlie Morin, a pool player he was backing in a $2,000 three-cushion tournament. He hoped that, in time, the Brittons would reconsider and that he'd have another chance to become a baseball boss. But that opportunity would have to wait. "I had two or three talks with representatives of Mrs. Britton, but there appeared to be no disposition on their part to come to terms for the sale of the club," Weeghman said. "I was told that Mrs. Britton would retain her interest in the team and that she would not at this time entertain any offers. It is a disappointment to me as I am anxious to get into the national game as a magnate, sincerely believing I could, 'make good.' I will bide my time and perhaps in the near future, there will be a change of heart on the part of Mrs. Britton in regard to the disposal of the club."[5]

Weeghman could take heart, though—the trip wasn't a total waste. On April 13, Morin did beat Pierre Maupome, winning the thrilling seven-game series in the finale at Weeghman's Madison Street pool room.

‡

If every story needs a hero, then when it comes to the story of the early days of Wrigley Field our hero is, no question, Lucky Charley Weeghman.

Despite the setback when it came to the Cardinals, for Weeghman, 1911 was a particularly good year in what had been a string of good years. Weeghman started by making a major investment, just before Christmas, 1910, in a double-store at 145 and 147 Randolph in the Loop. The property was located in the soon-to-be-opened Hotel Sherman, which would replace the recently demolished version of the hotel a few blocks away. Weeghman signed a ten-year lease at $80,000 total, and, as the *Tribune* reported, "Mr. Weeghman will expend considerable for remodeling and for fixtures." In September, he bought another piece of prime downtown realty, at Wabash and Van Buren, at a much steeper price—a ten-year lease at an estimated $250,000, including $40,000 for remodeling. On November 1, he bought a spot in a new building going up at Adams and Fifth (now Wells), with a $108,000, ten-year lease. A month later, he bought into the Grace Hotel building on West Jackson at $145,000 total over ten years. Weeghman was spending big. In the space of one year, he committed himself to more than a half-million dollars' worth of leases over the coming decade, covering four properties all within a six-block radius of each other.[6] And though Weeghman owned a pool hall on Madison Street and would open another (he also had interest in multiple Chicago movie theaters) there was no question what would be going into these new purchases: lunchrooms.

Weeghman's business would grow, but even then, he was known in Chicago as "the lunchroom king." That was a bit of an overstatement. He was certainly successful with his restaurant business, and at his peak, was running fifteen different lunchrooms in the Loop. That was no match for the city's real king of the lunchroom, though, John R. Thompson, Weeghman's rival. Thompson's empire numbered sixty-eight restaurants by 1912, many of which were in the Loop, and by 1914, he struck it rich by incorporating his chain.[7] Though commonly referred to as lunchrooms, the name is not entirely accurate—they were typically open twenty-four hours and did a healthy business among late-shift workers. But the bulk of the success of lunchrooms in Chicago did, in fact, come from the lunch crowd, who wanted predictable meals of standard quality churned out cheaply and quickly so that workers could return to the downtown offices. Customers in these establishments, who would pay about fifteen to twenty-five cents for a meal, were encouraged to get in and out without lingering because profits depended on volume. That meant tight quarters, no dallying over newspapers, and, in many cases, no coat racks. Diners would simply eat with their coats on.

These forerunners of fast food joints were an important development when it came to handling the concentration of businesses that were cropping up in Chicago's Loop. Weeghman estimated that, on average, his flagship lunchroom at 105 Madison (Thompson operated one next door at 107 Madison) fed 5,000 people per day, in 108 chairs, and never generated an annual profit less than $50,000.[8] Weeghman was fastidious when it came to cleanliness and convenience. As the historian Perry R. Duis wrote, "The Weeghman chain featured a white tile décor to emphasize cleanliness, a punched-check bill to minimize confusion and coffee served in special mugs to reduce both spilling and the number of dishes to wash."[9]

By his own account, Weeghman was a big success in business and was always expanding his interests. He would later estimate his peak worth at between $8 and $10 million, and if he was spending big on new places throughout 1911, it was part of his wider philosophy. Weeghman told an interviewer that when it came to locating a lunchroom, he had an "unfailing custom never to let the question of rent interfere with the location of a new place. Other restaurant men as experienced as I have made the mistake of establishing a restaurant a block or so away from the place where they would like to establish it solely because the rent was so much cheaper. My experience has been that the higher the rent I pay the better the location and the greater the volume of business, with its corresponding profits."[10]

Weeghman partook of the trappings of his success and carried himself very much like a man of means. He was an avid golfer and a member of the exclusive Exmoor Country Club and South Shore Country Club. He was tall and trim, with deep-set dark eyes and looked as carefully over his own appearance as he did the appearance of his restaurants. He was rarely seen outside without a good shave on his face and a bowler hat on his head. He wore three-piece suits accessorized with personalized cuff links and pocket watches with fobs—even when he was young, before he made it big, he took great care about his appearance. "Those of us who knew him back in the old days … when he was a good-looking young fellow with a penchant for natty clothes, do not find he has changed much with prosperity," wrote the *Tribune's* Harvey T. Woodruff in 1914. "He wears only slightly better clothes and the same size hat."[11]

The thumbnail sketch of Weeghman's life was oft-repeated over the course of his rise to business prominence, and given his predilection for good publicity, he surely bent the story in his favor when convenient. But his was the kind of rags-to-riches tale that Chicago seemed to be churning out in that era. Weeghman originally hailed from Richmond, Indiana, the son of Albert Weeghman, a German blacksmith born in Berlin with the name Veichman, which was Americanized when he arrived in this country.[12] When Charley Weeghman was eighteen and working in a jewelry shop, he—like so many young men and women in the Midwest and elsewhere—made the 250-mile journey from his small hometown to Chicago for the 1893 World's Fair. And, like so many young people of the day, he was impressed, allowing himself to get caught up in Chicago's big-city atmosphere. It was during the fair that Weeghman decided he wanted to build his future in the city. Upon coming to Chicago, Weeghman took a job as the night manager at Charley King's popular downtown diner. He started off making just $8 per week, and it was based in that humble background that Weeghman was given the nickname, "Lucky Charley." Not long after his initiation at King's, his boss promoted him, with a pay raise to $40 per week. It was at King's that Weeghman was able to ingratiate himself to Chicago's journalists, and to learn the complex ins and outs of the city and its politics, because the restaurant was located on the city's so-called Newspaper Row. Woodruff wrote, "While never a waiter in the sense of manning the coffee urn, he frequently donned the white jacket and apron during the 'midnight rush' hour, for King's catered to a newspaper and night-worker trade."[13]

In 1901, with King's blessing, Weeghman and two friends (Aaron Friend and Frank Conway, son of the city's fire marshal) pooled together some money and put up $2,800 for their own restaurant. It was, according to

Weeghman, an immediate success. At the time, Charley was just twenty-seven years old and as well-liked as he might have been in some circles, he did have a short fuse. In January 1903, ten of his waitresses went on strike because of Weeghman's controlling ways. "When I was eating my own lunch, he would 'rubber' to see what I had on my plate," one waitress complained. "I couldn't stand such treatment." The striking waitresses caused excessive noise outside the restaurant and Weeghman lost his temper, calling them "harsh names." The police came and Weeghman was arrested, charged with ten counts of disorderly conduct. After a teary session on the stand in court, Weeghman was ordered to apologize. He did.[14] This part of the tale never was mentioned in the retelling of the Lucky Charley legend.

Perhaps because of that incident with the waitresses, or perhaps because Weeghman simply preferred to work without partners (as he later put it), he was bought out by Friend and Conway later in 1903 and, as Weeghman said, "I was now free to launch out for myself, and with mature deliberation I decided to cast in my limited fortune with what was then a brand new idea. Arm chaired lunch counters, where waiters are eliminated and every patron shifts for himself, were just coming into existence. I thought the idea had a future and decided to launch on the tide while it was a flood."[15] For Weeghman, the foray into lunch counters most definitely proved to be a flood. After establishing his flagship at 105 Madison Street, he slowly bought up other Loop addresses. He got a place at 176 Adams in 1903. In 1906, he was given a lease for a double-store at 81-83 Clark. He leased 218 Wabash in 1909 and added another lunchroom at 90 Madison St. He brought on his younger brothers, Herbert and Albert, to help him as managers. Then, starting late in 1910 and through 1911, he went on the buying spree that greatly increased his lunchroom empire. In 1912, his wife, Bessie, had a daughter, named Dorothy. The following year, Weeghman moved his parents from Richmond into his place on the far North Side near Lake Michigan, at 5267 Sheridan Road.

As Weeghman established himself, he became a recognizable man about Chicago—in a bustling and growing city, a guy like Charley Weeghman would boast a wide cast of characters among his friends, including the famous, the powerful, and the utterly crooked alike. Weeghman was not, of course, at the level of Chicago families like the Palmers, Wards, Armours, and Pullmans, families that had built the city and were famous across the country, but he was firmly among Chicago's rising upper class and, it seemed, he knew everyone. When he was young, he would watch legendary ballplayer Cap Anson take the field for the Chicago Colts (who would later become the Cubs) at the West Side Grounds. After his baseball career, Anson was a champion pool player and made frequent appearances at Weeghman's for tournaments. Weeghman was also a friend of Cubs manager Frank Chance and was known to be a friend of one of Chicago's most notorious and violent gambling chieftains, Mont Tennes. One of Tennes's gambling outposts was located in the Loop near Weeghman's main restaurant, in fact, and at the tail end of a bombing war between gambling factions in Chicago, in 1909, an explosive device that was believed to have been meant for Tennes exploded in the Loop and blew out the back of Weeghman's restaurant.

And Weeghman counted among his associates the two men who ran the Cubs—Taft—the Cincinnati-based financial backer and brother of President William Howard Taft, and Taft's baseball viceroy, Charles Murphy. Weeghman and Murphy, at one point, even conspired against Thompson. In April 1909, the *Tribune* reported that "Charles W. Murphy, president of the Chicago National league baseball club, and John R. Thompson, county treasurer and owner of restaurants, have crossed bats with disastrous results." Murphy, it seems, was attempting to jack up Thompson's rent in a property at 130 Madison from $5,400 per year to $10,000 per year, after Thompson had been assured a raise in the rent of just $800 per year. Thompson had a hunch he knew what was behind the sudden spike. "[Murphy] attributed the raise in rent to the rivalry of Charles Weeghman and Mr. Thompson. Mr. Weeghman, besides owning several restaurants, has a billiard parlor in the Taft building immediately above Thompson's restaurant. Mr. Thompson insists there is an attempt to force him out by asking an absurd rental in order to let Mr. Weeghman in." Thompson knew how to hit back at Murphy and Taft. As a big baseball fan himself, Thompson knew that the West Side Grounds, also owned by Taft and Murphy, was not in good shape. He called on the city's building commissioner and told him of the numerous code violations at the ballpark. Inspectors responded, found violations, and though Murphy stated that there were no ordinances on the books govern-ing baseball grandstands, he would make the requested changes "in order that the park be as safe as money can make it."[16]

But there would not be all that many changes to the Cubs' park. Murphy much preferred money to safety. And if Weeghman seemingly knew every-one of importance in Chicago, he would soon put many of those relation-ships at risk, and the congeniality between the Taft-Murphy business pairing and Weeghman, their favored tenant, would not last much longer.

# CHAPTER FOUR

# Charles Webb Murphy

For Cubs pitcher Mordecai Brown, 1912 proved to be a disastrous year. Before the season, he had toyed with the idea of leaving baseball altogether and going into a café business with Al Tearney, president of the Three-I minor league.[1] He eventually dropped the plan, but he had kept the Cubs waiting before he signed a contract and was late getting to spring training because of it. When the year started, Brown wasn't in top form, and he had been working for Charles Murphy long enough to know that he would not be forgiven for that transgression. Still, arriving at his home on S. Ashland Avenue, just four blocks from the Cubs' field at the West Side Grounds, on October 12, Brown was met with a shock. He had received a notice on Cubs stationery. He had been released, and would be sent to the minor league American Association—or, in the words of the *Tribune*, "sentenced to the Cubs farm in Louisville." There, he was slated to be paid just $300 per month, and worse, he would continue to make money for Murphy, who owned a stake in the Louisville club.[2]

The timing was the worst part, just as the Chicago City Series was getting underway. The Cubs, after two rainouts and two ties, had just won the first game of their annual fall series with the White Sox, a hotly contested event that took place in Chicago each year that neither the Sox nor Cubs were in the World Series. These games roused extraordinary interest and talk in the city. In 1912, despite poor weather, the games would draw 160,000 fans[3], about one third of a good season's attendance. With so much attention focused on the teams, to let Brown go during the series was about as heartless as Murphy could get. Brown had not played since July 15, having wrenched his knee while sliding into second as a pinch runner on what was a decidedly rare stolen-base attempt—Brown played fourteen seasons, and had just eight stolen bases in his career. On one level, it was a worthwhile play because it propelled the Cubs to a thrilling win that helped keep them in the '12 pennant race. As I.E. Sanborn commented in *The Sporting News*, "His last act as a Cub, therefore, was to take a chance for the sake of winning, and it put him out of it."[4] As bold as the play was, on another level, it was not very smart. Brown was thirty-five and had torn ligaments in his knee while pitching an exhibition game in Cuba two years earlier, which had threatened to end his career. He had worn a brace to cope with the injury.[5]

With his conditioning off, Brown had started slow in 1912 but was just coming around at the midpoint of the season. He was 5–6 on the year, but before hurting his knee, he had won four of five starts and was looking like the Brown whom Cubs fans were accustomed to seeing. That Brown was special. He had been discovered playing for a semipro team in his hometown of Nyesville, Indiana, where he had been working in a mine since he was fifteen. That was the genesis of one of his nicknames—Miner—but Brown was also by his other nickname, Three-Finger. When he was a child and living on a farm, Brown stuck his index finger in a thresher and was left with a stump. The next year, he broke two fingers in a fall and the bones never really set correctly.[6] His middle finger was especially bent out of shape, so that to an observer looking at his pitching hand, Brown had just three healthy fingers. For Brown, this didn't turn out to be a handicap. His deformed right hand caused him considerable pain while pitching, but it also allowed him to make his pitches move in ways that traditional pitchers could not match, especially his famed, "down-curve." His breakthrough came in 1906, when he anchored a pitching staff that won the National League pennant. Brown was 26–6 that season, with a league-leading 1.06 earned-run average. He was 20–6 the following year, but it was in '08 that Brown truly established his legend as a "war-horse" appearing in forty-four games, going 29–9, and leading the Cubs to a World Series win. Brown and the Giants' Christy Mathewson were far and away the best pitchers of their time, and, as Frank Chance liked to point out, in head-to-head matchups in three of the seasons the Cubs bested the Giants for the pennant, Brown owned Mathewson—10 of Matty's 11 losses in those three years came against Brown, including a stretch of nine in a row. In all, by the end of the 1912 season, Brown had a record of 186–83 in nine years with the Cubs.

"Gentle, amiable, 'Brownie,' the greatest asset a baseball manager ever had and the greatest single aid in winning pennants and world championships the diamond ever saw or probably ever will see," his manager Frank Chance would later write. "Mordecai Brown, gentleman, kindly soul, born with a stout heart and a disposition possessed by few men, won pennants—and I speak literally of his winning pennants—because of these sterling qualities. 'Brownie' was a jewel of the first water among a galaxy of stars who formed the old Cub machine. … When I was short of pitchers, not knowing which way to turn and having no good, dependable pitcher to send into the box, Brownie was my life-saver. He was always willing to work."[7]

But now here was Brown, the most likable and hard-working of the Cubs, being dropped to the minors like a rookie. *The Sporting News* called it, "Another case of Murphy tact."[8] The *Chicago Daily News* reported that, at first, Cubs fans did not believe the report, but, "When they were assured it was true, they had many unkind things to say about President Murphy of the Cub team. They did not think the owner would send Brown to a minor league team after the wonderful work he had done for the club."[9]

‡

If every story needs a villain, then when it comes to the story of the early days of Wrigley Field our villain is, no question, Charles Webb Murphy.

Well before 1912, there were plenty of reasons for the Cub faithful to develop a deep disdain for Murphy and his handling of the team, even as the West Siders established themselves as baseball's most imposing dynasty between the years of 1906–10. In those days, the team was anchored by its legendary infield, with Joe Tinker at shortstop, John Evers at second base, and Frank Chance at first base, with Chance also serving as manager—he was highly respected in that role, most often referred to as, "Peerless Leader." The Cubs won the N. L. pennant four times in those five years, beating Ty Cobb and the Tigers in the World Series in '07 and '08, while falling to the White Sox in '06 and the Athletics in '10. They were a cantankerous, hard-driven group, and it was said that the double-play combo of Tinker and Evers so despised each other, they refused to exchange so much as a greeting. But they were also really good, all three earning spots in the Hall of Fame. They were immortalized in the 1910 poem, "Baseball's Sad Lexicon," by New York sportswriter Franklin Pierce Adams, which went:

These are the saddest of possible words:
Tinker to Evers to Chance.
Trio of bear cubs, and fleeter than birds,
Tinker and Evers and Chance.
Ruthlessly pricking our gonfalon bubble,
Making a Giant hit into a double–
Words that are heavy with nothing but trouble:
Tinker to Evers to Chance.

Whatever personal rivalries existed on the team, all Cubs players could agree on their hatred of Murphy, a fact that Chance used to his advantage, rallying his players around a common enemy. Murphy was notoriously cheap—he started out as a newspaper reporter in Cincinnati, became the press agent for the New York Giants, then borrowed money from Charles Taft (who was wealthy to begin with and would turn his editorship of the *Cincinnati Times-Star* into a media empire) in order to make his initial investment in the Cubs in 1905. Baseball was Murphy's only source of wealth, and it had paid handsomely, as the success of the Cubs drove up the value of the team while also bringing tidy annual profits. In his first full year of ownership, Murphy reportedly made $165,000. According to an estimate from Chance, who held 10 percent of the stock of the team, the other 90 percent of the stock made $198,000 in 1908 alone.

Taft wasn't much interested in running a baseball team, and no matter how personally objectionable Murphy might be, Taft didn't seem to care. Murphy made a lot of money for Taft in baseball, so Taft didn't see fit to question his methods. But those methods did not win him friends. Murphy took the running of the Cubs very personally, and, indeed, every dollar of profit helped cushion his bank account while every dollar spent came, in a way, out of his pocket. He acted accordingly. Wrangling contracts out of the Cubs boss, even when the team was winning pennants, became a sport in itself. As Chance said, "It's a dog's life to manage the team under Murphy. Why, I'd come in the spring to lead the players South (to spring training) and they'd all come to me showing letters from Murphy in which he had insulted them for asking for an increase in salary. Then I'd have to pacify them. ... He wouldn't loosen up any coin, you can bet on that."[11]

Murphy was an easy target, too. He was exceedingly round in every aspect, with a large head, a bulbous nose, and a portly frame, punctuated by a push broom moustache. He had a penchant for handing out hasty statements to the press that he would type up at his office in the Corn Exchange building on S. LaSalle Street, which one writer labeled "Murphy's famous interviews with himself." He claimed he engendered ill will from fellow owners because he refused to lend them money— though they'd be quick to point out that the many problems with Murphy began because he was too cheap to build a visitors' clubhouse at the West Side Grounds, that he routinely stood in opposition to whomever the National League put up for president of the league, and that he alienated reporters by moving their seats to the back of the grandstand during the World Series. Either way, Murphy was a prickly personality, not an active participant in the back-slapping world of baseball magnates, whose annual winter meetings revolved around late-night bar sessions spent telling old stories, being schmoozed by the press, and conducting business over cigars and snifters. "When I had the Cubs I was too busy for entertaining, or cultivating people," Murphy later wrote. "It is some task to run a championship ball club and cater to 25 'prima donna' ball players. When night comes you are all in and don't care for wine parties or bacchanalian revels—at least I did not."[12]

While players and fellow magnates had plenty of reason to dislike Murphy, so did the public. During the '08 World Series, it was alleged that Murphy conspired with scalpers to circumvent the set prices of the games. Originally, the Cubs put out word to the public that tickets could be bought at Spalding's Sporting Goods store in Chicago on the Friday before the Sunday and Monday games of the series. Fans lined up for tickets in the early morning even as tickets were being sold at the Cubs office without the public having been informed. Finally, at 1:30 PM, the crowd at Spalding's was told that no tickets would be available on Friday but they could be bought at the stadium box office on Saturday. The next day, fans again stood in a long line for hours, this time at the West Side Grounds. Again, tickets were being sold directly to scalpers at the Cubs office. Finally, fans in line were told that only those who had made arrangements for tickets in advance would be accommodated. According to the report of the National Commission, the team admitted to selling 630 tickets to one person. There was no direct evidence that Murphy profited from scalped tickets, and he responded to the censure of the Commission with his usual public vitriol, but, as Commission chairman Garry Herrmann wrote in a statement, "It has been clearly established from the personal knowledge that the commission had in this matter and the proof that was submitted that the Chicago baseball public was treated outrageously during the last world's series."[13]

If the anger and embarrassment that stemmed from the ticket-scalping scandal marked the starting point of anti–Murphy sentiment among fans, then the last few months of the 1912 season marked the starting point of Murphy's complete undoing in baseball—and, at the same time, paved the way for a series of high-impact events that would, within four wild years, lead the Cubs out of the West Side Grounds and into a new home on the North Side. Not only did Murphy and Taft have a hold on the Cubs, they also had an interest in the Philadelphia Phillies, which they'd purchased in 1909, putting up hapless sportswriter Horace Fogel as the front man, which permitted the N. L. the ability to deny that one group of owners held control of multiple teams. But Fogel, undoubtedly, was treated like a puppet by Murphy, and in 1912, at Murphy's bidding, Fogel wrote an article in the *Chicago Post* claiming that the National League race had been fixed for the

Giants and that St. Louis manager Roger Bresnahan, a former player for the Giants, had been pulling back on his team's effort against New York to help grant them the pennant. While Fogel took the fall and was booted out of baseball, most knew it was Murphy behind the entire fiasco. An editorial in *The Sporting News* said that kicking Murphy out of baseball "would be the greatest blow that could be dealt that gentleman; it would strike him doubtless in the only possible spot where he is tender."[14]

While the Fogel affair was distasteful and Three-Finger Brown's release, timed as it was during the City Series, was an egregious slap in the face to an all-time great, these were neither the first, nor the last, nor the most spectacular acts of self-destruction committed by Murphy in a surprisingly small window of time. On the field, beginning in late June 1912, the Cubs put on a mad charge, a stretch in which they went 45–15 and cut a fifteen-and-a half game Giants lead in the standings to just four games by August 22, rekindling hopes that there was another championship run left in the aging team. But by the end of October, just two short months later, things had taken a much different turn. Murphy saw to it that the Tinker-to-Evers-to-Chance dynasty was left in a smoldering ruin.

‡

It could be said that the final convulsions of the Cub machine first came in mid-August during a meeting of Murphy and Chance at West Side Grounds. Chance had been struggling with his health for the better part of two years, suffering from repeated headaches and dizzy spells. Over the course of his career, Chance was as good a player on the field as he was a manager in the dugout—he batted .296 for his career and led the league in stolen bases twice—but the headaches limited him to just thirty-one games in 1911 and only two games in '12. He had been diagnosed with a blood clot in his head and though surgery would be required to remove the clot, the prognosis was not serious enough to warrant immediate action. Chance would have the surgery after the season or, at least, when the Cubs were finally out of the pennant chase. With his headaches in full force on August 15, Murphy asked Chance if he would come back to manage in 1913. As Murphy remembered it, Chance said, "I would rather not," because of his health. But as Chance remembered it, Murphy added, "I would rather have you manage them sick than anyone else well."[15]

By the end of the first week of September, just starting a sixteen-game trip to the East, the Cubs had run out of steam, and the Giants pushed their lead back to eight games. While the team was in Cincinnati, Chance happened to catch outfielder Frank "Wildfire" Schulte returning to the team hotel well past the acceptable hour, and inebriated. On September 8, Chance suspended Schulte for the remainder of the season, without pay. Chance made the announcement regretfully because Schulte had been a good, loyal Cub since 1904 and, the previous year, led the league with 21 home runs and 107 runs batted in. Schulte accepted the punishment with dignity and was reinstated nine days later. But the suspension highlighted a problem that Murphy had been harping on with Chance for a while—that his men drank and cavorted too much and that the Cubs should follow a zero-tolerance policy for alcohol and cigarettes. Pirates owner Barney Dreyfuss had recently done so with his club, and though Chance was unsupportive, Murphy liked the idea.[16]

September took another bad turn on the tenth in Boston, when the hotheaded John Evers, who was given a surprisingly long five-game suspension for arguing with an umpire in August, again was suspended five games by National League president Tom Lynch, this time for his actions during a game on the eighth. Evers expressed his displeasure with a strikeout by vigorously dusting off his uniform so that the dirt went down the neck of the umpire's shirt. Because it was the second offense, the *Tribune's* Sam Weller wrote, "probably that's the reason the penalty is so heavy. If Johnny gets put out of the game another time this year, he may expect the electric chair or a life sentence." For Chance, Evers's suspension was about the end of his rope. Weller wrote that he was "so discouraged over the outlook that he refused to have anything to do with the game and turned the team over to Capt. Tinker, while he went off to the country to look for new material."[17] Indeed, Chance did say he was heading out to scout for minor league players. But he had other plans too—a week later, he checked into Presbyterian Hospital on East 60th Street in New York, where Dr. W. G. Fralick would remove the blood clot that had been causing him so many headaches.[18]

With Chance away, hell broke loose. Only four days after returning from his suspension, Evers' ongoing haggle with Tinker—as well as other internal tensions that were masked when Chance was around—boiled over. During a doubleheader in Brooklyn, Tinker called out Evers for failing to run hard on a ground ball. According to a report in *Sporting Life*, "When the last man had been retired, there was a sudden rumpus on the Chicago bench. Tinker was seen in the act of swinging a blow in the direction of Evers. In the mix-up, it looked as if these star players had clinched. Other members of the team grabbed Tinker's arm, and the next moment, a plain clothes detective jumped between the belligerents. ... Tinker and Evers indulged in several heart-to-heart talks while covering their positions on the field. On another occasion, [third baseman Heinie] Zimmerman caught a fly ball that [catcher Jimmy] Archer had called for. They came together with a bump. After some hard looks, Zim threw the ball down in a rage."[19] Those "heart-to-heart" talks, of course, were not particularly congenial.

While Cubs players were unraveling, Murphy saw Chance's absence as the end of the line for his manager. After all, in Murphy's mind, Chance had already told him in August he would not be coming back. On September 23, while Chance was laid up in New York, the seven-inch scar in his head still healing, Murphy put out a statement announcing that the Cubs would institute a complete ban on alcohol in 1913. In making the statement, Murphy indicated that the failure of the Cubs to win the pennant in 1909 and the World Series loss to the A's in 1910 could be traced back to the team's excessive use of alcohol and that the team should follow Dreyfuss's example in Pittsburgh. When Chance got word of Murphy's statement, he nearly popped another blood vessel. "If Mr. Dreyfuss or Mr. Murphy or anyone else says that my team lost the pennant in 1909 on account of drinking, he is a liar. If anybody says that the Cubs ever lost for that reason, he is a liar. I believe that I have the best behaved baseball team in either league. ... I feel these charges keenly. Reading them in the papers has set me back. I could hardly sleep last night. I cannot figure out what Murphy is trying to do. Apparently he is sore because I lost the pennant and wants to rasp somebody, but he is not going to rasp me."[20]

Chance was wrong on that account. Five days later, with Chance still recuperating in the hospital, Murphy let out another statement, this time telling the public that Chance would not be returning as manager, suggesting that Chance had retired. Now, Chance had truly had it with Murphy. He responded that he had not retired and that if Murphy wanted to be rid of him, he would have to release him. Chance "came back with a vigorous interview opposing Murphy's attitude and calling him various names of which 'ingrate' was the mildest."[21] The next day, Chance boarded a train and headed back to Chicago, ready to prepare his Cubs for the City Series against the White Sox and, incidentally, feeling much better after his surgery. What's more, he knew that he would return to the Cubs' field to a rousing ovation and that fans on the West Side would always side with the guy known as "Peerless Leader" over the guy known as "The Chubby One." In the meantime, he would put his fight with Murphy aside and focus on beating the White Sox.

The series was a nifty microcosm of the season for the Cubs. They won the first three games that were not ties, then lost the next three because they lacked enough pitching to hold off the South Siders. In the series finale, the Cubs threw in the towel altogether, losing, embarrassingly, 16–0. "What was the trouble with the Cubs?" the *Daily News* wondered. "Did the Cubs quit? Did the players refuse to work on account of President Murphy's attack on their reputation for sobriety? Were they out 'celebrating' after they had taken three games from the White Sox? ... Two answers were made oftenest. One was that the athletes failed to perform to the best of their ability because of Murphy's 'slam.' The other was that they were too confident over winning three in a row and went on an all night 'toot'" In the *Tribune*, the "toot" was detailed—Cubs players supposedly went to the Boston Oyster House until it closed, then drank more at the Edelweiss Café before moving on to the Drexel Café. At the Hotel LaSalle, "one was carried out in a helpless condition." The paper said that, according to rumor, "members of the club met in a downtown café and between bottles of wine denounced President Murphy for his reflections on the club."[22] Chance and his players denied all reports.

Whatever the case, Murphy wasted little time. Just after the series ended, he announced that he had chosen a new manager for 1913—without first telling Chance, and without giving Chance his release. The truce was over, and

Chance was, as the *Daily News* put it, "on the warpath, and at bay. He is more than peeved." That was evident. Chance said: "Murphy is not going to insult me. I do not think he had another man or even thought of one. He is trying to make the public believe that I have been a failure and did not take enough enthusiasm in my work. He never has been able to abuse me and is not going to do it now. I expected this from him after we were beaten by the White Sox. Had we won the series I do not think he would have said a word. He is not going to get away with it. Everything I say is the truth, and I am not afraid to say it, for he has nothing on me in any way. He cannot say that about himself."[23]

But Murphy had made up his mind. He had already released Brown, and now Chance was out. Murphy had decided to make Evers his manager and that meant Tinker would have to leave, too, because his relationship with Evers was so strained that "those on the inside in affairs of the Cubs club know that it would hardly be good policy to make one of those two boss of the team without getting rid of the other."[24] Tinker began negotiating with Cincinnati to take over its managership, which made sense—Reds owner Garry Herrmann, ever the peacemaker, was accustomed to cleaning up Murphy's messes, and this was one of his biggest. Herrmann later signed Brown, too, and claimed Chance on waivers, not because he intended to use Chance, but because he knew he could lessen the black eye Murphy had given baseball by having Chance's rights and finding a good new situation for him. Chance, who owned an orange ranch in Glendora, California, told the press he would be happy to simply retire and live off the profits from his oranges. Eventually, Chance was coaxed off his ranch to the only city outside Chicago to which he was willing to accept a deal: New York. He would take over the Yankees, joining his hated rival, the Giants' John McGraw, as a new tenant in New York's Polo Grounds.

Murphy might have been right to make changes, because his team was aging. But he couldn't have picked a more caustic and repulsive way to go about making those changes. "He has stirred the resentment of the patrons of his club," an editorial in *The Sporting News* suggested, "and he may be brought to the realization that if the club's popularity has waned it is not because of suspicion held against the players, but from dislike of the man who is the club president. In this way, he may have paved the way for his own effacement."[25]

Through all of the 1912 tumult, one thing Murphy did was dangle in front of fans the possibility of a new stadium to replace the rickety wooden West Side Grounds—it was his favorite carrot, something he routinely brought up to boost his image among fans. Back in January of 1912, Murphy said that a new park was coming, and the news was treated with sarcastic cheer. According to *The Sporting News*, "he turned loose the information that when everybody else in the big leagues had erected steel and concrete palaces, he would have a corps of experts in architecture and construction go over the whole lot of them, then build a new home for the Cubs that would beat anything yet provided for the public. Consequently, when the other fifteen club owners have their steel stands finished, look for the beginning of the realization of the West Side fans' dream."[26] In other words, it would be a long wait.

And in the heat of his public back-and-forth with Chance in late September, Murphy told reporters that a new stadium would be started shortly, saying, "It may be next fall before the plant is completed, but it will be constructed in pieces, so that the games can be played next summer just the same. ... The plant will have every modern convenience for the patrons of the game and will seat 30,000 persons comfortably when completed." Again, there was some cynicism about this claim. In one of Chance's part-ing shots at Murphy, he said, "If he wants to please the public and do the right thing by them, let him build his new ball park as he says he will. I'll bet $1,000 he never will do it. That is how much he cares for the public." Chance was right. By November, Murphy was claiming he could not yet build a new stadium because he didn't have the right permits to build so close to the Cook County Hospital, which was just across the street from the West Side Grounds.[27]

Had Murphy not been so penurious, had he been more willing to provide his West Side patrons with "every modern convenience" and a new ballpark, who knows where the Chicago Cubs would be playing their home games more than a century later?

# CHAPTER FIVE

# Joe Tinker and the Federal League

Early in the winter of 1913, the long, slow process that would produce what is now known as Wrigley Field had reached its critical moment. There was an available plot of land, once the centerpiece of a plan to create a third major league, on the North Side of Chicago, owned by baseball magnates with little interest in keeping it. There was a wealthy, popular young restaurant owner—Charley Weeghman—who was eager to have a team of his own. And there was Charles Murphy, who had torpedoed the popularity of the Cubs with repeated scandals, with his refusal to upgrade his ballpark, and, finally, with his poor treatment of the team's beloved star players the previous year. Under Evers, the Cubs had played respectably, winning eighty-eight games and finishing third, but largely because of Murphy's unpopularity, attendance on the West Side plummeted from about 514,000 to 419,000. The conditions were ideal for the North Side. All that was needed was a credible league to back a third team in the city, and a well-liked man to head up the operation.

As it happened, Joe Tinker was in the midst of a strange month. Following his trade to Cincinnati in December of 1912, he had taken over the Reds, and the stint did not go well. The Reds went 64–89, finished in seventh place, and at the end of November, Tinker was let go by Cincinnati, a move he welcomed. For all the dysfunction of the Cubs during his time in Chicago, at least the authority of Frank Chance was unquestioned and when there were battles, they were between Chance and Murphy directly. In Cincinnati, Tinker dealt with an owner, Garry Herrmann, who was undermined by his board of directors. Tinker tried to get better players and Herrmann would approve, only to have the board veto his attempts. When Tinker put it to the board that either he alone should make personnel decisions or they should find another manager, the board opted for another manager. In the days that followed, rumors of Tinker's next destination cropped up from every corner. Boston, Philadelphia, New York, Brooklyn, and Pittsburgh all wanted him. So did the Cubs. Tinker had, a year earlier, said that he would never play for the Cubs again. But even with Murphy in charge and with his old rival John Evers as manager, Tinker would have accepted a return to the West Side—he had two sons, after all, and had just bought an interest in the Garfield Plating business near the ballpark.[1] He could navigate Evers and Murphy if it meant spending most of the year at home in the nearby suburb of Oak Park. Murphy, having felt the sting of declining attendance, needed a boost like the return of Tinker.

Knowing he had some star power on his side, Tinker let it be known that he did not want to play for any of the four teams in the East, and since the penny-pinching Cardinals expressed no interest, that left only the Pirates and the Cubs as prospective trade partners for the Reds. Tinker had spoken with Pittsburgh manager Fred Clarke ahead of the National League's meeting in New York, which was to begin on December 10, but Murphy was traveling with his wife in Europe and wasn't able to begin a negotiation for Tinker until he returned. When the N. L. meeting opened, Murphy made a surprise appearance, having cut short his European jaunt. He did so without regret—he didn't much like Europe because he had to give out too many tips. "Everybody had his hand out and you could not take a step without giving someone a bit of change," Murphy said. "In Paris I asked for a second piece of toast and it took four waiters to bring it. Each had his mitt out for the money."[2] He was in a more generous mood when it came to Tinker.

He was informed that Brooklyn's Charles Ebbets had offered the Reds $25,000 for Tinker but Murphy told a reporter, "Say for me, that I will give more real money for Tinker than any other man."[3]

He wouldn't get the chance, however. On the evening of December 12, with the league meeting over and Murphy asleep on a train back to Chicago, Ebbets and Herrmann were still among those socializing at the Waldorf-Astoria in New York. Egged on by reporters and probably a few drinks in, they came to an agreement, with Pirates owner Barney Dreyfuss signing on as a witness. Ebbets would purchase Tinker for $25,000, with $10,000 of the sale price to go to Tinker as a bonus "on condition of that said Tinker accepts terms with said Brooklyn Base Ball Club and reports for services."[4] At the time, it was rumored that the deal was the result of a joke, but actually, it was more of a dare—Ebbets was angry that Herrmann said he didn't think Ebbets had $25,000 with which to buy Tinker, and he went through with the deal, basically, to protect his pride.[5] It would be the highest such bonus given to a player, and, despite Tinker's objection to playing in the East, he was flabbergasted by the potential for a bonus of that size, to the point that he wasn't necessarily going to believe it until he saw it—he, too, had to wonder whether the deal was a joke. His doubts were confirmed a few days later, when the Reds board of directors, once again, became a thorn in his side, declaring that it repudiated the Tinker deal because the Reds didn't receive any players in return. More than that, the *Chicago Daily News* reported, "The inside of the whole affair is that the directors simply could not stand for Tinker getting $10,000 as a present for going away."[6]

In the meantime, Murphy registered his objection to not being allowed to work out a deal for Tinker, who said, "I am going to do all I can to swing the deal to Chicago. If President Murphy wants me and is willing to bid for my services, I am going to demand that the Cincinnati club give him the chance."[7] It wasn't until December 20, when Ebbets and Herrmann got together in Cincinnati and worked out a further exchange of players to go along with the Tinker sale, that the Reds' board finally agreed to the swap. The next day, a Sunday, Tinker was to meet with Ebbets and manager Wilbert Robinson in Indianapolis to negotiate a contract. But Tinker's real interest in the meeting was to ensure that Ebbets would make good on the $10,000 bonus. When he was told on Saturday, then, that Ebbets was returning to Brooklyn and only Robinson would go to Indianapolis, Tinker was unhappy and stayed in Chicago. There was no point in seeing Robinson alone, he figured, since Robinson would have nothing to do with paying the bonus.[8]

Robinson, when it was clear that he was being stood up in Indianapolis, called Tinker on the telephone. Tinker told Robinson that he wanted a raise from his old Cubs salary, which had been $7,000—in all, Tinker wanted three years and $7,500 per year, plus the $10,000 bonus. He had already made clear to reporters that he wouldn't go to Brooklyn without a raise, so this wasn't news to Robinson. But, Robinson said, Ebbets would not go for that, saying that he had a figure in mind and would not pay one cent more than it. Considering he had already agreed to spend $25,000 just to get Tinker's rights, Ebbets's hard line on salary was understandable. But Tinker wasn't budging. "Well," Tinker would later recount telling Robinson "you have lost the $15,000." Two days later, Ebbets sent off a letter to Tinker, reminding him that $7,500 was more than he made playing for the Cubs— Ebbets's logic was that he should not pay Tinker more than he was paid when the Cubs were champions. Ebbets added, "Then, too, Joe, there is another angle that cannot be ignored, which is that men on our team with ability equal to yours are not receiving the money you ask for; as a second division club, we are paying these men first division salaries which is exactly what we shall do with you but cannot pay any in excess of same." Then Ebbets got to the heart of the matter. He'd grant a three-year contract, but at $5,000 per year. He closed by writing, underlined, "I believe nothing further should be said to the members of the press relative to salary."[9]

Tinker was frustrated. As far back as December 3, it had been reported that he had been contacted by representatives of the Federal League, a revamped independent league headed by a new president, James Gilmore, and seeking to make itself a third major league operating outside the auspices of Organized Baseball—the same sort of outlaw organization that the American Association would have been had the war plans of Charles Havenor and Mike Cantillon been actuated. Tinker met with the Federals at the Blackstone Hotel on Michigan Avenue in Chicago on December 26, and after the meeting, speculation held that he had been offered a three-year deal, worth $36,000 total, which the league would put in the bank for him up front. This was big money. Even if Ebbets gave Tinker the $7,500 per year he was seeking, that deal would be worth $32,500 in total. Besides, Tinker could not be blamed for having tired of the antics of National League owners, not after he had been lowballed by Ebbets, undermined by the Cincinnati board of directors, and denied a chance to return to the Cubs.

Thus, the new league did not sound so bad. Making things all the sweeter for Tinker, he would be given charge of the Federal League's team in Chicago. He wouldn't have to move east, or move anywhere at all. He could not resist the offer. "The proposition they have made me is a good one," Tinker said. "I know I can make more than if I stayed in organized ball. They have offered me some stock on which I have an option, and if arrangements can be made, I will take it." And Tinker added this: "There will be a dandy new park here, too."[10]

‡

On Christmas Eve, Murphy—technically the landlord for some of Weeghman's restaurant sites—was quoted in the *Chicago Daily News*, saying, "This Federal League is a huge joke from start to finish. It lost money last year and I know no money is back of it next season. The report has been going around that Charles Weeghman is to finance the local club. He is not, for he told me so himself just the other day. He knows it is a losing venture and would not invest his money that way. ... Millionaires do not like to lose money anymore than a poor man."[11]

Weeghman either never actually said that to Murphy, or he flat-out lied. Not only had Weeghman already agreed to join up with the fledgling Federal League, he had been working with Gilmore for nearly a month and had been with him when the Federal League secured a one-month option on the North Side seminary property in early December. After that, he was actively trying to get both Joe Tinker and Mordecai Brown to commit to the new league, knowing full well that they would be good targets because of the treatment they'd received recently from Organized Baseball in general and Murphy specifically. It would be a gamble for both players because there was no telling what was in store for the Federal League. Any player leaving the stability offered by O. B. ran the risk of a blacklisting. For Tinker (age thirty-three) and Brown (age thirty-seven), that would mean the end of their careers.

The Feds were an especially risky proposition. In contrast to the move of the American League to major league status a decade earlier, or even the A.A. plan, the Federal League was working from virtually no history and no sense of identity with hometown fans—the American League had been an established minor league for years before it declared war, and it would have been the same had the A.A. gone on with its war plans. The Federal League, though, had been in operation beginning in 1913, the brainchild of John T. Powers, who had been labeled "Don Quixote John T. Powers, titular head of one of the 'third major' leagues" as far back as 1912.[12] At that point, Powers was running a fanciful fight against Organized Baseball with what he was calling the Columbian League, which wilted within a month and never actually played a game. Powers bounced back the next year with some of the same financial backers and a new league name, the Federal League. But the new league didn't register at all as a threat. There were six teams, including one in Chicago that was based at the small athletic field located at DePaul University, on Sheffield Avenue, two miles south of Addison Avenue. There was a team in St. Louis, a city that already had two big-league teams. Three teams—Cleveland and Pittsburgh, and Covington, Kentucky, across the Ohio River from Cincinnati—were in markets that had only one big-league team. There was a team, too, in Indianapolis, which had a strong American Association club.

By the high point of the Federal League's first season, though, the league's owners had tired of Powers' quixotic approach, and Powers was ousted. Gilmore, who owned part of the Chicago team, took over as a temporary replacement, and later was elected head of the league. Gilmore was no less fanciful than Powers in terms of his outlook for the Federal League, but he was more practical and credible in terms of his ability to fulfill that vision. "The Federals have admitted that there is but one chance for them," an article in *The Sporting News* stated. "They must get away from the 'bush' stage on which they operated last year at a cost to their angels of a sum running into five figures and show the fans some real 'major' base ball if they would get enough support to keep them going."[13]

This is where Gilmore proved a big upgrade over Powers—a wealthy man himself, and a good talker, Gilmore was very adept at identifying and persuading the biggest of potential backers to sign on to the new league. That made Weeghman an obvious target. As he recalled in *Baseball Magazine*:

> Spotting me as a likely victim, [Gilmore] came to me with the proposition. 'Now, Weeghman,' he said with the bland expression of a disinterested friend. 'I have a fine business opening for you, but we need more financial resources. We are going to reorganize the club with a capitalization of fifty thousand dollars. If you will take twenty-six thousand dollars' worth of stock, that will give you control of the club. Even I had the intelligence enough to see if I owned fifty per cent of the stock I would get control, but I didn't grasp the subsequent details quite so clearly. 'Are you sure fifty thousand dollars will be enough to finance this thing?' I asked. 'Won't there be other expenses that crop up when the club gets under way that will be likely to cost a lot of money?' But Gilmore smiled indulgently at my childish ignorance. 'Oh no,' he assured me, 'all we want is fifty thousand dollars. There won't be any other expenses. That will be all the money we shall require.'[14]

Gilmore could offer a simple, clear-minded plan for getting a foothold among fans for the new league. The first challenge was to hire managers, and that meant bringing in recognizable veteran players, ideally one per team. The second challenge was to place five major league players on each of the teams in the league, which would expand from six to eight franchises. In that light, waging war against O. B. didn't seem so difficult—all they would need for a credible start was forty players plus eight managers. The Feds had their first public success in November when they signed recently deposed St. Louis Browns manager George Stovall to manage the Kansas City team, which had been moved from Covington. Stovall was a difficult character, known for smashing a chair on the head of his manager, Nap

Lajoie, during a fight in a hotel lobby when he was with Cleveland. But he was an able talent evaluator and had a lot of connections within the game.

At a meeting of the insurgent league on November 29, a list of more than fifty names was compiled; credible big league players who were to be approached by the Federals. These players were carefully chosen. The plan of the Feds also included minimizing antagonism toward O. B., and that meant they would not sign players who had contracts already. Among those were some star-caliber players like Cubs sluggers Heinie Zimmerman and Frank Schulte, as well as Lajoie, first baseman Hal Chase, and pitchers Rube Marquard and Smoky Joe Wood. Athletics second baseman Eddie Collins admitted that he had been offered a three-year, $50,000 contract, but turned it down. It was estimated that for the Federal Leaguers to sign the majority of the players on the list, they would need $250,000. That was a sizable outlay but within Organized Baseball, the new league was causing some concern—players who would normally sign contracts before Christmas were holding off. "The fact that none of the National and American League clubs have been able to sign the players under reserve for next season is beginning to worry some of the magnates in spite of the fact that they cannot make themselves believe that the Federal promoters are able to dig up enough money to obtain a good share of the available playing talent," one report stated.[15]

Besides players, there was also the need to exploit as many weak markets as possible. With the Cubs' unpopularity, Chicago was the ripest fruit on the baseball map for the Federal League. On the same day that Murphy was claiming Weeghman was not involved with Feds, the *Tribune* reported on Tinker's dalliance with the new league. "Tinker's hesitation also is believed to be one of the reasons for the delay in making public the plans of the Federal League," the paper noted. "It apparently is the desire of the new organization to make Tinker the centerpiece of its first real volley of fireworks in the coming scrap with the forces of organized baseball."[16] The delay didn't last. On December 27, it became official when Tinker signed on with the Federal League to be the manager and shortstop of the Chicago team. Brown, his friend and teammate, signed, too, also taking a three-year contract, and he would be at the head of the new team in St. Louis.

At the same time, the Chicago team announced the reorganization of the franchise, which would place Weeghman as the team president. Alongside him would be Bill Walker, the owner of a fish distribution business on South Water Street in Chicago (said to be the biggest such business west of the Atlantic coast) and Weeghman's closest associate—they had come up through the ranks of the food business together. Walker was strictly on board as a financier and shied away from the public attention that Weeghman so loved. Indeed, Walker seemed to know something that "Chubby Charley" Murphy did not. "Nobody loves a fat man," he told *Baseball Magazine*, "so I keep in the background and let Weeghman do all the talking. I am interested in the venture as much as he and we both think we have a good proposition, but I don't understand the publicity part of it so well. He handles all that. ... They say it's a show business, and an owner is in the public eye and, I suppose he is, but I had rather be back with my fish—I know more about them."[17]

The addition of Tinker and Brown brought immediate legitimacy to the Federal venture—days later, the Feds also signed Philadelphia Phillies infielder Otto Knabe, who would be the manager in Baltimore. But for the magnates of O. B., the loss of those players was not nearly as concerning as the presence of Weeghman, who had already made an impression among baseball men when he nearly bought the Cardinals. Among the rest of the league's owners, only St. Louis brewer Otto Stifel (whose partner, Phil Ball, owned a multimillion-dollar cola business) was perceived to have the financial backing to run a professional baseball team. Having a man of Weeghman's wealth, in a city as open to third-league support as Chicago appeared to be, gave the venture sudden heft.

The North Side site was another problem, because it was an ideal locale. The Cantillons, despite their insurrectionary leanings in the past, were still part of Organized Baseball as the owners of the A.A. Minneapolis Millers, and were pressured by their fellow magnates not to let the property to Weeghman. But the Cantillons bought the spot for the purpose of erecting a park and the land would have more value for that purpose than if it were to be broken into residential lots—something that didn't really interest the Cantillons, who were baseball men, not real estate barons. If Weeghman put a park on the spot and the Federals failed, as most assumed they would, the Cantillons would be quick to offer an A.A. team. Besides, they were able to dodge a disloyalty charge from their friends in Organized Baseball by putting their shares in the land in the name of their brother-in-law, Edward Archambault.

Murphy was especially distressed by the possibility of a new park in the Sheffield-Addison location. As reporter R.G. Tobin wrote, "President Charles W. Murphy, of the Cubs, seems to be quite excited over the proposed entry of the Federals in Chicago. He has oiled up his old No. 4 Remington and is grinding out page after page of interviews with himself on the case. In one of the last of these efforts he went so strong that some of the Chicago papers would not even print his communication for fear of drawing a libel suit. Murphy has attacked the promoters of the Federal circuit, the Chicago officials and most everyone connected with the proposition." Murphy went even further. He brought to light—and most likely encouraged—some neighbors who threatened legal action against Weeghman and Gilmore if they built a park in the area. Murphy's statement, the *Chicago Daily News* noted, "claimed that H.D. Moreland, William Sampson and a Mr. Wickes are said to be the ones making the objections. In fact, Mr. Wickes called up President Murphy today advising him that such action would be taken."[18]

Still, Weeghman gave out his plans for the new park and its location. "I propose to build a grandstand of steel or concrete to cost about $100,000 or $125,000, if necessary," he said. "I have asked for bids and within forty-eight hours the contract will be let. We have leased the grounds at the corner of Sheffield Avenue and Addison streets running west to Clark Street. The lot is 600 feet by 598, runs along the Clark Street car line and the Northwestern elevated has a station at Addison Street which is half a block from the lot. We want to have the main entrance at the corner of Sheffield Avenue and Addison Street. The grand stand will be built to seat 15,000. It will be so constructed that we can add wings to it at any time when patronage demands it."[19] The following day, Weeghman joined Tinker and the architect Zachary Taylor Davis (who had designed Comiskey's new park, which opened in 1910) at the North Side site. With just three days to go before the option on the land expired, Mike Cantillon boarded a train from Minneapolis to Chicago that night. On New Year's Eve 1913, he and Weeghman signed a preliminary lease—though, by the time the deal became final in late January, Archambault had acquired the other interests.[20]

It had all come together. In the course of a month, the new Federal League team in Chicago had acquired a popular new owner, a new set of backers, and a star shortstop who would serve as the team's manager. They also had a piece of seminary land on the North Side. Now they needed to turn that into a baseball park, and do it in time for Opening Day.

# CHAPTER SIX

# Weeghman and the War

The signing of Tinker and Brown might have been, as the papers declared, the first shots of the Federal League's new baseball war, but Organized Baseball's initial battle strategy was not player-focused. Indeed, there were few actual players on the Federal League roster as 1913 turned to 1914, but the league did have one thing going for it—the labor movement was gaining strength across the nation and globe and the national game was not immune. In baseball a fledgling players union, called the Baseball Players' Fraternity and led by lawyer and ex-ballplayer Dave Fultz, had come into being in 1912. The Fraternity didn't have the power to negotiate collectively but it did present Organized Baseball with a list of seventeen demands after the 1913 season and the Fraternity had advised players not to sign contracts until after January 1. Fultz had two reasons for this: He wanted to see whether the magnates accepted his demands and see whether the new Federal League (which offered him leverage against O. B.) would survive the winter and get legitimate backing. While baseball dealt with Fultz, it also pursued a divide-and-conquer approach, the idea being that if O. B. could somehow peel off Weeghman from the outlaws, the Federal League would quickly wither. Weeghman obviously wanted a team of his own, so the trick for baseball's magnates became finding a team for him, one that would supplant his interest in the Federal League and pave the way for his departure.

First up: The Browns. American League president Ban Johnson felt he could pull off a sale of his St. Louis club with some personal arm-twisting. The Browns were owned by Col. Robert Hedges, who had built up his wealth in the buggy-manufacturing business in the late 1800s. After he sold his company in 1900—he avoided becoming a cliché by recognizing that the automobile would doom the buggy industry—Hedges was approached by Johnson about entry into the American League. He arranged for Hedges to buy the Milwaukee team and its players for the bargain sum of $30,000 and move it to St. Louis. Hedges lost money on the team in 1902, his first year of ownership, but had pretty much cleaned up on the Browns since. One estimate in *The Sporting News* in 1915 held that, in thirteen years of ownership, Hedges personally had made more than $700,000 off his initial $30,000 investment and that in the 1913 season, the team made $50,000 (Hedges held a 66.5 percent stake in the club).

Those profits came despite the fact that the Browns were awful and pretty much always had been. They finished eighth in the eight-team American League in 1913, losing ninety-six games, which marked the third eighth-place finish in four years for St. Louis (the one year they didn't finish eighth, they finished seventh). The Browns had finished among the top four teams in the A. L. just twice in Hedges's tenure, but the years of 1910–13 were especially unbearable—they lost an average of 103 games per year in that stretch and posted a winning percentage of .330. Hedges was making a profit, and because he wasn't being punished on the balance sheet, he wouldn't spend money on quality players. The 1913 season was a particular embarrassment because Hedges had tolerated irascible manager George Stovall, in the opinions of his fellow American League bosses, too long. Stovall had drawn the ire of the A. L. when he spat in the face of an umpire in May, but Hedges kept him on as manager until he finally fired Stovall in September.

This was why, in the third week of January, Johnson traveled to St. Louis to see Hedges. It was also why Johnson brought back Hedges to his office in Chicago with him on Friday, January 16. That happened to be the day before the Federal League would hold a meeting at the Hotel LaSalle in the Loop, just six blocks away from Johnson's office at the Fisher building.[1] Johnson knew that Weeghman had been prepared to buy the Cardinals in 1911 and he knew that there were several scenarios in which he could wind up with the Browns—either he could buy Hedges's stock outright, or buy enough to take a controlling interest, or pair with St. Louis Feds owner Otto Stifel in a joint venture for the team. In either case, the Federal League would be left neutered and, as a bonus, Johnson would strengthen a weak spot in the A. L.

There was another scenario: the American Association. Weeghman's landlords, the Cantillons, would happily arrange for Weeghman to get control of the St. Paul franchise so that he could move it to the North Side. Johnson also had Cleveland Naps (they weren't yet the Indians) owner Charles Somers on his side. In addition to the Naps, Somers owned the A.A.'s Toledo franchise, and that could be made available for Weeghman. Given the reality of having Joe Tinker leading a team with major league aspirations on the North Side, Charles Comiskey would assent to having a minor league team under the auspices of Organized Baseball located there instead.[2] It would work out best for the Cantillons, who would finally get the A.A. team in Chicago they so long wanted, and the possibility of removing the drain of the St. Paul team from their market in Minneapolis would be a bonus. Whether Weeghman got St. Paul or Toledo, though, they would benefit because the value of their league as a whole would spike by having a Chicago team playing in a first-class ballpark.

There was a third option, too, which would call for simply paying off Weeghman, allowing Joe Tinker, Mordecai Brown, Otto Knabe, and others who had signed with the Federals back into O. B.'s good graces and forgetting the whole thing ever happened. After Weeghman, it was obvious that the choicest target was Joe Tinker, who was the biggest name and sharpest talent on the roster of the Federal managers. On the morning of January 16, just ahead of the Federal League meeting, Ebbets asked Tinker to meet him at the LaSalle—he was still willing to give Tinker the $10,000 bonus plus the three-year contract at Tinker's $7,500-per-year demand, reminding him he had paid $15,000 just for his rights. "I have a Brooklyn contract in my pocket and have come to see if you will sign it," Ebbets said. Tinker told him, "I couldn't sign a Brooklyn contract, for I'm bound to a contract for three years with the Chicago team of the Federal League." According to the *Tribune*, the meeting lasted two minutes and "when it was over it seemed Mr. Ebbets had purchased $15,000 worth of experience."[3] But the effort didn't stop there. According to the *New York Times*, Johnson, Ebbets, and Garry Herrmann "were all day attempting, it is said, to induce Joe Tinker to sign with Brooklyn, despite his contract already made with the Chicago Federals. Their attempts in this direction were futile."[4]

For Charles Murphy, the buyout attempt was the way to go, because the Cubs boss wanted no team on the North Side, even a minor league outfit. A few months later, a friend of Weeghman's was quoted saying that Weeghman "had been offered $500,000 for his Federal League holdings. The outstanding stipulation was that he literally speaking, abandon the Feds."[5] The friend might have been exaggerating the figure but not on the thrust of his claim—buying out Weeghman was O. B.'s best option. He had a lineup in Chicago and a North Side site, making the prospect of owning a team in St. Louis a lot less attractive, especially with his restaurants running at an all-time high. He was, however, amenable to taking an American Association team, and with Comiskey and the American League on board with that plan, all that was required was a unanimous vote by the National League. But Murphy wouldn't budge. Later, a story in *Sporting Life* cited a *New York Sun* report that said, "It is understood that the action of C. W. Murphy, owner of the Cubs in opposing an American Association club in Chicago has precipitated a crises in major league circles." It quoted an N. L. magnate: "It is true that the constitution of each league calls for the unanimous consent of club owners when one's territory is to be invaded by another league in Organized Baseball, but it will have to be amended. There is no use beating about the bush."[6]

Still, Murphy was certain enough that Weeghman was about to land elsewhere that he issued a statement saying, "Mr. Weeghman had secretly retired from the Federal League, which is on a hunt for another angel. ... The Federals have shot their wad and are practically dead, and it is only a question of a week or two before the obsequies will be held." That, Weeghman responded, was "absurd and silly." But, really, Murphy was right. Weeghman's willingness to abandon the Federal League wasn't all that absurd and silly, as the new league's other owners would soon find out.[7]

‡

When Weeghman showed up at the LaSalle for the Federal League meeting on the morning of January 17, he was agitated. He was only three weeks removed from the triumphant signing of Tinker and less than three weeks from the equally triumphant acceptance of the option on the North Side lease, but already the temptation of abandoning the Feds for the security of a spot within the American League or American Association was beckoning. The more he ascertained the state of his own league, the more disheartened he became, and it was at this meeting that he wanted his questions answered completely. For Weeghman, the problem boiled down to money—he didn't feel as though his fellow owners were risking as much as he was and, worse, he was not sure they could afford to risk all that much even if they were so inclined. Weeghman didn't want to put in his lot with men who would not be able to absorb the losses that would surely come in getting the league off the ground. Stifel and Ball in St. Louis were not a problem, and Baltimore, being run by veteran baseball men Ned Hanlon and Harry Goldman, appeared to be running well too.

But the rest of the teams—Pittsburgh, Buffalo, Indianapolis, and Kansas City—had dubious backing, and no one was quite sure whether the proposed team in Toronto (which did not even have a manager three months before the season was likely to start) had any hope of surviving. There were no first-class ballparks in any of the cities, and in some cases, teams hadn't even identified where their grounds would be. Populating the league with credible big league players was a bigger problem. By Weeghman's estimation, only Chicago, Pittsburgh, and Baltimore had signed up any major leaguers, and those were precious few. League president James Gilmore claimed that thirty-three big leaguers had gone over to the Feds, but Weeghman knew that the Feds would need far more than thirty-three quality players to yank themselves out of their bush league past and start winning over real fans. All teams had accepted that when they signed up for Gilmore's league in November. "We are eager to see just what every team has done up to date," Gilmore said. "Every club is under agreement to sign five star players and a deposit of $25,000 (per team) as evidence of good faith. Now we want to see if every club has kept its word."[8]

No matter what Weeghman did next, Organized Baseball's honchos were satisfied that they had created significant enough havoc within the Federal League to cause the venture to unravel. They had made offers to Weeghman and floated rumors (through one of their favorite instruments, veteran *New York Sun* writer Joe Vila) about those offers so that Weeghman's fellow owners were sure to be upset, and even stirred up the rumor that Gilmore would soon be replaced.[9] They had created enough doubt in Weeghman's mind to nudge him into being confrontational when put into a room with the Federal League magnates. Add Weeghman's temper to the mix and the Feds were in for a difficult day at the Hotel LaSalle. If Weeghman backed out—to accept an A.A. team, to buy the Browns, or to take a buyout—the whole league would collapse and the future of his North Side land would be thrown into flux.

The Federal League magnates took a break at 2 PM. at the LaSalle, and Weeghman was immediately accosted by reporters. "Would you buy the St. Louis Browns?" he was asked.

"How much do they want?" he answered slyly.

Told that wasn't an answer, Weeghman said, "That is too pointed a question to answer at this time. You must excuse me for the time being. I have told the other backers just where I stand and they know I am not bluffing. I have heard three reports [from Federal League teams] and they are stronger than horseradish."[10] Later in the day, Weeghman did acknowledge that he had been approached about the Browns but that he wasn't sure if the offer came from a legitimate representative of the A. L. or a "nut." Weeghman was then asked about the report that the National Commission "had offered the Federal league a price and you in particular had been offered a certain sum with the understanding that the slate was to be wiped off, all ball players were to be restored to good standing, and the managers like Tinker, Brown, and Knabe satisfied financially and restored to their original place in organized baseball. Is this true and would you sell?" Here Weeghman offered a white lie and a dodge. "I have not been approached by any member of the national commission or anyone else offering me a price," he said, "but I am a business man and would sell the suit off my back if I got what I considered my price."[11]

At 3 PM, Federal League president James Gilmore told reporters, who had been gathered in the hotel's anteroom since morning, that they should probably tell their wives they'd be missing dinner and tell their editors they'd be missing deadlines. "This meeting will not be over before 5 o'clock this afternoon."[12] That bit of news delighted the esteemed gentlemen gathered at Ban Johnson's office in the Fisher building. According to the *Tribune's* Sam Weller, "while the Federal League craft was weathering the storm in the Hotel LaSalle," Johnson, Herrmann, Hedges, and Navin were "holding a chuckling meeting," keeping in touch with Ebbets via telephone. "The coterie had assembled there earlier in the day, but met again at nightfall and had a big league repast served in the office of the American league head," Weller wrote. "A visitor called upon them soon after 7 o'clock while the feast was at its height. He found them jovially celebrating the downfall of the outlaws."

"The Federal league will never start the season," Johnson said.[13]

‡

There was evidence that Johnson was right. The Federal League was teetering and Weeghman was on the verge of bailing out before the crash. The $25,000 per team just didn't seem to be enough, and as a matter of simple math, that should have been obvious. Average salaries in baseball in those days were in the $3,000-$4,000 range and $25,000 put up by eight teams gave the Federals a pool of $200,000 with which to sign players. Even if they used that money to sign average major leaguers, they'd only get about fifty players. That's six per team and doesn't count the managers' salaries and the rest of the roster. It also doesn't take into account the pay raise necessary to get even average players to forsake O.

B. and risk joining up with an outlaw organization that might fold before the season started and could cost that player a five-year suspension. Take, for example, shortstop Al Bridwell. He earned $4,000 with the Cubs in 1913, and hit just .240 on the year. He was a decent player, but nothing special and at thirty years old, probably headed into a decline. To get him to sign with the Federal League, he was given $6,500. With those kinds of pay bumps, $200,000 would only get the Feds in the range of thirty big-league players. And they would be thirty very average players.

This was the disheartening reality for Weeghman. He wanted to sign on to a first-class league, but he did not have first-class peers within that league. Weeghman realized that the Federal League needed not only $200,000 to sign players, but a $200,000 reserve fund to help attend to whatever matters might arise for the league—if, say, they made an outrageous offer to an O. B. star and he actually accepted, there had to be a fund from which to guarantee that player's contract. But he wasn't convinced his fellow magnates had the stomach to put up that kind of fund. As Weller commented, "For hours the gale raged and a little craft labeled, 'Federal League,' was in great distress. ... At 4 o'clock in the afternoon, it looked the small craft was lost and sympathizers began to mourn. But between the hours of 4 and 7, something happened and no one has been able to explain it."[14]

Two things happened. For one, Baltimore's Ned Hanlon spoke. Among the men gathered for the Federal League meeting, there was virtually no one with actual experience in major league baseball, as a player, manager, or front-office executive. Tinker and Three-Finger Brown were there, but the only other managers present were Bill Phillips of Indianapolis and Doc Gessler of Pittsburgh. Phillips had pitched in the majors for seven seasons, winning seventy games. Gessler was a better player, but his career was something of a disappointment—he was only thirty-three and had a degree in medicine, so, unlike his peers, baseball was not the only way he had available to make a living and the Federal League was far less of a do-or-die situation. Hanlon, though, was a baseball lifer, as a player and manager, and was dedicated to getting big league baseball back into Baltimore. The city had been deserted by Ban Johnson's American League in 1903 and few of the city's baseball-loving citizens ever forgave Johnson for it (Hanlon included). Hanlon had been in the game since 1880, so his voice carried special weight among the Federal League ingénues, even the wealthy ones. "The Feds nearly blew on Saturday," Cincinnati reporter Jack Ryder wrote, "and were held together only by the manly eloquence of Ned Hanlon, the Baltimore impresario, who spellbound the other delegates into holding on for a week or so longer."[15]

After Hanlon's speech the Federal magnates began to put up more money. According to *The Sporting News*, "One report came out that Otto Stifel, the wealthy St. Louis brewer who is backing the Federal League club of that city, had come to the rescue at the league meeting ... by tossing his check for $100,000 on the table and telling President Gilmore to go ahead and spend it for the immediate needs of the league. However, it is thought others besides Stifel had a hand in making up the bundle of coin to hand out to players."[16]

It was almost 10 o'clock on the seventeenth when Gilmore opened the door to the meeting to the waiting newspapermen, emerging from the meeting, smiling. "Instead of reading the obituary of the Federal League, he announced that it had been the greatest base ball meeting in 10 years and that the Federal League was sure to go through," *The Sporting News* reported. But the paper also said that the Fed owners were so jubilant as to draw suspicions that "the happy and joyous front was all a bluff."[17] Indeed, word was that there were teams, still, that had to show they had the money to stick in the league and Ryder reported they would have a week to do so. By month's end, Weeghman would create a stir when he sent out his personal attorney to Federal League outposts in Toronto, Buffalo, Baltimore, and Pittsburgh to ascertain the health and viability of those franchises and their parks because "the Chicago backer is not satisfied with the rosy reports that President Gilmore and others have made him and he is to find out for himself if he is being misled."[18]

But when the reporters walked into the LaSalle meeting room what mattered most was that the day had passed and Weeghman was still there. Asked by a crowd of reporters if he had heard what he needed to hear in the meeting, he declared, "I am for the Federal League, hook, line and sinker."

When reporters scurried over to the Fisher building with Weeghman's declaration fresh in their notebooks, they found Ban Johnson's office dark and empty.[19]

# CHAPTER SEVEN

# Crisis Management

Weeghman had his concerns about the health of the rest of the league and its far-flung circuit, but when Organized Baseball failed to pull him away from the outlaws, it was assured that the downtown Loop would take the mantle as the epicenter of baseball's war. As one writer would later observe, "Chicago men, Chicago capital and two well-known Chicago ball players are chiefly responsible for making the Federal League. James A. Gilmore, president of the league and Charles H. Weeghman, president of the Chicago Club, developed the organization. Joseph Tinker and Mordecai Brown, veterans of the Chicago Cubs, were the first real ball players to go to the Federals, and their example brought other players from the forces of Organized Ball."[1] Once the league withstood its internal battle at the Hotel LaSalle, it was able to redirect its attention on the crucial battle to be waged against O. B. To do that, the new league, bolstered by the influx of capital that had been demanded by Weeghman, needed to sign players, and as January wore on, the league headquarters in the downtown Old Colony building began to bustle with player visits, deal-making, and eager reporters. Perhaps the Federals would need even more capital eventually—Weeghman obviously thought so—but the meeting had produced enough cash to get the attention of players.

"From the way business was rushing in the offices of Gilmore, Weeghman & Company," Chicago sportswriter James Crusinberry commented, "it seems someone interested in the welfare of their adventure must have emptied a barrel of gold in the treasury. One thing is absolutely certain. Since the meeting of the Federals here (on January 17th), money has been spent by them with reckless abandon that has caused some of the wealthy men of organized ball to gasp in wonder."[2]

Weeghman, meanwhile, tried to smooth over his public agitation, issuing something close to a formal apology. The seventeenth had been a Saturday, and his annoyance with his compatriots at the time was obvious, but on the eighteenth, he said, "I never felt better over the prospects of the Federal League than I do today. I wanted the other fellows who were going into this thing with me to show me some money and players, and they showed me so much money right up in that meeting room Saturday afternoon that I felt ashamed for having asked it of them." Weeghman understood that he was the bellwether of the new league and if he continued to show any public indication that he was wavering on the Feds, he would give O. B. fodder to scare off potential investors as well as players interested in jumping.

Those players were badly needed. The Federal League claimed to have signed thirty-three major league players before the meeting, but as an article in *Baseball Magazine* pointed out, "According to a census made at the same time by the majors, the only way in which the Feds could claim 33 big leaguers was by counting in every recruit that had ever had a short trial in fast company, and every has-been yanked from obscurity for the new show. Of the 33, so they stated, seven were players who had already been passed back by the waiver route and felt sore about it; five were youngsters who had been hired and fired by major teams; ten were antiques or dead ones, some of them out of the big circuit for three years ... and of the survivors, at least two were shaky on their pins."[3]

But busy days at the league office had yielded results. One week after the Hotel LaSalle meeting, the Federal magnates met again, this time in secret at the Chicago Athletic Association. They had much different numbers to report. When the meeting adjourned, Weeghman met reporters and gave out a stunning update: There were now 127 players under contract for

the Federal League, and of those players, eighty-three were major leaguers. Among them were two players Tinker had landed for the Chicago
club—pitcher Claude Hendrix, who had fallen out of favor in Pittsburgh
because of an injury one year after posting a 24–9 record, and Rollie Zeider,
a long-time White Sox infielder who had been traded to the Yankees the
previous year. If the major league credentials of some players the Federals
signed were questionable, those of Hendrix and Zeider were not. Each was
an established player in the prime of his career.

Weeghman was the most important man on the business end of the
Federal League, but Tinker was the most important man when it came to
luring players to jump to the new league. Baltimore manager Otto Knabe
made some successful runs at his former teammates with the Phillies, and
Kansas City's George Stovall provided a steady stream of recruits from his
familiar stomping grounds among the West Coast's minor leagues, but
Tinker was by far the most effective recruiter the Federal League had. Tinker
might not have had much success in his tenure as the manager of the Reds
in 1913, but he inspired loyalty among his men. There were forty-five players who came through Cincinnati that season, and including himself and
Brown, thirteen of those players wound up in the Federal League, including
the top three pitchers on that Reds staff, Gene Packard, George Suggs, and
Chief Johnson—they'd combined to go just 29–42 in '13, but each threw
more than 190 innings. Tinker nearly got another Red, longtime Cub teammate Jimmy Sheckard, to manage in Pittsburgh, but the team backed out
when Sheckard made shifting demands on a contract. Tinker was also adept
at using his hometown sources in the Topeka-Kansas City area to drum up
players. Tinker signed three of the top stars (most notably popular outfielder
Dutch Zwilling) from nearby St. Joseph of the Western League, which was
owned by Jack Holland. Of course, Holland was not pleased and though
Tinker and Holland "are old-time friends, they have been near enemies"
after the player raid.[4]

Even when Tinker failed to close deals with his former players, he had hit
O. B. hard by forcing teams to give players raises. Tinker estimated that he
cost the Reds $100,000 in contracts and multi-year deals and that Murphy's
Cubs were down an extra $25,000.[5] He also helped lure Charley Williams,

secretary of the Cubs, over to the Feds. That might not sound like a big hit to the West Siders, but Williams was one of the most popular men in baseball, a man who "often has been declared by his associates to be the world's champion secretary."[6] Some of Tinker's signees would wind up elsewhere, but the roster he and Weeghman were assembling in Chicago created a problem—it threatened to dominate the league and, perhaps, kill interest in the pennant drive. "In doping out the chances of the Federal League, it begins to look as if President Weeghman might bust up the organization before the middle of the season simply by being too live a wire," a dispatch to *The Sporting News* commented. "He surely appears to be the livest wire of the outlaw circuit and so far as known has corralled a team which outclasses the others in playing strength. If the Tinker team goes out and wins too far off, there will be nothing to the race and interest will not be sustained and attendance will drop off."[7]

Tinker had signed sixteen players, and while four were from the semi-pro ranks, four were credible minor league performers from top leagues and eight were major leaguers. In the infield, Tinker had himself and Zeider, with Al Wickland, one of his Cincinnati players, in the outfield. His pitching crew was impressive, with Hendrix, Packard, and ex-Phillie Ad Brennan, plus former Cub King Cole. And at catcher, there was former Phillie Bill Killefer. At least, he was a former Phillie as far as the Federal League was concerned. Killefer had other ideas.

‡

Whenever the United States Congress sees reason to get involved with Major League Baseball—whether it was the players' strike in 1994–95 or the steroid investigation in 2005—it claims the authority to do on the basis of the protection of the reserve clause. It's a legal construct that causes the eyes of many fans to glaze over, but the reserve clause has been, since the inception of professional baseball, the backbone of the organization of the game and its various leagues. Without it, the structure of the game as we know it would crumble. As the war between the Federal League and Organized Baseball began to slowly get rolling, the reserve clause moved to the forefront of the minds of magnates on both sides of the issue.

It had already become a preoccupation for Organized Baseball. In March of 1912, another Chicagoan threatened to upstage the order of baseball with an attack on the reserve clause. That was Rep. Thomas Gallagher of Illinois's Eighth District, who, spurred by the holdouts of star Tigers outfielders Ty Cobb and Sam Crawford, put forth a resolution to begin an investigation into the business practices of baseball—specifically, Clause No. 10 in the standard player's contract. It read: "The player will, at the option of the club, enter into a contract for the succeeding season upon all terms and conditions of this contract, save as to clause 1 and 10, and the salary to be paid the player in the event of such renewal shall be the same as the total compensation for the player in clause 1 here of, unless it be increased or decreased by mutual agreement." According to the clause, then, by signing a contract for the upcoming season, a player was also agreeing to the same salary and terms for the following season, unless both sides agreed to alter the pay, which was handled in Clause 1.

That meant a player was not just signing with a team, but he was signing for as long as that team wanted to keep him on the roster, and that the team had no obligation to negotiate a raise. What's more, there was Clause 7: the ten-day rule. That allowed a team to cut any player, for any reason, as long as it gave the player ten days' notice. The player, however, did not have the same right to terminate his contract and go sign elsewhere. That put the legality of baseball's standard contract on very dubious ground. Teams controlled their players absolutely, with no obligation to complete a contract as long as they gave notice. But the players had no reciprocal rights.

Cobb's case, the one that inspired Gallagher's action in 1912, provides a good example of the players' plight. Cobb had won five consecutive batting titles, and in '11, he had batted .420—that's right, .420. Yet Cobb had not gotten a raise in three years. He was making $9,000 and wanted $15,000. But because of the reserve clause, his only option was to play for the Tigers again at $9,000 or find a different line of work. He refused to report to spring training, and his holdout generated enough negative publicity for the Tigers that owner Frank Navin eventually compromised and gave him a raise to $11,000. But the holdout was Cobb's only recourse. Because the contract he signed included a team reservation for the following year, the only tool at a player's disposal was to conduct a PR battle against the team. "The public and players are victims of this baseball trust," Gallagher said. "The agreements between the two principal leagues and the minor leagues constitute a clear violation of the Sherman law. They are subject to the anti-trust act because they engage in interstate commerce when transporting their chattel, these purchased and enslaved players, from one state to another for the purpose of giving their exhibitions. Players also are held in reserve to their employers from year to year. Each club sends to the national commission each year a list of reserved players and no other club is allowed to seek to sign such reserved players."[8]

This was the age of trust-busting and it is the reason that baseball was nervous about the standing of the reserve clause. In 1904, the Supreme Court had upheld the government's argument that Northern Securities railroad holdings company violated Sherman Anti-Trust law, and in 1907, federal judge Kenesaw Mountain Landis fined Standard Oil a massive $29 million, a penalty that was overturned but eventually paved the way to the breakup of the company. While many who listened to Gallagher rail against baseball magnates thought he was joking, he produced sheaves of telegrams from ballplayers to show he was quite serious. Ultimately, Gallagher's resolution was brushed off, his investigation never taken up.

But considering the attitude toward big business at the time, Gallagher had gotten the attention of the magnates. Before the 1913 season, the commission changed the first clause of its contract to divide a player's salary into a 75-25 proposition—75 percent of a player's pay was to go toward his salary for the year and 25 percent was pay that counted toward the option on the next year. That didn't mean a bonus, it simply meant that if a player was to get $4,000, the contract was written so that $3,000 was for '13 and $1,000 was for the team's right to keep the player in '14. The contract now held that players were being paid for the following season's option, and even if that was dubious in reality, the commission felt it strengthened their position legally and with the public. Who could complain about the reserve clause when the contract clearly stated that he was being paid for the team's right of reservation?

When the Federal League began to sign players after the 1913 season, Gilmore vowed that they would not interfere with anyone already under contract—players in the middle of two-year deals were off-limits, then, and the Feds would not attempt to get players who signed in October or November to jump their contracts. But the Players' Fraternity had advised players not to sign until January, and Federal League had made clear it would not respect the validity of the reserve clause. "We maintain that the reserve clause is illegal and not binding upon players, lacks mutuality and is against public policy," Federal League attorney E. E. Gates said.[9] Moreover, Gates stated that it would not be in the best interests of the National Commission to go to court because it would be fairly easy to show that baseball, with the reserve clause, is a trust. It should be pointed out, though, that running professional baseball without a reserve rule, conceivably allowing players to become free agents each year, was an untenable way to run the game. As much as the Federal League officials opposed the reserve clause, one of their dirty secrets was that they, too, had a reserve clause (and a ten-day clause) in their contracts. They were slightly different, allowing for a minimum of a 5 percent raise per year and requiring the team to inform players about their reservation in September, rather than February as A. L. and N. L. contracts held. But a reserve clause is a reserve clause, and the Feds had one.

When Weeghman and Tinker signed Bill Killefer on January 8, paying him a $500 advance on a three-year, $17,500 contract that would pay him nearly twice as much as he had received from the Phillies, they had no idea that Killefer would become a reserve clause poster boy. Signing Killefer was a coup. Though he wasn't much of a hitter, he was a master at handling pitchers and his defense made him the best position player in the Federal League. But Phillies president William Baker was not going to give him up. He wrote to Killefer's father, a probate judge in Michigan, explaining the reserve rule, and enjoined the senior Killefer to persuade his son that, legally, he belonged with the Phillies. Bill Killefer acquiesced, first denying he was ever with the Federal League, then re-signing with the Phillies on January 21, getting a raise in the process. Weeghman was stunned and Gilmore was incensed. The Federal League had not pursued players who had already signed, but here was a National League team pursuing a player who had signed a Fed contract. "There is a vast difference," Gilmore said, "between a contract to play for the seasons of 1914-1915-1916 at a salary agreed upon, and the unconstitutional reserve clause covering future service without a definite salary agreed upon between both parties as contained and submitted in contracts signed by players in organized baseball in 1913 and prior thereto. The reserve clause is merely an agreement that the player will agree to play with the reserving club providing he agrees on terms. Killefer, by his action in signing a Federal league contract, did eliminate the possibility of agreeing upon any terms with the reserving club."[10]

Gilmore vowed to sue. The reserve clause was heading to court, and much more than Killefer's catching ability was at stake. In the weeks that followed, several other players coaxed into signing with the Feds were reminded of the reserve rule barrier and jumped back to O. B. Others simply looked at the outcome of Killefer's case—he basically used the Federal League to secure a raise from the Phillies—and did likewise. Now, the Federal League not only had a problem signing players, it had a problem keeping them. As Stovall later said, "I can go out and get these ballplayers, but I can't chain 'em down."[11]

‡

While the reserve clause fight went to the legal system, Organized Baseball kept up its shadowy war on the Federal League, publicly assuming the stance of annoyed indifference against the upstarts while using an array of underhanded, behind-the-scenes tactics to throw off whatever progress the league might have made. A report in *The Sporting News* highlighted a top-secret meeting that was held in Pittsburgh on January 31 "the object of which was to devise ways and means to give battle to the death of the Federal League, the new organization which has sprung into the limelight, and not admittedly threatens the strongholds of organized sport." The meeting was attended by the National Commission—Ban Johnson, Garry Herrmann, and N. L. president John Tener—as well as Pittsburgh owner Barney Dreyfuss on the N. L. side and Cleveland's Charles Somers, Philadelphia's Connie Mack, and St. Louis's Robert Hedges for the American League. The purpose of the meeting was to hammer out the legal defenses and attacks that baseball would conduct, assuring that what happened in the courts was coordinated through the National Commission and not a haphazard series of suits.[12]

Meanwhile, O. B. had other tactics. They disseminated rumors that Weeghman again might abandon his Fed brethren, including a rehash of the American Association possibility and a new rumor that Weeghman had been offered a controlling interest the Cubs for $400,000. Additionally, magnates made a series of outreach efforts to Federal League men in the name of baseball peace—though, more often than not, these were attempts by O. B. to assess the health of the Federal League rather than actual peace ploys. The O. B. men still had their eyes on Tinker too. Though the matters were settled for nearly a month, Brooklyn owner Charles Ebbets still sent Tinker a copy of his contract and a letter, dated January 26, 1914, saying, "We have determined to tender to you the compensation which you demanded, Seventy five hundred ($7500.00) dollars per year with a three year contract and we herewith enclose to you revised players contracts in duplicate originals for the seasons of 1914, 1915, and 1916."[13] As *The Sporting News* reported, "Ebbets has been advised by counsel that as he exercised the option on Tinker's services at the price requested by the player, the Federals never had any legal grounds for tampering with him. The option on services could not expire until February 1, the time specified for renewal of contract. Thus, argues Charley, Joe Tinker's Federal League contract is null and void."[14]

There also was the crown jewel of the new league—Weeghman's North Side park. On January 22, after wrangling with Archambault and the Cantillons, Weeghman and Bill Walker finally signed a ninety-nine-year lease on the land, paying $16,000 annually for the first ten years, $18,000 for the next ten years, and $20,000 for the remainder of the lease, an average rent of $19,393 that would run to more than $387,000 over the life of the lease. But other obstacles popped up repeatedly. On January 28, a petition had gone around the North Side neighborhood opposing the building of a park on the seminary lot and 2,000 locals had signed. There was a strip of land, too, near the park site that measured about 16 feet by 100 feet, but mysteriously was not part of the lease. As it happened, the land was owned by a friend of Weeghman's and the friend told him that a mystery agent had offered $25,000 for it. Weeghman shrugged and told his friend that if someone was going to pay that much for the strip, he should take it. When Weeghman's friend showed up for a meeting to discuss the $25,000, the alleged buyer was not there. "I knew organized ball was behind that offer," Weeghman said.[15]

Ban Johnson, naturally, harrumphed that he knew nothing of Weeghman's strip of land but he wasn't very believable. At first dismissive of the Federal League, Johnson was increasingly belligerent toward it. "I don't think Mr. Weeghman and his associates are going to be able to build a ball park on their north side site," Johnson said. "I understand the property owners adjacent to the grounds are objecting, and yet I can't understand how a smart business man would go into a thing without having investigated those points previously. Mr. Weeghman is not experienced in baseball, and it's just as inconsistent for him to jump into the baseball business as it would be for me to start a lot of restaurants in the Loop. Getting a lease on a piece of ground isn't all there is to it. Building a ball park on that ground is quite another matter."[16]

Weeghman was learning that lesson the hard way. He had been drawn into the Federal League by Gilmore on an assurance that only $26,000 was needed to make the Chicago team viable, but on February 5, he claimed he and Walker were already into the league for $125,000 and expected that to be $250,000 by the time his park was finished. He was close. Weeghman had already committed $40,000 to players, and the final cost of the park would be $219,000, as was reported in April. There was some good news for Weeghman in mid-February, though, when Gilmore persuaded millionaire businessman Robert Ward—owner of the Tip-Top bread company—to come into the Fed fold, taking over the very weak Toronto team and moving it to Brooklyn. Weeghman and the St. Louis owners had money themselves, but Ward was even wealthier, and just as enthusiastic about the game of baseball, if somewhat ignorant of the business end of it. Still, money was the biggest concern for the Federal League and with Ward's wealth added to the pool, no longer could the removal of Weeghman by the forces of O. B. guarantee the failure of the new league. But a new front for baseball's mounting war, this time within Organized Baseball itself and again within the Chicago city limits, was about to open.

# CHAPTER EIGHT

# Murphy and Evers

It was late January of 1914 and Frank Chance was in Los Angeles, speaking with a reporter. The entire baseball world was closely watching the spark started by the guerilla Federal League and the efforts of baseball's behemoths to stamp it out. When Chance came to the subject, he observed, "Charles W. Murphy is responsible for the organization of the Federal League. The president of the National League Club is to blame for the large number of major league baseball players who are jumping to the outlaw organization. Charley Murphy has done more to hurt baseball than any other man who has been in the game in all the years the sport has flourished. He is going to continue to be an objectionable figure just as long as he is allowed to have any connection with any club."[1]

On Sunday, February 8, Murphy and Hank O'Day boarded a train in Chicago bound for New York, where the National League was to hold its meetings. O'Day was an N. L. umpire and was on the rules committee, so he had to get to New York in time for the committee's meeting on Monday morning. He was also a good friend of Murphy's—he lived on Chicago's West Side and, famously, had made the ruling in the pivotal 1908 Cubs-Giants game in which John Evers recorded an out because New York's Fred Merkle had not touched second base as required, a call that helped propel the Cubs to a pennant and a World Championship. It was bound to be a big week for baseball, because, in an unprecedented show of unity, the American League meeting would be held later in the week and they would overlap so that the two circuits could hold a joint confab for the first time in their history.

The joint meeting was called with the Federal League in mind. "This is taken to indicate either that organized ball is somewhat worried over the activities of the enemy or has arrived at some definite plan of campaign to where it is necessary to wean over a few magnates whose personal interests stand in the common good of all," a *Sporting News* writer noted. The magnate whose interest stood in the way of the common good was, of course, Murphy, as Organized Baseball was still pushing a plan which would give Weeghman a team in the American Association to put into his North Side park. One A. L. magnate told the writer, "Murphy wouldn't stand for the deal because since his trouble with Chance, he is very, very unpopular. He was afraid that on the days when his Cubs conflicted with the Association team, his attendance would be greatly affected. … But Murphy will be brought to his knees pretty quickly, I can tell you, and by his own colleagues."[2]

Little did those colleagues know that, while sitting with O'Day en route to New York, Murphy was providing an unexpected trove of ammunition to be used against him. About a week earlier, Murphy had received a letter from Evers, the manager he had picked to replace Chance. Evers wanted his contract redone to eliminate the ten-day clause, or else he vowed not to manage in 1914. At the time, this was a common move—the threat of a holdout was the first weapon a player had when seeking a change of contract. The second was an actual holdout. As with Ty Cobb in 1912, those were the only two arrows in Evers's quiver. But when Murphy saw the letter, he decided to wash his hands of Evers altogether. Murphy claimed that the letter was proof that Evers was quitting, though any magnate who had done the holdout dance would have known that Evers was merely starting a negotiation. Evers later said that Murphy's real problem with him dated back to the previous fall's City Series, which the Cubs lost to the White Sox. On the day before the final game, Evers dropped by the office of *Chicago Tribune* sports editor Harvey Woodruff, and discovered

White Sox manager (and former anarchist) Jimmy Callahan there. The two arranged to have a late dinner with their wives, and when Murphy got word that Evers was dallying with the enemy manager, he was incensed. In Evers's mind, Murphy had been looking for a reason to overthrow him since October, and the ten-day clause request was simply an excuse to make it happen.[3]

Murphy had sounded out O'Day about the possibility of managing the Cubs, and on the ride to New York, they firmed up the proposal. It wasn't unheard of for umpires to pass through to the ranks of manager at that time—O'Day, for example, had already done so, serving as the predecessor to Joe Tinker in Cincinnati in 1912. Murphy had it in his mind to trade Evers and rid himself of that last vestige of the Cubs' glory days, with Chance off to manage the Yankees, and Tinker and Brown in the Federal League. Murphy would then have a younger team and a banal manager who would not challenge Murphy's authority.

At 3:30 on Tuesday afternoon, before Murphy had let out the news about the managerial change, he walked through the lobby of the N. L. meeting headquarters, the Waldorf-Astoria, accompanied by O'Day. One reporter cracked to him that he should be careful, lest he get in trouble for tampering with an umpire. "I wasn't tampering with an umpire," Murphy said. "I was talking with the new manager of the Chicago Club. Ha! Ha!"[4] The assertion was so preposterous that none of the gathered newsmen considered that Murphy was giving them a scoop. Instead, it was taken as a joke—no one would make a managerial change just weeks before the start of spring training, and no one would let loose of a star like Evers in favor of O'Day, especially not in the midst of a war with a surprisingly resilient upstart league.

Even when the news broke that Murphy had, indeed, dumped Evers and hired O'Day, the reporters "refused to believe that it was not even then a joke. When they finally did realize that the story was true they were dumbfounded." Evers himself had not been informed. Murphy claimed that Evers had resigned, and when Braves owner Jim Gaffney asked Evers whether he planned to stay in Chicago under O'Day, Evers had no idea what he meant. Gaffney explained that he had resigned as manager of the

Cubs. "I told Mr. Gaffney that if it was true that O'Day had been appointed in my place, I hadn't resigned, I had been fired," Evers said.[5]

The A. L. and N. L. were supposed to meet in a joint session to deal with the Federal League crisis. But Murphy, as he had done so often, handed them an entirely different crisis.

‡

For Ban Johnson, the Evers case was just about all he could stand from Murphy. The two had a long-standing dislike for each other, and Evers himself thought he knew why. Both Johnson and Murphy had come up in Cincinnati as newspaper reporters, but now, years later, they were both among the elite of baseball. Except Johnson was a little more elite, as the ruler of the American League. "Both had gone into baseball and made a fortune," Evers explained to *Baseball Magazine*. "But Johnson had won more than a fortune: He had won power in baseball councils which has never been rivaled. And Murphy, with all his financial success, was but an individual magnate in a rival league. It was a plain case of one doing a little better than the other and the other resented it. Hence, more or less mutual recriminations and ill-will."

Johnson had also long lamented the inability of the National League to put aside its internal squabbles and behave as a unit. Of course, it was those internal squabbles that allowed Johnson's American League to come into major league prominence more than a decade earlier, but Johnson was forever annoyed that in the years since the end of the A. L.-N. L. war, the Nationals had not found a strong commissioner who could keep his teams in line the way Johnson did in the American League. He had some hope for the current commissioner, John Tener, the former governor of Pennsylvania who replaced the overmatched Tom Lynch, who was a mere umpire and lacked the gravitas for the job. While Johnson's ability to move his league as a unit is often credited to the loyalty A. L. owners felt toward him after he'd led them to major league prominence and to the force of Johnson's personality, Tener would later point out that Johnson had a distinct advantage in his league that wasn't afforded to National League presidents—he (or, rather, the league) owned a majority stake in every team. "The National League is a little differently situated in that respect than the American, where the head of the league holds 51 percent of each club's stock in escrow," Tener said. "With us each club is a private corporation."[6]

Even in his position with the National Commission, Johnson had limited power over Murphy, but the reaction to the deposing of Evers was so strong, Johnson had no choice but to force the N. L. to do something. It wasn't just that Murphy had behaved badly, it was that he had chosen the worst possible moment to pull the Evers stunt—in the midst of a war against a third league that was gaining steam, a war that had Murphy's ill treatment of Frank Chance at its roots. Evers rubbed salt in the wound by saying to reporters, "Take it from me that if Mr. Weeghman had tried to sign the Cubs every one of them would have deserted Murphy. I know what I am talking about. I stuck to Murphy through thick and thin. I never showed any disrespect for him. I was loyal and painstaking. But after the deal Chance got I might have known I would get the same."[7]

The backlash was strongest in Chicago. Evers, though always a hothead, was popular among fans and the press. Northwestern League president Fielder Jones, who had managed the White Sox to the 1906 World Series championship and maintained a lofty reputation in Chicago, was quoted saying, "It was worse than the Chance release for the reason that it came at a point when baseball is at an acute stage and the Federals appear to be gaining ground all the time. Let there be a few more affairs of this kind in the National League and it will just about be through as a drawing power among the baseball fans, who are getting sicker all the time of the outbursts of the older organization."[8]

This was also a golden opportunity for the Federal League. Evers viewed Murphy's action as an outright release and claimed he was a free agent— he would not go along with Murphy's scheme to trade him to the Braves. He was a perfect fit for the Federal League, a disgruntled Cubs star who wanted to hit back at O. B. Weeghman, Gilmore, and Walker happened to be already in New York to talk with new Brooklyn owner-to-be Robert Ward, but when Evers was let go, they pounced. Weeghman wired Tinker on Tuesday night, telling him to be ready for a trip to New York. When

Tinker walked into the Old Colony office at 9:30 on Wednesday morning, he found the phone already ringing. It was Weeghman. Evers had met with Gilmore, but they knew they needed Evers's old teammate (and one-time nemesis) to close the deal. Tinker and Charley Williams got on the next train and reached New York in the afternoon.

Johnson, meanwhile, watched in horror as it appeared the National League would take the crisis Murphy incited and bungle it further by losing Evers to the Federal League. As the N. L. saw things, Murphy had taken one of the league's umpires and, according to league rules, was required to give compensation. The compensation, the league declared, would be Evers—he and his contract would essentially become N. L. property. "It was decided that if lots were drawn for the player, he might go to a club that really was not in need of his services," the *Chicago Daily News* reported. It is not difficult to imagine steam shooting from Johnson's ears on hearing that the N. L. was considering drawing lots to determine Evers's destination.

With so much at stake, Johnson stepped up his efforts to strong-arm the Nationals. In the wake of Murphy's defiance over moving the American Association team to the North Side and shutting down the Federal League altogether, Johnson had pushed N. L. magnates to grant Tener the kind of unilateral power that Johnson had been granted. That was no easy task, because N. L. owners felt no special reverence for Tener and were not partially owned by the league. On the Saturday before the Evers blowup occurred, *Daily News* writer Oscar Reichow commented that the rift between Johnson and the National League—Murphy especially—over the North Side of Chicago threatened to split baseball apart altogether. The spat, Reichow said, was "more serious than many people think. If the American League votes for it and the other does not, it is not unreasonable to believe that the two major organizations will separate and renew the war they engaged in more than ten years ago."[9]

Johnson didn't do much to quell that notion. He wanted Murphy out. He had met with some N. L. owners in New York and later said he "gave them an ultimatum that unless the National League can give the same absolute authority to its president, Gov. Tener, or to Tener and a couple other men in the league, the American League no longer can dovetail its business with the National and work in harmony with it. We have had a complete understanding and most of the National League magnates are upset over the doings of Murphy and eager to get rid of him. … This upheaval of Murphy's upon his return to Chicago is the last straw and should only help to adjust the conditions we are after. I can say now that we will go to any extreme to eliminate Murphy from Organized Baseball."[10]

The National League did settle the Evers deal, pulling him from Tinker and Weeghman, and arranging for him to get an unheard of $25,000 bonus and a $10,000 per year salary to join owner Jim Gaffney, who badly wanted him for the Braves. Murphy wanted two players in exchange for Evers, but one of the stipulations Evers had before he would accept the arrangement was that Murphy get no benefit from the deal, including players. It was just the final insult in a week in which Murphy was pilloried by the press and in which his fellow magnates were moved to call for his ouster from the seat as the head of the Cubs—none having done so quite as loudly as his archenemy, Ban Johnson.

‡

Murphy's mood was probably not boosted by the fact that on his way home from New York that Friday, his train, the Wolverine Express, was delayed. For three hours. When he got to his office at the Corn Exchange building, it was after 5 PM. O'Day was there, as well as Murphy's secretaries and a handful of reporters who had been waiting on him. Murphy said nothing as he removed his hat and coat—it was just sixteen degrees outside—and calmly turned to face the reporters. "I'm going to give you an interview," he said. "Now, listen, and get these exact words. I'm going after that big _____ _____, Ban Johnson, tomorrow morning for conspiracy and slander. Be sure to get those words—big _____ _____. There's a suit of clothes in it for every fellow who gets them in his paper." (*Tribune* writer Sam Weller, obviously, did not get them into his, and Murphy's exact insult is lost to history.)

Murphy stepped into his office for a moment, spoke with O'Day, and emerged again. "Now I'm ready to answer any and all questions," he said, according to Weller. "The Cubs are not going to be sold. I'm in baseball to stay and no _____ _____ _____ is going to force me out of the game. I am not going to stand for Ban Johnson's methods any longer, either. I'm going to sue him for conspiracy and slander right away. I'm going to find out if there's any justice in the courts. He's a big, arrogant, fourflushing, double crossing _____ _____. Ban Johnson is a bad man to have in baseball and I am going to try to put him in a penitentiary. I don't care if it costs me $100,000 or $200,000, and I say this while I am perfectly calm and dispassionate."[11]

Murphy's diatribe continued. He claimed Johnson was helping the Federal League, and that it was Murphy, not Johnson, who was protecting Comiskey (presumably by blocking the A.A. team on the North Side). He claimed that he had no choice but to hire O'Day because Evers had insisted on striking the ten-day clause from his contract. It might have been easy to sympathize with an owner who didn't have Murphy's reputation. He was right that Johnson was out to get him and even Johnson had conceded that Murphy was within his rights to let Evers go—but Murphy's recent history had pretty much exhausted any goodwill toward him among magnates, fans, or the press. Additionally, it was Murphy's own action that gave the National Commission a cudgel to wield against him. In the wake of the Fogel affair, the constitutions of the two leagues had been changed to allow the National Commission to remove owners who publicly questioned the integrity of the game. Murphy was clearly doing just that.

On Friday, February 20, Murphy was called to Cincinnati to join the National League meeting being held there. Murphy knew that he would be walking into an execution. He came down with a sudden case of lumbago and failed to show up on the twentieth in an effort to place one last thorn in the sides of his O. B. superiors. "I have it from one of his best friends— yes, Murphy has some friends—that he stayed in Chicago with the idea of embarrassing Governor Tener and the other club owners if it was decided to put him on trial," a source who was at the Cincinnati meeting said, according to *Sporting Life*.[12]

In his place, Tener, met with the Cubs' two other stockholders. Harry Ackerland, who had purchased Chance's ten shares when he left the team, was present but the main cog was Charles Taft, who still owned 37 percent of the Cubs and who was in with Murphy on the lease of the West Side Grounds as well as other properties around Chicago. After a four-hour meeting, Murphy finally agreed to accept a buyout offer by which Taft would pay him $9,500 per share, for a total payment of $503,500. And that was it. According to Tener, "Mr. Murphy has resigned as president of the Chicago club and will have no further connection with its affairs." Ban Johnson was asked for his thoughts, and said, "There's no use in saying anything of Charley Murphy now; he's out of baseball."[13]

Taft, a Cincinnatian who had no interest in running a baseball club and was strongly tied to Murphy in other business ventures, was now the team's owner. "This action to wipe Murphy off the baseball map may not have been as positive as all might desire," a *Sporting News* column noted, "since Murphy and Taft have been so friendly as to excite a suspicion that there may be an understanding between them."

In the end, Charley Weeghman and the Federal League gained nothing tangible out of the Murphy-Evers episode. But two months removed from the opening of the North Side ballpark, Murphy's dismissal of Evers, and the perception that Murphy was still entangled in Cubs business, gave even the most die-hard Cubs fans yet another reason to switch loyalties to the up-and-comers. As Tinker said of Murphy, "[He] is the best little press agent the Federal league could get. We are much obliged to him."[14]

# CHAPTER NINE

# Groundbreaking on the North Side

It was just about thirty degrees near Chicago's Lakefront on March 4, but still, even before 10 AM, a crowd of thousands had gathered near Clark and Addison, awaiting the big event of the late winter—the groundbreaking that would kick off the building of the Federal League ballpark, one that team owner Charley Weeghman promised would rival any grounds in baseball. While a crowd of more than 100 workers and civil engineers from the Blome-Sinek construction company leaned on their shovels, waiting, somewhat annoyed, a movie crew recorded the event, and the baseball-loving locals got a thrill when manager Joe Tinker appeared from across the lot, along with Bill Brennan, the Federal League's chief of umpires. Weeghman, though, looked impatiently at his watch. Mayor Carter Harrison, Jr. was expected to turn the first bit of ground but he had not shown, and soon after ten, Weeghman was off in search of a phone. Meanwhile, a brass band blurted out "The Gang's All Here" and other tunes. Weeghman's partner, William Walker, was there with his five-year-old son, nicknamed Buster, while Federal League president James Gilmore and league lawyer E. E. Gates stood with Chicago Federals secretary Charley Williams.

Things did not go quite as expected, and considering the lurching start that the Federal League itself was off to, maybe that was fitting. By 10:30, Weeghman had given up on Harrison—he was told that the mayor had already left his home but it was also known that Harrison was recovering from an illness. In his place, the city's building commissioner, the architect Henry Ericsson, took hold of the spade. Ericsson was no politician and apparently lacked the gift of gab. Not to mention the gift of shoveling. As John O. Seys (who would later work as the Cubs' team secretary at the very park that was being built) wrote in the *Daily News*, "Ericsson was there to take the mayor's place, without making any speech or saying a word of cheer to the magnates, he dug deep into the earth and threw it to the winds. He had gathered up a shovel full of ashes and the dust created a cloud that ruined the pictures of the various photographers when they sprung the shutters. It was then necessary to do it all over again."[1]

More successful on the second effort, Ericsson held up the shovel for Buster Walker, who was armed with a bottle of champagne and needed multiple tries to finally get the bottle to break, pouring the contents into the hole left by Ericsson's spade. Weeghman, wearing expensive kid gloves, was induced by his friends to take up a shovel and dig some ground for the cameras—even after the photographers stopped clicking pictures, his friends, pulling a prank on him, got Charley to keep going, unaware that he was no longer being photographed. He "dug lustily into the frosty ground as if he would build the entire stand himself."[2] As soon as the revelers wrapped up their little shindig, the hundreds of members of the construction crews cleared them out and began work on turning over the ground in earnest.

They would have to move quickly. The contractor, John P. Agnew, had agreed to execute architect Zachary Taylor Davis's plans by a deadline of April 25, leaving just fifty-two days to complete an entire stadium that would be able to seat 20,000 fans. About ten days earlier, Agnew had secured the work permit for the new park and even then he had said that "time is too short to permit concrete construction of all the buildings which will be necessary for grand stands, bleachers and other buildings in the park."[3] Davis planned a curved stand that would measure 800 feet in length, and measure 100 feet wide and 56 feet high. The crew had ordered 160,000 bricks for the project, and would require 42,500 cubic feet of concrete, 1,900 cubic feet of hollow tile, and 1,700 yards of plaster.[4]

To that point, the only work that had been done at the site had been the razing of some of the seminary buildings that were on the property. It would take about two weeks before the ground was even ready to begin erecting the steel needed for the grandstand and the brick needed for the outfield bleachers. The foundations would be laid by March 23, and by March 29, the skeletal framework of the grandstand roof was built and part of the roof itself was complete. What would later be the outfield was littered with piles of debris and stacks of lumber, but the structure that has for so long been known as Wrigley Field was taking shape—a shape that would be surprisingly familiar to North Side fans of more modern vintage. In all, the cost of the new park, Weeghman said, had risen to about $250,000, twice as much as he had originally expected when he leased the grounds from Archambault and the Cantillons.[5] But laying out that extra money probably seemed worth it to Weeghman as he was roundly feted on this day.

A new ballpark would, in the eyes of most area residents, put the North Side on par with the West Side and the South Side at long last. Over the history of Chicago's stunning boom, from the Great Fire of 1871 to the early years of the twentieth century, the North Side lacked the character and identity of the South Side, site of the 1893 World's Columbian Exposition, the landmark fair that helped elevate Chicago to a world-class city. The city's elite had built their mansions near Lake Michigan, blocks away from renowned vice districts and clusters of working-class housing. The South Side was not separated from the Loop by the Chicago River the way the North Side was, so the city's expansion in that direction only made sense.

But as bridge-building and transportation advances were made, the West and North sides began attracting residents. The West Side was especially attractive for the waves of immigrants who were arriving from Southern and Eastern Europe, because it had plenty of cheap rental property available— one study conducted around the time found that half of West Side residents had been in their current residences two years or fewer and that a quarter had been there six months. Only 9 percent owned their homes. Overcrowding affected at least 300,000 Chicagoans, and "the worst areas were on the West Side, where congestion had been an enduring problem but where the spread of commercial and industrial areas into formerly residential neighborhoods had magnified the consequences."[6]

The North Side, though, represented a step up. As the South Side became increasingly intolerable, the city's elite—starting with the move of the renowned Potter family to Lake Shore Drive—began to pack up their mansions and move to what became known as the Gold Coast. Many of those old South Side mansions are still there, a hollow remnant of the area's former status as the capital of Chicago society. The Near North Side mansions on or near Lake Shore Drive are still there, too, and remain the homes of many of the city's elite. The move of Chicago's best-known families to the North Side granted the area as a whole some periphery prominence. The building of a railway line, the expansion of Chicago's streetcar system, and the spread of the elevated train increased accessibility to the Loop. The results were noticeable and "nowhere was the impact of the new transportation more quickly felt than the North Side. Because of poor facilities, its connections with the downtown had never been as good as those of other parts of the city. With the opening of the Northwestern Elevated Railroad in 1900, this handicap disappeared. The original terminus was at Wilson Avenue where the Uptown shopping center and hotel complex grew up. In 1907 a new branch, the Ravenswood line, made possible the development of Albany Park, another important commercial concentration."[7]

Albany Park was only about four miles northwest of the site of the new park. The Wilson terminus of the Northwestern El was a little more than a mile north. The Loop lay just a little more than four miles to the south. Even then, on the cold March morning that saw the first work on the park being done, there was a sense that Weeghman wasn't just building a ballpark, he was creating a centerpiece for the North Side. "Weeghman was elated over the reception given unto him on the occasion," one report stated. "Many north side residents stepped over the police line in order to get a chance to shake hands with the young man who had the nerve to buck organized baseball and give the north siders a baseball park which, he says, will outshine any in either the National or American league with the exception of the one at the Polo Grounds in New York."[8]

‡

There was, strangely enough, another longtime baseball man present at the North Side groundbreaking—that was Charles W. Murphy, only ten days removed from his departure as boss of the Cubs. There was some irony and coincidence connected with Murphy's showing at the groundbreaking. It was the very existence of that stadium which paved the way for Murphy's exit on the West Side, and yet, it was Murphy's existence on the West Side to begin with that inspired and gave Weeghman enough hope to build that stadium. Murphy, in a way, both started the Federal League and was undone by it. Murphy would spend a lot of time around the Federal Leaguers— whom he had labeled a "joke"—in the early part of the season, feeling out the strength of the league and whether he should get involved with the Chicago club as an investor. He did not.

Later, when Weeghman met Brooklyn's Charles Ebbets—whose back-and-forth with Tinker inspired Tinker to jump to the new league—Ebbets told him, "They blamed me for causing the Federal League." To which Weeghman replied, "It was an injustice, for it was Charles Webb Murphy who really caused the Feds. He gave Mordecai Brown such a raw deal that I agreed to subscribe $5,000 to put a new Chicago club in the field and, by the way, I've been putting up money ever since."[9]

But here in early 1914, though he officially had sold out his stock in the Cubs to Taft under pressure from the league, Murphy was not exactly through. Once it became known that Taft would take over Murphy's stock, offers for the team came pouring into Taft's office, at least twenty from around the country—among the inquirers were Broadway impresario George M. Cohan and famed New York hat maker Truly Warner. The most fervent and serious bids, though, were the ones coming from Chicago itself. One of the first bids was from a syndicate headed by Charles McCulloch, who ran the Parmalee Transfer Company, and "Commodore Jim" Pugh, a developer who would be instrumental in the building of Chicago's Navy Pier (which was nearly called Pugh Pier). Also on board was William Hale Thompson, known as "Big Bill," a politician and businessman who had been elected alderman of the city's second ward. As he was bidding for the Cubs, Thompson was a little more than a year removed from being elected mayor, a post he would hold for twelve years in total. If Thompson had gained control of the Cubs, he might have gotten out of politics, and, perhaps, Chicago would have been spared the tenure of a mayor who, as the *Tribune* would put it in 1931, "has given the city an international reputation for moronic buffoonery, barbaric crime, triumphant hoodlumism, unchecked graft, and a dejected citizenship. ... He made Chicago a byword for the collapse of American civilization."

There were also a pair of West Side syndicates hoping to gain consideration. One, headed by a former minor league ballplayer named Frank McNichols was said to be willing to pay $1 million for all of Taft's ninety shares of stock. Another, under the guidance of John P. Harding, a hotel owner and friend of Charles Comiskey, hinted that they'd offer $775,000 for a controlling 51 percent interest in the team. Taft, of course, knew very little about Chicago and offered only tepid responses, if any response at all. "There are rumors of new offers," *The Sporting News* pointed out, "and all a man has to do to get his name in the paper is to announce that he has money with which to buy out Mr. Taft."[10]

That was borne out on February 25, when Taft had agreed to meet with attorney Louis Behan to discuss the sale of the club. Behan had, very mysteriously, announced that he was representing four men who were willing to pay $750,000 for a 51 percent interest, but refused to give out their names. He said he was taking a certified check for $100,000 to Cincinnati and would hand it over to Taft as a down payment if a deal could be reached.[11] There was much speculation as to the identity of Behan's backers—a rumor had it that one was millionaire restaurant owner John R. Thompson, Weeghman's biggest Loop lunchroom rival[12]—but Behan remained tight-lipped. When it became known that Behan was meeting with Taft, the other bidders said that they, too, would be heading to Cincinnati, and a *Tribune* headline claimed, "Chicagoans Rush to Redville with Bids to Buy Cubs."

Except there was no rush at all. On the morning of the twenty-fifth, Taft went into his office and met with only one bidder, Behan. For all the talk of hundreds of thousands of dollars being forwarded for the Cubs, there was obvious reluctance to actually pay that much money, and there was, similarly, some reluctance on the part of Taft to sell—McCulloch later said that Taft never responded to any of his seven telegrams. Even Behan, when he got into the meeting with Taft, proved to be a disappointment. He said the men he represented wanted certain conditions met before they would complete the deal, including the return of John Evers to the Cubs or compensation from the Boston Braves, the removal of Taft from interests in any other teams (his wife and Murphy were still leaseholders for the Phillies' park) and, most stunningly for Taft, either a settlement with the Federal League or the placing of current standard National League contract in front of a "court of last resort" to determine its legality.[13] The meeting lasted five minutes before Taft showed Behan the door.

Behan was asking much more than Taft could or cared to deliver and, later, some—including Charles Murphy—speculated whether he secretly was making his offer on behalf of the Federal League. Taft, who was sixty-six and had never gotten involved with the operation of the Cubs, seemed somewhat bewildered by the entire episode. After the brief meeting, and with none of the other prospective buyers having actually shown up, he invited the gathered Chicago reporters into his office. "The impression one got from the interview was that he wasn't one whit enthusiastic about the game, but that he had a broken toy on his hands and wished to good-ness that someone would come along could take it and fix it up."[14] But Taft's naïveté was probably somewhat forced. He was making some unre-alistic demands of his own, and it was later revealed that Taft had asked for nearly $1 million for the purchase of the Cubs.[15]

At the same time, questions about Murphy's ongoing relationship with Taft resurfaced. Seeing as the Cubs had not been sold by Taft, and as Murphy had not yet been paid for his share of stock, he kept showing up to his office in the Corn Exchange building. It was fair to wonder whether Murphy had really sold the stock at all, and a March story in *The Sporting News* said Murphy "still figures in the public prints in connection with the game. He still occupies his chair in the office of the Chicago National League Club and says he means to keep it until the club stockholders, of whom he is not one, get together in meeting and elect a new president."[16]

In the background, too, were simmering rumors about the Cubs being used as a bargaining chip to end the war with the Federal League. As a story in the *New York Times* noted, the Cubs were on the market and the Cardinals probably could be had, too—Helene Britton was still the primary owner and she allowed her husband, Schuyler, to run the team, but they were clearly out of their depth as magnates. Because Weeghman and St. Louis Federal owner Otto Stifel were two of the Feds' biggest backers, the National League could resolve the entire Federal League crisis. "Weeghman has an ambition to buy the controlling interest in the Cubs from Charles P. Taft, while Stifel would like to buy the St. Louis Cardinals. Weeghman is said to be willing to pay what Taft gave Murphy, but no more."[17]

That proposition did not get much traction, though—at least, not yet. As things stood, the last and best chance to get the Cubs into the hands of a new, Chicago-based owner, appeared to be John T. Connery, who had just about every characteristic imaginable for a new owner of the Cubs. He was wealthy and connected politically, having had a long and successful career in business in Chicago. He was the president of the Miami Coal Company, with one brother who was city clerk and another who was county recorder. He was a good friend of both Ban Johnson and Charles Comiskey and knew National League president John Tener. On March 7, a Saturday, the sale of the Cubs to Connery was so close that the *Chicago Daily News* actually reported it to be completed, citing a "man high in baseball ranks," under the headline "C. P. Taft Accepts Terms for his Stock."

Connery and Taft could not come to a deal. Taft, not wanting to get mired in the muck of haggling over a sale, had given Tener a price and charged him with doing what was necessary to find an acceptable buyer. Over the course of two days, with a heap of other issues also on the docket, the National League magnates sought to work out a deal for the Cubs—Tener even held a secret meeting with Ban Johnson who was acting on behalf of Connery. Taft's price was high, and he was not budging from it. Connery would later say that Taft had asked for $875,000, a fortune for a team that Taft had secured with an original investment of $105,000 less than a decade earlier. The highest offer Connery would make was $770,000, a full $100,000 below Taft's price.[18] Connery could not get Taft to acknowledge a basic fact: the Cubs' park was in utter disrepair. In addition to the $750,000 to buy the team, Connery would have to put up "an additional outlay of approximately $500,000 for a new grandstand and field in Chicago, which we have promised the Cubs fans."[19]

On March 18, Taft made a trip to Chicago, where he had a morning conference with Charles Murphy. Taft emerged from that conference and announced that he would no longer look to sell the Cubs for at least a year and that he would run the team himself. Further, he was appointing thirty-eight-year-old Charles Thomas—Murphy's secretary, who had ranked as only an associate secretary before Charley Williams's departure the previous month—as Murphy's replacement as Cubs president. This drew almost immediate fire from Tener and other National League owners. One article connected the very obvious dots: "Messrs. Taft and Murphy are connected in various business enterprises, it is said, and as Murphy is the experienced baseball man, it is a cinch that directly or indirectly, he will control the club as long as Taft owns it. ... It is ridiculous not to suppose that he was picked for his present position by Murphy rather than Taft."[20]

In a very Murphyian twist, Taft had something to add after his meeting: "One other bit of news was furnished the assembled scribes. There will be no new grand stand in the Cub ball park this year. Mr. Taft will make a few improvements and may erect a stand next year."[21]

And so the Cubs would continue playing their home schedule in their ramshackle park, with Murphy's puppet technically running the team. Connery did not get the chance to buy the Cubs and build a new $500,000 stadium. If he had, the Cubs might still be playing at Connery Field—on the West Side—to this day.

# CHAPTER TEN

# The Battle of the Dock

For the Federal League, there was no time to spend congratulating themselves on the groundbreaking at the North Side park. As soon as the construction crews began their work at Clark and Addison, Weeghman, James Gilmore, and attorney E. E. Gates scurried back to the Loop, where Gates and Gilmore would catch a train to New York—Weeghman was originally slated to go, too, but pulled out, with other business to attend. Gates and Gilmore probably should not have been surprised to find Ban Johnson on their train too. After all, baseball was getting ready for a day in Gotham on which, the *New York Times* would say, "More events of history-making significance in the realm of baseball [would] happen than in any day since the game became endeared to the hearts of the American sport-loving public."[1]

Back on October 18, Giants manager John McGraw and White Sox owner Charles Comiskey gathered together a group of players—including stars like Tris Speaker, Sam Crawford, Buck Weaver, Germany Schaefer, Hooks Wiltse, Fred Merkle, Hans Lobert, Lee Magee, and Larry Doyle—in Cincinnati, where they began one of the most remarkable and ambitious projects baseball has ever undertaken. They went on a tour of the world, first through twenty-seven cities in the U.S. and Canada, then to Asia and

Australia, around through Africa, and finally to Europe, staging baseball games for the mass of humanity on the planet that was utterly unfamiliar with the American pastime. Throughout the trip, dispatches from abroad appeared in the sports pages, titillating fans with stories of perilous seas in Japan, games of catch and photos taken at the Sphinx, a meeting with the Pope, and news that the eleven-inning game the teams played in London had so thrilled King George V, he ripped his hat off and shook it in the air when the winning hit was made.

On Friday, March 6, five months after their departure, the tourists were slated to come home, and long before their boat was to dock, plans had been underway to put on an audacious welcoming gala that would attract hundreds of fans, magnates, and officials seeking to celebrate McGraw, Comiskey, the players, and the game in general. Moving among the revelers though, would be a small contingent of Federal League representatives who were heading to town with business more than pleasure in mind. The world tourists featured eight players of special interest—players who had not yet signed contracts for 1914, players who were bound to their teams only by the reserve clause and thus were, in the eyes of the Federal League, free agents. The eight targets: Speaker, Crawford, Magee, Ivey Wingo, Dick Egan, Lefty Leverenz, Mike Doolin, and Steve Evans. The Federal League had, to this point, been frustrated in its attempt to land star-quality players and had watched Killefer and others sign on only to jump back to their original teams. With teams readying for spring training, these players represented the Feds' final chance to land big names.

Even before the players' ship was to dock, the battle between the Federal League and Organized Baseball had made its way on deck, through telegrams and personal entreaties. Jimmy Callahan, the one-time battler of the reserve clause now in the good graces of O. B. as the White Sox manager, had been trying to persuade American League stars like Crawford and Speaker to sign their contracts on the boat and have them sent back to the team. McGraw, meanwhile, had been telling the National Leaguers that if they did not jump to the Federals, he would work out trades for them to get them to play for him in New York—a dream for many players. The Federals had their allies at work too. One of Speaker's good friends, his ex-manager in Boston, Jake

Stahl, had nearly joined up with the new league weeks earlier but pulled out. Still, he wired Speaker repeatedly, telling him not to sign until he saw what the Federal League would offer. Similarly, Gilmore sent messages to the available tourists throughout the winter, advising them hold off on signing until they had spoken to him.

"They will be crazy if they don't accept what we are willing to give them," Gilmore said. "If we do not get every one of the eight unsigned players, it will be because some of them don't know what money is. [They] can have contracts that will give them an idea of how far the Federal League has progressed since they left these shores."[2]

Two days before the scheduled arrival, with New York still digging itself out of one of the worst blizzards in the city's history, which had dumped ten inches of snow and brought eighty-mile-per-hour gusts earlier, the Federal League outlined its plans. Since the league was little-known when the tourists departed, the players would have no idea who Jim Gilmore or other league officials were. Instead, the league would send more familiar faces—managers Mordecai Brown, Larry Schlafly, and George Stovall, to be joined by Baltimore's Otto Knabe—onto the boat to greet the players, make offers and set up meetings. Presumably, players would be more likely to trust former teammates and other fellow players than bespectacled businessmen. All the while, though, "the league officials will simply stand back with the bank rolls ready to live up to the promises of their managers."[3]

It was no secret to the heads of Organized Baseball that the Feds were gunning for the unsigned tourists—that could have been gathered on the boat by McGraw and Callahan, who surely heard rumors about the Feds' growing influence from the players. But what was odd was that the Federal Leaguers let the media know their plans in such detail, exactly which players they would push to sign, and where all the representatives of the league would likely prefer to be stationed. That gave O. B. officials plenty of time to orchestrate its defense. Every owner of a team with an unsigned player on hand was ordered to New York. When the tourists' ship—the Cunard liner Lusitania, which would gain notoriety the following year when it was sunk by a German U-boat and helped push the U.S. into World War I—came into New York harbor, Germany Schaefer pointed to the Statue of Liberty and joked, "That, ladies and gentlemen, is Jim Gilmore, the man who is fighting to free the baseball players with a smile and a bankroll as his only weapons."[4]

There was some good luck on the side of the O. B. magnates. The only way to get on board the Lusitania between the time it hit quarantine and the time it made it to Pier 56 at 14th Street was to gain access to one of the revenue boats from the Port of New York that were to meet the ship. That required special passes from Dudley Field Malone, the Port collector. Malone was a special case in the field of New York politics of the day in that he was notably uncorrupted by the local machine politics, but still, he was the son of a Tammany Hall operative and was himself a Tammany Hall politician. He was at the time heading a battle against the head of Tammany Hall, Charles F. Murphy (no relation to the Cubs boss), a baseball fan whose brother-in-law happened to be James Gaffney, the owner for the Boston Braves. Despite the Murphy-Malone rift, Gaffney surely would have had a history with Malone and his father, William, and could call on a favor from him.

When it came time to allot passes for the revenue boats that would meet the ship, then, O. B. had well-placed friends. The Feds did not. Ban Johnson, Frank Farrell of New York, Joe Lannin of the Red Sox, William Baker of the Phillies, and Charles Ebbets of Brooklyn would be among the first to greet the players. Malone granted them passes on the promise that no contracts would be signed on the ship, but that wouldn't stop them from making their cases, and indeed, "before the newspaper men had even begun to talk to the players, the magnates had several players cornered talking contracts with them."[5] Ebbets went so far as to hand shortstop Dick Egan a three-year contract on the boat, which Egan slipped into his pocket and carried around with him throughout the day, unsigned. Baker pulled his shortstop, Mike Doolin, out of the crowd and promised a $4,600 contract, with an extra $200 for back-money Doolin was owed, and claimed he shook hands with Doolin on it.[6]

While the O. B. owners were getting face time with players on the boat, the Federal League managers could do no better than passes to the pier, where they would be among hundreds of other baseball dignitaries and fans greeting the players. That left Knabe, Schlafly, Brown, and Stovall struggling to shout their meeting requests to the passing unsigned players, which was hardly the way the Fed plan was supposed to go. But Gilmore had been able to get telegrams to the eight players the league was after, informing them that he had a suite of rooms at the Knickerbocker Hotel on Broadway and 42$^{nd}$ Street. After leaving the boat, the players were scheduled to check into the Biltmore Hotel on Madison and 43$^{rd}$ and with the N. L. headquarters at the Waldorf-Astoria on Fifth Avenue and 34$^{th}$ Street, most of the most powerful and famous men in baseball were stationed within a triangle of luxury hotels, all within a square half-mile.

Of the eight players the Feds sought, only four showed up at the Knickerbocker to talk with Gilmore, though others weighed Federal offers. Dick Egan had his contract from Ebbets and would eventually sign it after considering a Federal League proposal. Lefty Leverenz, who had been all but committed to playing for Stovall in Kansas City for $6,000 per year, was persuaded to stay with the Browns by owner Robert Hedges, who took Leverenz to dinner with a girlfriend of the pitcher and "the host of the little dinner party made so good with the fair member of the trio that she loaned him her wiles and argued for him that Leverenz's place should be with the Browns."[7] Ivey Wingo, just twenty-three years old, was given a raise to $6,000 by the Cardinals' Schuyler Britton. Outfielder Sam Crawford quickly agreed to a contract with Detroit owner Frank Navin. The Feds were prepared to offer Crawford a huge raise and make him the manager of the Brooklyn team, but Navin boosted his salary from $5,000 to an estimated $7,500 and Crawford accepted. If Crawford had waited to see what happened with Boston's Tris Speaker, he might have at least gone to see Gilmore.

Speaker was one of the four (Evans, Doolin, and Magee were the others) who did see Gilmore. After Ty Cobb, Speaker was the greatest player in the game, only twenty-five years old and coming off a year in which he batted .363. It was widely reported that he would re-sign with Boston, but Joe Lannin was taking no chances with his star—he stuck by Speaker's side as he came off the boat, creating the strange spectacle of a baseball magnate sycophantically attending a player's needs. Lannin boasted he had once been a bellhop as he carried suitcases, arranged for Speaker's bags to get to the

Biltmore, and "volunteered service on a half-dozen errands and otherwise made Speaker's homecoming noteworthy."[8] Still, Speaker knew he had the baseball world's attention. He was going to bask in it, and maximize his contract at the same time. His insistence on giving the Federal League a hearing "may only be an indication of Tristam's keen sense of his own dramatic value, but it rather looks as if he had an even keener sense of his own advantage."[9] There would not be much dramatic value in quickly signing with the Red Sox, and there would be considerable financial advantage in listening to Gilmore.

Up in the Federal League room at the Knickerbocker, Speaker sat down with Gilmore and Gates, plus Brooklyn owners Robert and Walter Ward, and John Montgomery Ward, a star player of the late 1800s who was the Brooklyn team's business manager (and no relation to his employers). The Feds offered him a three-year deal at $15,000 per year, with an added bonus of $15,000. And it was in cash. Spread out on the table before Speaker were fifteen bills, $1,000 each, and if he signed the contract, he would walk out with them. "Tris found it a difficult matter to get out of the room," the *Boston Globe* reported.[10] He did leave, though, without signing a contract, telling Gilmore that if the Federal League would offer a five-year deal with no ten-day release clause, Speaker would consider it. Gilmore and Gates were "staggered" by the proposal. They had been prepared to add ten more $1,000 bills to the bonus, but Speaker was essentially asking for a five-year guaranteed contract, unheard of in baseball at the time.

In the late afternoon, Speaker went back to the Biltmore and met Lannin to begin contract discussions with the Red Sox. Team vice president John I. Taylor was called in. After some discussion, they broke for dinner, Lannin and Speaker continuing to work out details of his new deal. By the time dinner was over, Speaker had agreed to sign, and shortly thereafter the announcement was made—the Red Sox had given Speaker a two-year deal. Details were not released, but the *Globe* put the total deal at $40,000, while the *Times* claimed it was $37,000. "We had to give Speaker the money, but he is worth it," Lannin said.[11]

In the end, Magee turned down a three-year offer from the Federal Leaguers too, taking a one-year, $6,000 contract from Britton to stay with the Cardinals, claiming that McGraw had told him he would make a trade and Magee would be a Giant.[12] (McGraw never made the trade and probably never intended to.) The Feds were able to sign Doolin, who backed out on his handshake deal with Baker and was rumored to have had an agreement already in place with Baltimore manager and ex-Phillies teammate Otto Knabe. And after keeping Wingo and Magee, the Cardinals let speedy outfielder Steve Evans sign with the Feds with little resistance— Britton said Evans was on the verge of being sent to the Pacific Coast League, but that was a dubious claim given that Evans was only twenty-nine and had been in the big leagues for five straight years.

Overall, the battle for returning tour players was another disaster in the Federal League's player hunt, the outlaws getting just two of the eight players they were after, and the two—Doolin and Evans—were not top-tier talents. The fact that the magnates of Organized Baseball had been forced to pay hefty salaries to keep their players was of little consolation. It appeared that players had successfully leveraged the Feds' cash against their old teams in order to get new contracts, and little more. "The failure of the Federal League to get more than two of the eight players sought was not relished by the promoters of the new league," an article in *Sporting Life* commented. "The charge was made by one of the Federal League managers that the players had been using the new league as a 'goat.'"[13]

‡

With no unsigned major league players left, the rosters of the Federal League were set, and as the rag-tag lineups prepared to head to spring training, gloom set in over Fed quarters. Over the course of the winter, the league had made offers—some serious, some strictly for publicity—to a list of stars who might have immediately changed the perception of the circuit and inspired others to join them: three years, $50,000 for Eddie Collins; three years, $30,000 for Jake Daubert; two years, $15,000 for Honus Wagner; two years, $16,000 for Gavvy Cravath; three years, $40,000 for Walter Johnson; three years, $30,000 for Smoky Joe Wood; five years, $75,000 for Ty Cobb. There were the offers made to Speaker and Magee, too, and just a few days before the battle of the dock, the Feds had been turned down by Giants ace Christy Mathewson, who got an offer to manage the Brooklyn team for three years and $65,000.

It was bad enough that all the top stars had rebuffed the Federal League. Making matters worse was that other players followed the example of Bill Killefer, jumping to the new league and then flopping back to Organized Baseball. Still, if the goal of the league back in late November 1913 had been to acquire five major leaguers for each team, then, overall, the Feds had been successful. An article dated April 1 appeared in *Sporting Life* counted fifty-nine major league players populating the Feds. According to *The Sporting News*, which, as the printed mouthpiece of Organized Baseball, was naturally skeptical about the quality of players the Feds claimed, the count was more like twenty-four players, after eliminating the quasi–major leaguers and those who had flopped back to O. B.[14]

The Federal League had money behind it. That was one area in which Gilmore, affable and successful in business, had proven adept. Otto Stifel in St. Louis had been a holdover from the 1913 season, but Gilmore brought in Weeghman, Robert Ward in Brooklyn, and, in March, persuaded Edward Gwinner—son of one of the wealthiest men in Pittsburgh—to take over the franchise in that city. Soon after, Gilmore claimed that the league's backers were worth $50 million, a questionable figure, but one that still had O. B.'s attention. As N. L. president John Tener said, "I believe that man Gilmore not only can convince a millionaire the moon is made of green cheese, but he can induce him to invest money in a cheese factory on the moon."[15]

That money hadn't been converted into players, however. The high point of the Federal League's winter had been the first shot of the war against Organized Baseball, the signing of Tinker and Brown. Players had dabbled with the Federal League and universally hoped for its success, especially when it came to the reserve clause and player treatment in general. But few actually wanted to risk jumping to a still-unknown venture. Speaking to J.B. Sheridan of the *St. Louis Globe-Democrat*, Brown summed up the sour mood: "All the ball players told us they were for the Federal League, for it every way; that it was a great boost to baseball; that it was making them money, etc. Then they took the money it made them and signed with

National League and American League clubs. It was, 'Brownie, we are with you, old boy,' and to Tinker, 'Joe, we are for you,' but when it came to signing contracts it was back to the old bosses and the old spot. I'm pretty sore on ball players. Tinker and I got out and took a chance and got these fellows 300 percent increase in salaries. They come in and salve Tinker and me and tell us what great work we are doing. But do you suppose they'd offer us a hand? Not on your life. They'd sell either or both of us for a nickel apiece."[6]

The setbacks, though, only seemed to get Gilmore—nicknamed "Fighting Jim" for his service as a lieutenant in the Philippines during the Spanish-American war and in the Illinois National Guard—fired up. Increasingly, Gilmore was doing more of the public talking for the league, and as the rhetoric from baseball's entrenched powers got more heated, Gilmore followed suit. But Gilmore had a personal reason for his increasing animosity toward O. B. officials. Gilmore confessed to reporters that in late February, just before the battle of the dock, he and Ban Johnson had held a secret, four-hour conference at the Chicago Automobile Club during which the two discussed the baseball war. Gilmore said of Johnson, "He said he was opposed to going into court. I agreed with him. We both agreed that such a proceeding meant thousands of dollars spent by all three leagues for attorneys and court costs. We fully agreed that peace was preferable."[17] Gilmore, encouraged by Johnson's show of goodwill, suggested that he and Johnson meet again, with John Tener attending, too. Johnson wanted the third National Commission member, Garry Herrmann, to be involved, too, but Gilmore said no, he wanted to meet with Johnson and Tener as equal heads of their respective leagues, not with the National Commission as a whole. Johnson told him that he'd call Tener, arrange a time and place and get back to Gilmore the next day. That's where things went sour. "I never heard from him after that," Gilmore said.

Gilmore, insulted by being stood up and certain that Johnson had merely used the meeting to get a sense of the state of the Federal League, began a public verbal assault on O. B., and Johnson in particular. When talented young Naps pitcher Fred Blanding signed a contract with the Feds and then went back to Cleveland on March 3, the news "caused President Gilmore to fly into a rage," according to the *Tribune*, before he sent out a telegram to Johnson and Tener warning that if they did not stop signing players under Federal League contracts, his league would respond in kind and go after major league players who already had contracts—in other words, not only would the Federal League regard the reserve clause as worthless, they'd regard any contract as a whole as worthless. Johnson gave out a long statement saying that he would not negotiate "with representatives of this 'joke' league" and labeled the Feds "pirates." Johnson went on: "I haven't answered Gilmore's telegram relating to tampering with players. Why should I? Why, it's a joke. They steal our players, and then they have the cheek to threaten reprisals if we do not stop trying to get back our men."[18]

Gilmore was floored by Johnson's tactics, how he could have been so reasoned during their meeting just weeks earlier, yet so full of bluster and bile in the press? He went after Johnson's hypocrisy. "Is this the same Johnson who encouraged contract-jumping when he was making his league leap to the front as president of the struggling young American League?" Gilmore asked. "If it is to be a war with contract-jumping and that sort of thing, which I have been opposed to from the start, I will show Mr. Johnson a few points he was the first to teach and then improve some on his original methods. ... He says he wants war, well, he is likely to get all he wants. And the fireworks will start before the Fourth of July. The fireworks may start within the next few days and Ban had better look out. He might get singed."[19]

Now Gilmore was guaranteeing that baseball's war would head to the courts. Technically, no player had jumped a contract just yet, not until he failed to show up for spring training. Gilmore would be traveling to Shreveport with Tinker and Weeghman's club and let it be known that if Bill Killefer were not on the train with his would-be teammates, he would be considered a contract-jumper and an escalation of the baseball war would ensue. He knew full well that Killefer would not be there, but the context of Killefer breaking his Federal League contract to sign a contract with Organized Baseball gave Gilmore justification for breaking his promise not to sign players who already had contracts.

At 5 o'clock on Sunday, March 8, Tinker herded his team onto the seven-car special train at the Illinois Central depot on Chicago's South Side amid hundreds of cheering well-wishers. There were twenty-eight players on board, and Gilmore officially noted Killefer's absence. He sent telegrams to all owners and managers in his league, telling them they were free to sign any player, no matter his contract status. If O. B. would freely violate Federal League contracts, the league would respond in kind and court proceedings would be started against Killefer the following day. Just as the train was pulling out, Gilmore shouted, "It's war to the end. We will show the public that the Federal League is not a piker and that Ban Johnson of the American League is a four-flusher. ... We have acted on the square in all our relations with the players and club owners and we intend to go through with this war to the bitter end."[20]

In a little more than a day, the Chicago Feds would be in Shreveport, and the morning after that, they would take to the field for their first-ever spring training under Joe Tinker.

# CHAPTER ELEVEN

# "The Fellows from the North Side Were Actuated with Pride"

On March 9 at just about 10 PM, Joe Tinker gathered his team at the Hotel Youree in Shreveport and gave out the first official speech of his career as a Federal League manager. He laid out the ground rules of camp—two practices per day, at 10 AM and again at 2:15 PM, all players in bed by 11:30 PM—but emphasized that this team, of all, had the most riding on it for the coming season and he expected them to act accordingly. "The eyes of the baseball world are centered directly upon you," Tinker said. "Chicago practically made the Federal League, because it furnished James A. Gilmore, president of the new organization, who furnished the nerve to buck organized baseball and he has started an organization that made the two big leagues sit up and gasp for breath."[1]

But the only heavy breathing the two big leagues had done so far had been to overpay to keep players who had made overtures to the outlaws. It was obvious that the Federal League, for all the money its backers supposedly had, was still an operation held together by chicken wire and bubble gum. The league's owners had been so focused on fighting for players and preparing for court battles that major problems like outfitting the league's stadiums and working out the season schedule had been put on hold. Even the team names had been an afterthought. Baltimore would, fittingly, be known as the Terrapins, Indianapolis would be the Hoosiers, St. Louis the Terriers, and Kansas City, the Packers. But Tinker's bunch had no name and was simply called the Chifeds. Pittsburgh was eventually named the Rebels but only after the team fired Doc Gessler eleven games into the season and hired thirty-year-old Rebel Oakes to replace him as manager. There was a stir among the dyed-in-the-wool baseball media a month earlier when Brooklyn owner Robert Ward announced that he would call his team the Tip-Tops. Ward had made his millions running the Tip-Top bakery in New York and his blatant commercialism was pilloried.

Then there was spring training. Even in the majors, training trips to small towns in the South could be grueling. But the trip to Shreveport would be brutal, and that was obvious from the moment Tinker's team got to the field the next morning. Because Organized Baseball had shut the Feds out of all desirable facilities, teams had to scramble to find places to work out. For the Chifeds, this meant the infield of the horse racing track at the Louisiana State Fairgrounds. The grounds were soggy and bumpy, unsuitable for baseball practice. Beyond that, the weather was not exactly Southern—it would prove to be cold and rainy for the bulk of the trip. Nice weather might have drawn the locals to watch the team practice and scrimmage, but with the cold and wind, few were interested in the Federal League's training games and might not have been interested even if the heavens had complied. (The revenue generated from fans at those games went a long way toward covering spring expenses, which were considerable. The bill at the Hotel Youree wound up at $4,800.[2]) Tinker frequently brought his troops inside and practiced at the Fairgrounds Coliseum, though even that was a problem because there was no heat. Tinker's men played two indoor games on March 20, but they were not sharp because "the rain and chilly weather of yesterday were the cause of about fifteen members of the 'Fed' party catching colds, and today they are all sneezing. Several of the athletes were affected, but not severely enough to keep them out of practice. 'Doc' Brady, the trainer, was busy last night and tonight making the rounds of the rooms of the ailing ones and handing out pills and something warm out of a bottle."[3]

It was a blessing, then, when the Chifeds packed up their trunks and got out of Shreveport in early April to begin playing games in other spots around the South before heading back to Chicago, but things were not much better elsewhere. In New Orleans on April 6, Tinker was "disgusted" by the fact that O. B. had frozen his team out of the use of any good fields, to the point that he refused to allow his starters to play on "an impossible field" in a scheduled game against the New Orleans Eddys. They arrived at Gulfport, Mississippi, the next day, happy because they would have use of the field that the Detroit Tigers had been using for training, marking the first time the team would practice on a real diamond that spring. But on April 8, the game was called off because of cold weather. "It wasn't any bluff, either," the *Tribune* reported, "for the wind was whizzing down from the north at a terrific pace and it was cloudy."[4] When the team reached Knoxville, Tennessee on April 10, they were finally able to put on a good intrasquad game at a "pretty suburban park" in front of 1,000 fans. Among the fans was Weeghman, who had gone back to Chicago nearly a month earlier to look over the progress of the North Side park but rejoined the team in Tennessee.

Weeghman had originally arrived to help settle a dispute over star pitcher Tom Seaton. In yet another sign that the league was still far from operating smoothly, Seaton had provided some embarrassment when he refused to join the Brooklyn Federals—he had been one of the game's best pitchers in 1913, with a 27–12 record and had agreed to leave the Phillies only because he would join with teammate Ad Brennan in Chicago. He finally consented to heading back east only when he was plied with perks, including traveling expenses for his wife when the Tip-Tops were on the road. With the Seaton matter settled, Weeghman thought he might actually get a chance to take in a game with some peace and satisfaction. He arrived at the park early, bought a bag of popcorn and took his seat. His peace didn't last long, though, as one of the local reporters let out the news that the Killefer case had been decided. He was staying with Philadelphia. "This sort of spoiled the afternoon for the worthy president," the *Tribune*'s Sam Weller wrote.[5]

Indeed, Judge Clarence Sessions, in Grand Rapids, Michigan, issued a perplexing ruling in the Killefer case, one that allowed both sides to claim a win. Sessions agreed with the Federal League lawyers that the reserve clause in player contracts was not legal and not enforceable, which had been the basis for the league's approach to signing players, including Killefer, all along. Therefore, Sessions said, the contract Weeghman signed with Killefer was "in form, valid and binding upon the parties thereto." But Sessions also claimed that the Federal League approached Killefer with "unclean hands," a doctrine stating that a party is not entitled to legal remedy if it has behaved unethically. There was some paradox in this decision. Sessions was saying that the Federal Leaguers had unclean hands when signing Killefer, because they knew he was property of the Phillies. But the only thing that made him property of the Phillies was the very reserve clause that Sessions ruled invalid. How could the Feds legally sign anyone under that logic? As long as O. B. kept the reserve clause—admittedly illegal—in the contract, wouldn't the Federal League have unclean hands every time a player was approached?

Weeghman was confused by the ruling. But as for his team without Killefer, he tried to put things in a positive light. "I don't know that we need Killefer," he said. "We have a star catcher right now in (Art) Wilson. We need a star first-sacker and a hard hitting outfielder more than a catcher, and when we get them, we'll have a team fit to fight any world's champions. I just can't understand how the judge could call the reserve clause illegal and then at the same time say we went after Killefer with unclean hands."[6] Weeghman wasn't done with the Killefer affair—the Federal League appealed the decision—nor would it be the end of the long legal slog that the Feds and O. B. had ahead. "Seems to me," Weeghman would say, "these fellows are trying to make us split our profits with the lawyers. If they can stand it, so can we."[7]

But in the days after the Killefer ruling, concerns about jurisprudence faded quickly. Despite cold and rainy weather in training camps across the South, it was spring and ball clubs were, like the Chifeds, winding down the exhibition season and preparing for the real thing. Opening Day was here.

‡

Between the years 1909 and 1912, seven of the eight American League teams replaced their rickety old wooden parks—prone to fires and stubbornly dirty—with glistening new concrete-and-steel structures. The one exception was New York, which had a lease to play at the Giants' Polo Grounds home, a concrete-and-steel park that opened in 1911. In the National League, Philadelphia's Baker Bowl was the original jewel box park, built in 1895, and when Charles Ebbets opened his new park in Brooklyn in 1913, the number of teams in the league with concrete-and-steel parks was up to five. That didn't include the Braves, who would play part of their season at the Red Sox's new Fenway Park and were planning a huge new stadium that would open in 1915. The only two major league teams still playing in antiquated wooden parks were the sad-sack Cardinals, perennially short on money and having finished in the league's second division for twelve straight years, and the Cubs, the best team in baseball over the previous decade and one of the game's biggest moneymakers.

The Federal League had six teams playing in wooden parks, and of those, only one (Pittsburgh's Exposition Park) had been a big league park that was recently abandoned for a new field. The grounds that would house the other teams were decidedly minor league in quality—in St. Louis, for example, Handlan's Park had been a circus grounds just months before its Federal League tenants opened play. The park in Kansas City, Gordon and Koppel Field, was far too small to be considered big league and was built in a low-lying field on Brush Creek, making it susceptible to flooding. A concrete-and-steel plant had been built in Brooklyn, at the Dodgers' old Washington Park, but that was poorly located and needed much work even after it opened. The great hope of the league was the Chifeds' gleaming new North Side park, and as the April days slipped away, the race was on to complete the park in time for the home opener on the twenty-third.

On April 3, Weeghman and Gilmore took Chicago sportswriters on a tour of the new park. Embarrassingly, there was a strike of Teamsters at the park that day but Weeghman said he expected a delay of only a day or two. The progress the crews had achieved in just a month was remarkable. The steelwork was entirely finished and the roofing was to be done by noon on the fourth, leaving the stands completed. Weeghman had chafed at reports that the new park was to be smaller than the Cubs' park and pointed out that the left-field line measured 310 feet, and the right-field line was 345 feet. He also said the park would hold 20,000 fans, 2,000 of which would be bleacher seats for the "two-bit" fans (tickets at big league parks across the country were divided into seventy-five-cent seats, fifty-cent grandstand seats, and twenty-five-cent seats in the bleachers). "The president is planning an addition to his grand stand next year so that it will sweep far into left field. ... An enormous space has also been set aside for automobiles, but some of this extra room probably will be occupied by store buildings next season."[7]

In the meantime, despite the miserable and money-draining spring training for the Feds and in the wake of the Killefer blow, there was finally some good news for the league. On April 13, in Baltimore, the league opened its season with the Terrapins hosting Buffalo. It was an enormous event for the city, which had stewed with bitterness for more than a decade over its abandonment by Ban Johnson and the American League. The status of the Federal League's legitimacy as a major league was a common question in baseball circles, but jilted Baltimoreans, headed by local hero Ned Hanlon, rushed to give the outlaws their stamp of approval. When the first pitch of the game was registered, the *Baltimore Sun* reported, "28,000 fans of the baseball denomination let loose a shout that promised to give tremors to any seismographic instrument within 100 miles of Baltimore. ... It was a glorious thing to think when one looked out upon the Terrapins' playing field that the men responsible for putting this city back on the baseball map were men who live here and who know the people here."[9] When Jack Dunn's Orioles, of the International League, put on their Opening Day the following week, they drew a crowd of 619 fans. If Baltimore fans were voting with their wallets in a battle of the Federal League against one of baseball's best minor league franchises, the initial tally had the Feds ahead by a 45-to-1 ratio.

The Chifeds would open three days later in Kansas City, and the showing was similarly strong. Only 9,000 fans attended, but that was because the Packers played at a particularly small stadium—regardless, the *Tribune* reported that the crowd was "more than double in numbers the one which attended the opening game in the American Association here two days ago. Consequently, it is taken that Kansas City is for the Federal League."[10] Across the state, in St. Louis, Miner Brown's Terriers opened in front of 20,000 fans. "Viewing the situation from that point, the Federal League looks like a great big and glorious success," *Sporting Life* reported. "The opening day attendances in the various cities speak volumes. They constitute the verdict of the real judge of all, Mr. Fan. After all, it is what he says which plays the real part and he certainly has spoken favorably."[11]

A week later, the Packers were in Chicago and already, things had shaped up well for Weeghman's club. If part of the Federal League's success as a whole depended on the ability of the Chifeds to pull fans away from the Cubs—staggered as they were by the foibles of the only half-deposed Charles W. Murphy and compounded by the ineptitude of Charles Taft—then Weeghman and Gilmore were surely ecstatic to see that Opening Day on the West Side had drawn just 4,000 fans. Weeghman had also done well in the run-up to his opening, to sell his new park to middle-class Chicagoans who were fed up with the ramshackle park on the West Side, one of the worst fields in major-league baseball where the first-base stands had been burned out by a big fire twenty years earlier. The West Side Grounds were known, too, for rude ushers and pushy vendors selling cigars, popcorn, and programs in the aisles, blocking fans' view of the game. When discussing his new park, Weeghman was careful to contrast what the experience would be like on the North Side against the miserable experience had at a typical ballgame. He didn't need to name the West Side park specifically—fans in Chicago would have recognized his meaning immediately.

"It is my belief that in order to draw and keep the fans, a club management must show plainly that the first thought is for the fan's comfort," Weeghman told the *Chicago Post* in February. "I have been a baseball fan for years ... and many a time, I have gone to a park all dolled up in my very best regalia, only to find that in order to occupy the seat, I must either buy a cushion or ruin my clothes. The dusty and generally dirty condition of several of the parks is not the only undesirable feature that the fan has been forced to tolerate. The retiring rooms for men and women are generally a disgrace to the park. We will have the best that is to be had in all branches, and we will spare nothing in making the park one solid comfort. There will be no abusive ushers to insult fans and there will be no dusty and dirty seats and filthy aisles for the fans to complain about."

Weeghman's park would feature small but popular changes. He would sell refreshments behind the seats rather than in the aisles (the first ballpark concession stands) to cut down on vendors. He would employ a team of men to clean the park each morning "to have our plant in a condition that would be a credit to Spotless Town."[12] He created a Ladies' Day, and marketed heavily to Chicago's women, who were increasingly filling jobs in the downtown Loop and feeling more empowered after having just won suffrage in the city. For the team's first game, he gave out caps and pennants with the team's logo, the kind of freebie that is common now but was unheard of at that time—many major league teams were so protective of their logos in those days that they would not allow caps to be printed at all, even for sale, let alone give them away to fans. Before Opening Day, Weeghman ran an ad in the city's newspapers asking readers to "Be a Fed Fan," and again contrasting the Feds against the Cubs and Taft, their Cincinnati owner:

"Tomorrow the Chicago Federal League (Weeghman Park) opens its gates to the Chicago sports-loving public. This great park, dedicated to clean sport and the furtherance of our national game is *yours*, not ours. Its destiny is in *your* hands. Believing that Chicago Fans are champions of fair play, believing that the great North Side of this city needs a Big League Ball Park, believing that the baseball public will respond to a Chicago Ball Team Owned By Chicagoans, I have devoted my time, my energy and my money to help bring this project to the point where it stands today."[13]

Notably, the words "Chicago Ball Team Owned By Chicagoans" were set apart, underlined, italicized, and in 24-point font.

Weeghman's pitch had worked. On April 23, despite poor weather, the *Chicago American* reported that 300 fans were in line at the park at 9 AM and "when fans will stand in line for three hours, with a raw and chill wind blowing, there must be enthusiasm." When the gates were opened at noon, spectators were pouring off the five-cent streetcar lines and the 'El' stop at Addison, and according to the *Daily News*, 2,000 fans rushed in to grab seats. By 1 PM, the circus seats ushers had placed on the field to handle the overflow spectators were filling up. (The park was said to hold 18,000, though Organized Baseball officials, always seeking to downplay any Fed successes, claimed it was actually 14,000.)[14] With the park beyond capacity, the gates had to be closed at 2:30, a half-hour before the scheduled first pitch, leaving thousands of fans locked out. Many of them, unwittingly, foretold an area tradition by crowding onto the rooftops of nearby apartment buildings to watch the game.

There had been festivities at every park opening in the Federal League, but Weeghman topped them all. There was a parade to the park from the Loop that stretched a mile. Once at the park, there were ten bands playing at varying times. There were a half-dozen booster clubs on hand, including one group of 3,000 North Siders known as the Bravo el Toro Club (of which Weeghman was a member), who marched from the popular local tavern, the Bismarck Garden, and took the field at 2 PM in their red-and-gold sashes intent on putting on a choreographed faux bullfight. It might have been a nifty show, except the bull in question was feeling lethargic and despite multiple efforts, "the fatted steer refused to get mad, and the bullfight was a fizzle."[15] With the field cleared of cattle, the Ladies of the Grand Army of the Republic followed, accompanied by a fifty-piece band that marched all the way out to center field, where the Ladies made a presentation of a giant American flag, struggling against the wind to hold it aloft. That was punctuated by a 21-gun salute and a rendition of "Columbia, Gem of the Ocean." The bunch then tramped back to home plate for the presentation of flowers, a cup, and a handful of—oddly enough—neckties to manager Joe Tinker, who was limping badly from having been spiked by a cleat during a game the day before.

At long last, Weeghman went to the mound for the ceremonial first pitch. Mayor Carter Harrison, Jr. was supposed to do the honors but, as he'd done at the park's groundbreaking, he stood up the Feds and counsel William Sexton filled in. Harrison was one of the few powerful Chicagoans not in attendance. Illinois Supreme Court chief justice George Cooke had a prominent seat and Judge Charles A. McDonald was nearby—McDonald would go on to become a significant figure in baseball history, presiding over the grand jury that began the investigation into the 1919 Black Sox scandal. Cubs bidder John T. Connery was in attendance, as was William Hale Thompson, who would replace Harrison as mayor the following year. George Busse, brother of former mayor Fred Busse, had a seat, though he was probably uneasy at the sight of "el toro," because three years earlier he had been gored within inches of his life by an angry bull on his farm in Fox Lake. Warren Wright, president of Calumet Baking Powder, was there, and generations of horse racing fans would recognize his company name because Calumet Farms later became the world's most renowned horse breeding operation. Other sporting stars were present, including first-ever professional football coach Sport Donnelly, soccer Hall of Famer Peter J. Peel, and race car driver Arthur Greiner (who made history by finishing last in the first Indianapolis 500, completing only twelve laps before crashing).

Oh, and there was another familiar face: "Charles W. Murphy was present. He was clad in a bright green hat, a tie to match, and announced that he was looking for a job. The only fault to find with the former president is that he doesn't carry out his color scheme. His automobile didn't match his hat and tie."[16]

After Sexton's first pitch to Joe Tinker, "while everybody yelled and while three or four bands were playing at the same time and a male quartet was megaphoning a popular song, the real ball game was begun."[17] Spitballer Claude Hendrix, probably the best pitcher and arguably the best player in general in the Federal League, took the mound. Just after 3 PM on April 23, 1914, with a crowd estimated between 18,000-25,000 fans on hand, he threw the first pitch in the history of professional baseball at Sheffield and Addison on Chicago's North Side.

The new park was only about a mile-and-a-half away from where the Chicago Federal League contingent had played in 1913, at DePaul's athletic field. As the writer J. G. Davis noted, "It is not a long jump from DePaul field, where the lowly Feds played last year, to their modern home at Addison Avenue, but a glance at the wonderful setting for yesterday's combat brought the thought that someone must have rubbed Aladdin's lamp to effect such a magical transformation."[18]

Weeghman was nearly in tears, "beaming smiles on every one who entered the gate."[19] Those entering beamed smiles right back. This was not just a big day for Weeghman and the Federal League, it was a defining day for the entire North Side. As one report put it: "They came in pairs, in groups, in crowds, some came with a marching band at their head. … You could tell the fellows from the North Side. They were actuated by pride. They were rooting feverishly, in the hope that the hope which had been held out to them was not a false one, but that they were to take rank with the South and West Sides in this national game."[20]

# CHAPTER TWELVE

# A Promising Start for the New League

Opening Day at Weeghman Park was met with fanfare, but it was not much of a game once it did get started. Spitballer Claude Hendrix was dominant, giving up just five hits on the day for one of what would be a Federal League-best 29 wins for him that year. But catcher Art Wilson was the hero of the day, knocking a two-run home run in the second inning, and following it in the fourth with another home run, this one "going clear over the score board, landing in the middle of Waveland Avenue."[1] (It was Wilson's second two-home run game vs Kansas City in four days; he had two at KC four days earlier.) It was a cold at the park, with winds swirling off Lake Michigan and, in another foreshadowing of a future park feature, Wilson's long drives were likely aided by the park's swirling wind. In another bit of Clark-and-Sheffield foreshadowing, kids who were not actually at the game were lining up on Waveland to chase home run balls. The Chifeds posted fifteen hits in the game, winning easily, 9–1.

The new park received great reviews. The *Post* reported that fans "went away tickled to death with the treatment they had received. Each was made to feel that he was welcome. Nothing in the park was too good for him.

The fun was clean and amusing and the general effect was that of a huge family having a good time. This tone reflected Charley Weeghman's good fellowship, and it is significant because it indicates that those who went to the opening game will go again and again, and they will bring others with them. In other words, the North Side has good reason today to stand up and holler. It has something."[2]

After the strong showing on Opening Day, the North Siders were idle on the next day. Tinker called off practice and instead headed over to the West Side, where he and some players—first baseman Fred Beck and shortstop Leo Kavanagh of the Chifeds, and Cad Coles of Kansas City (who had been traded by the Chifeds in spring training)—went to watch the Cubs play Tinker's old team, the Reds. Cubs president Charles Thomas offered to allow the players in for free, but Tinker, on the front lines of the politics surrounding the baseball war, insisted that they pay. Sitting in a field box near third base, Tinker drew much attention, as "the camera boys helped themselves to some new snapshots of the Fed manager."[3] The Cubs, however, drew very little attention. Even though it was a Friday, here were fewer than 2,000 fans on hand.

The early returns suggested that the Federal League's goal of crippling the Cubs with the new stadium and Tinker's managership was well met—Charles Murphy's treatment of John Evers, Taft's inability and/or unwillingness to sell the club to local men, and his hiring of Thomas, Murphy's right-hand man, were bonuses to the Feds provided by the Cubs themselves. When the Federals got back to work on Saturday, they drew 12,000 fans, while the Cubs had a crowd of 5,000. It wasn't a friendly crowd on the West Side, either. The Cubs lost, 13-1, to Cincinnati and by the third inning, "the small crowd jeered efforts of the Cubs. A derisive cheer went up every time a Red was retired to the bench."[4] The Cubs drew better on Sunday, getting a crowd of 13,000, but 22,000 showed up at Weeghman's park on the North Side. Including Opening Day, the Chifeds drew 54,000 fans for three games from April 23–26. The Cubs played four games and yet drew just 21,000.

Even up against the much more popular White Sox and their relatively new stadium, the Chifeds were holding their own. On Sunday, May 10, for the first of four times on the schedule, the Cubs, White Sox, and Chifeds were at home on the same day. The Cubs were playing Pittsburgh and

Honus Wagner while the Sox had Ty Cobb and the Tigers—two of the biggest stars in the game. But the Feds, wisely, had scheduled the Terriers to be in Chicago on that date, which meant it was Mordecai Brown Day on the North Side. Brown was in St. Louis now and had been in Cincinnati the previous season, but he was still a hero to the fans of Chicago and a sympathetic figure given the poor treatment he had received from Murphy and the Cubs. Brown and Tinker drew about 20,000 to the North Side, and Cobb helped the Sox attract about 21,000. The Cubs lagged badly, drawing about 10,000 fans, and already, it was obvious Taft had made a big blunder in not accepting John T. Connery's offer for the team. "Joe Tinker's team is making a joke of the Cubs in Chicago, and that is not a very comforting situation for a man in Mr. Taft's position," Ban Johnson observed.[5]

With its mid-April successes, the Federal League established credibility with players in the National and American leagues. In his syndicated column, Giants pitcher Christy Mathewson—who had spurned a $65,000 offer from the Feds the previous month—wrote, "You would be surprised by the number of sensible players in the business who are beginning to take the Federal League seriously. I know one man who has been on a club that has taken three world's championships who made this remark to me recently: 'If the Federal League makes me an offer next fall like the one it did last, I'm going to consider it a long time. If I don't take it I'll worry somebody anyway.'"[6]

But in order to keep fans coming back, the league would have to show it was playing quality baseball, and that led to an early concern about Weeghman Park. The first three games featured a burst of scoring and home runs—the Chifeds followed their Opening Day rout with a 7–2 win the next day, and Kansas City closed the series on Sunday with a 12–4 win, in which they whacked three home runs and five doubles. In all, thirty-five runs were scored in the first series on the North Side, and while modern fans tend to delight in the home run ball, back in the deadball era, with its emphasis on speed and strategy, such slugging was viewed as bad baseball. Weeghman summoned team secretary Charley Williams and said, "Have that left field fence moved in the morning." Williams replied in the affirmative and *Chicago American* writer Bill Bailey (whose given name was Bill Veeck) reported, "He said it just like that, as if moving a brick wall was as easy as moving a trunk." Weeghman also had concerns about the liveliness of the Federal League ball, made by Victor Sporting Goods in Springfield, Massachussets. He summoned Jim Gilmore, too, and said, "There's too much rubber in those balls. You'll kill a couple of my infielders."[7] Effectively, then, Weeghman wanted his fences pushed back and the balls un-juiced.

Sure enough, a crew of 100 workers was out the next day, moving the fence back. By one measure, the left-field foul line went from 302 feet to 327 feet. Left-center field was pushed back by fifty feet. There was a brick house beyond the left field fence that could not yet be torn down—the resident had until May 1 to move out—but the fence was placed as far back as possible. "Even the porch was torn off the house to make more room for base hits," the *Tribune* reported. The plan was to eventually tear the house down and move the fence back more, with a new set of bleacher seats to be erected in left field. Additionally, Victor Sporting Goods reported that a new set of balls would be shipped to every team, with 15 percent less bounce. This was bad news for poor Art Wilson, who had been dubbed, tongue-in-cheek "Home Run" Wilson by local writers. One writer joked that in the apartments out beyond left field, residents moved away from their windows when they heard Wilson's name announced. In a missive from Wilson's perspective, writer Ring Lardner waxed poetic:

> Weeghman, spare that wall!
> Don't move it back, I pray.
> Cut out the lively ball,
> But let that short fence stay.[8]

The moving of the fence did coincide with some bad fortune for Wilson. After the deed was done, "it was learned that Art Wilson, who has gained such fame with his home run clouts, was sick in bed and required the attention of a doctor. Art had heard about the fence moving, but upon investigation, it was learned that was not the cause of his sickness. He has a severe attack of tonsillitis."[9]

‡

Certainly, when Cincinnati manager Buck Herzog saw Joe Tinker, his predecessor with the Reds, in the West Side crowd on April 24, he had to cast a wary eye in Tinker's direction. Tinker had already been successful in pushing players to jump from the Reds to the Federal League, but when the team's former clubhouse boy, Joe Schreckel, asked for a big raise and was fired before the season, Tinker gained an ally. He promised Schreckel a job with the Chifeds' grounds crew on the North Side if he would work as an agent for the Federal League, helping persuade even more players to leave the Reds.[10] Schreckel obliged and put Kansas City president C. C. Madison in touch with two players—Cuban outfielder Armando Marsans and pitcher George "Chief" Johnson (a member of the Winnebago tribe, Johnson, like most Native Americans in baseball, were usually called, "Chief," or "Indian.") While the war between the Federal League and Organized Baseball had a very public audience among media and fans, there was also a hefty amount of backroom dealing. Tinker, with his strong and recent connections to the National League, was often somehow involved.

Earlier, just as the baseball season was getting underway, on April 20 at the Sinton Hotel in Cincinnati, Madison first met with Marsans, who turned down his offer to leave the Reds for the Feds (he would later reconsider and join Brown's team in St. Louis). Madison next met with Johnson at the hotel, offering him a $2,500 bonus. Johnson initially turned that down too, but when Madison reached into a valise and pulled out a stack of $100 bills, counting out twenty-five of them and adding five more, topping it with an offer of three years at $5,000 per year, Johnson was swayed. He packed his belongings and would head to St. Louis where the contract would be signed the following day before heading to Kansas City. But Madison wasn't finished tapping Tinker's sources when it came to players. Larry Cheney, who had led the league in wins with 26 back in 1912, Tinker's final year with the Cubs, was also said to be unhappy. He, too, was in contact with Madison. Madison had spirited Johnson out of St. Louis and was taking him back to Kansas City, stopping in St. Louis on the twenty-first. While there with Johnson, Madison figured he'd keep trying his luck and go for another pitcher—the Cubs had just wrapped up a series against the Cardinals and Madison called Cheney on the phone several times, but couldn't connect.

The Cubs were wise to Cheney's unhappiness, though, and knew he was being pursued by the Federal League. At two o'clock that morning, in fact, Cheney had been awoken by the sound of the telephone. It was Charles Thomas, frantically calling because he had heard Cheney jumped to the Feds.[11]

At 8:45 that night, a squad of reporters went to Union Station with Madison and Johnson, whose train to Kansas City left at 9:00. The Cubs' train was scheduled to depart at 9:10. Madison searched for Cheney and was able to locate his wife and son—but Cheney was not with them. Charles Thomas had outsmarted Cheney. "Finally," the *Tribune* reported, "a scribe spied Larry coming in. He had been enticed into a motor party planned to keep him away from the independents."[12] Madison did chat with Cheney at the station but not long enough to make the kind of financial pitch that had moved Chief Johnson to ditch the Reds. Cheney announced he would not make a decision until he sat down with both Madison and Thomas and heard them out, which he planned to do on Thursday, the twenty-third, with the Packers in Chicago to open Weeghman Park against the Chifeds. Before Madison's dalliance with Cheney, players on both the Cubs and the White Sox had been relatively unaffected by the Federal League. This was by design. For one thing, both Weeghman and Gilmore were friends with White Sox owner Charles Comiskey, and were fellow members of the Chicago Athletic Association. For another thing, there was the fear that Federal raids on Chicago players would undercut the league's popularity among baseball fans in the city. Weeghman repeated that he had a "hands off" policy[13] when it came to Sox and Cubs players, but with the season started and the Killefer case having been decided, his fellow Feds had Chicago ballplayers in their sights.

It wasn't just Cheney, either. Before the drama with Cheney at the train station in St. Louis, Mordecai Brown was in his office with two of his former Cubs teammates, infielder Heine Zimmerman and catcher Jimmy Archer, potential Federal League targets. Meanwhile, catcher Roger Bresnahan, a famed disciple of John McGraw with the Giants before going to the Cardinals as player/manager, then to the Cubs in 1913, was reported to have agreed to join the Feds if he could be made a manager again—he was not happy playing for Hank O'Day and splitting catching duties with Archer.[14] Federal League approaches also were made to two other Cubs, pitchers Jimmy Lavender and George Pierce. It seemed as though the bulk of the pitching staff as well as the meat of the lineup on the West Side, where the situation was deteriorating by the day, was being pursued by the Federal League. The Feds were taking chances on the South Siders, too. In Cleveland, agents for the Brooklyn Federals were talking with a pair of White Sox, infielder Buck Weaver and pitcher Jim Scott.[15]

Across baseball, Organized Baseball was scurrying to keep up with rumors of players ready to jump their current teams, despite the fact that, in the wake of the Killefer ruling, the Federal League would obviously have "unclean hands" if it pursued players already under contract. That's because the Feds had developed a new legal tack in their pursuit of players—in a twist, they would use the hated ten-day clause against Organized Baseball. The ability of a team to release a player on ten days' notice was a foundation for baseball, allowing teams to keep their payrolls clean by dropping under-performing or injured players. But in the Killefer decision, Judge Sessions expressed some doubts about the ten-day clause, and the Feds ran with it, basically stating that in a valid contract, any such clause must be recipro-cal. If teams can cut their players for no reason, then players can cut their teams. The assertion was that if players had no right to notify their teams that they were ending the deal within ten days, the entire contract was void. This would be the league's main argument in fighting the Chief Johnson injunction.

There was irony in this. Just months earlier—even weeks, at the battle of the dock—teams had fought players who wanted the ten-day clause out of their contracts because Organized Baseball wanted to maintain its right to cut players. It was Murphy's justification for firing Evers in February, after all. But now recognizing that the lack of reciprocity in the ten-day rule might left them vulnerable and might well cancel the entire contract, teams scrambled to remove the very clause they'd fought so hard to protect. The Cubs, for example, reportedly paid Jimmy Lavender a $3,000 bonus to remove the clause[16] from his contract, and when Cheney finally agreed to stay with the Cubs on a new contract, he got $8,000 per year for three years and had the ten-day rule stricken from the deal.[17] On the South Side, Comiskey reportedly had gotten the clause removed from all of his contracts, except the one belonging to first baseman Hal Chase.

All of the wrangling over contracts and clauses started to move a gloom over the season. Before Opening Day in the three leagues, there was hope in the press that once real baseball was played, the war chatter would fade and the Feds and O. B. would let the fans decide whether a third league could be a moneymaker based on merit. *The Sporting News* groaned when two National League teams—the Phillies and Braves—sued the Federal League for damages, saying, "It rather shocks our faith in the judgment of those in control of organized ball to learn that they have decided to make their fight on the Federals in the law courts, instead of at the turnstiles."[18] But yet, here was baseball, not even two weeks into the season, again mired in a hectic and ugly player war, with Federal League agents seemingly lurking in every hotel lobby, restaurant, and train depot, and O. B. magnates frantically handing out gaudy raises to thwart them.

And the Killefer case was only the beginning. The peak of all the April maneuvering came at Weeghman Park on Opening Day, that glorious first showing of the North Side park. Buried in the lead of the stories about Weeghman's pride and joy was a disturbing sidelight for the Feds—Madison's new prize from Cincinnati, Chief Johnson, took the mound for Kansas City against the Chifeds. Reds owner Garry Herrmann sought an injunction to keep Johnson from pitching for Kansas City, and, as an article in *Sporting Life* (rather unsubtly) described, it was in the third inning of the game that "a stalwart deputy sheriff strode upon the field and hissed: 'Curses, here are the papers!' The Indian emitted a disgusted war whoop and moccasined his way to the tepee of the Kaw tribe, whereupon [Dwight] Stone took up the Red Man's burden."[19]

Johnson would have a hearing but would be unable to pitch for Kansas City until a judge made a ruling on his contract. Stovall was served papers, too, enjoining him from interfering with any other Reds players. Madison—who had met with the Reds' Marsans again in Chicago, as well as his teammate, pitcher Rube Benton—would have been slapped with an injunction, too, but once he saw Johnson getting his papers, Madison was "said to have taken the secret passage used by the players and successfully to have run the blockade of the sheriff's posse. Before he could be intercepted, Madison had escaped without the state boundary and consequently, the jurisdiction of the Illinois courts."[20]

The season was underway and fans were ready to focus on pitchers, hitters, and pennant races. But as a whole, in the early weeks of the 1914 season, the game itself had been reduced to one of the least important aspects of baseball.

"Fighting Jim" Gilmore (left) and Charles Weeghman were the driving forces of the Federal League's challenge to Organized Baseball, and the main reasons that the league's epicenter was located in Chicago. The two had a sometimes strained relationship, however. While Weeghman was more diplomatic and wanted eventually to own a major-league team, Gilmore frequently antagonized—and was antagonized by—the baseball establishment. *(Library of Congress)*

The treatment of ace pitcher Mordecai "Three Finger" Brown by owner Charles Murphy in 1912 helped lead to the disenchantment of Cubs fans. When Brown was given the chance to jump to the Federal League in the winter of 1913, he did so, and was named manager of the St. Louis Terriers. *(Library of Congress)*

This cartoon from the *Chicago Daily News* in October 1912 depicts owner Charles Murphy, having just severed ties with popular manager Frank "The Peerless Leader" Chance, presenting a battered Cubs franchise to new manager Johnny Evers. *(Chicago Daily News)*

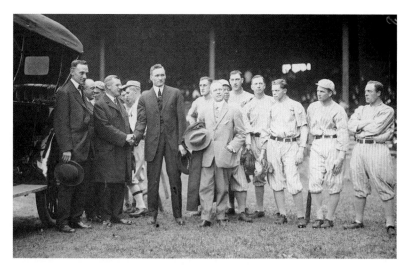

Walter Johnson being presented with an automobile as his prize for winning the Chalmers Award, the equivalent of the MVP, for going 36-7 with a 1.14 ERA in 1913. The Federal League pursued Johnson heavily over the course of its two years of existence, and Chicago manager Joe Tinker actually signed him—briefly. *(Library of Congress)*

White Sox first base-
man Hal Chase was one
of the biggest names
to actually jump to the
Federal League, which
needed to go to great
lengths to keep him in
Buffalo. *(Library of Congress)*

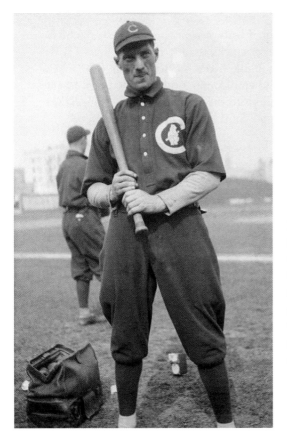

No player better summed up
the shifting fortunes of the
Cubs in the post-Tinker-Evers-
Chance era than Heinie Zimmerman, the eminently talented
slugger whose repeated fights
with teammates and managers
alienated fans and ruined team
chemistry. *(Library of Congress)*

American League owners pictured with league president Ban Johnson (seated, front middle). With Johnson, clockwise, are the White Sox's Charles Comiskey, the Tigers' Frank Navin, the Senators' Ben Minor, the Yankees' Frank Farrell and the Red Sox's Joseph Lannin. While the National League was more willing to give concessions to the Federal League, Johnson's A.L. magnates held out strong against the third league. *(Library of Congress)*

Cincinnati publisher and brother of President William Howard Taft, Charles P. Taft was an absentee owner of the Cubs after the alleged departure of Charles W. Murphy, but had little interest in baseball. *(Library of Congress)*

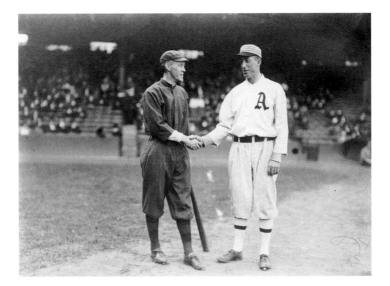

Johnny Evers (left) wound up with the Braves after he was abruptly fired by Murphy in the spring of 1914 and resisted overtures from the Federal League. He helped lead Boston to the 1914 World Series against the Athletics. Here, he is pictured with Eddie Plank, who would join the Feds in 1915. *(Library of Congress)*

Roger Bresnahan was initially unhappy when he arrived in Chicago in 1913, but that changed when he was made manager for the 1915 season. After a good start under Bresnahan, the Cubs unraveled thanks to tensions between Bresnahan and star Heinie Zimmerman, further weakening the team's standing among Chicago's baseball teams. *(Library of Congress)*

By the end of the Federal League's first season, the financial backing of Brooklyn Tip-Tops owner Robert Ward was essentially keeping the venture afloat. Ward was a big baseball fan, but was unable to lure major stars to his team. *(Library of Congress)*

Judge Kenesaw Mountain Landis faced a dilemma when the Federal League chose to bring its antitrust suit against Organized Baseball in his Chicago court in January 1915. Landis was known as a trust-buster, but was also known as an avid baseball fan with close ties to major-league magnates. *(Library of Congress)*

A baseball card depicting Cubs manager and first baseman Frank Chance. After his ouster by Charles Murphy in 1912, Chance wound up with the Yankees in New York, but never enjoyed the kind of success he had on the West Side. Chance was out of major-league baseball after 1914, returning to manage the Red Sox for just one season, in 1923. *(Library of Congress)*

LETTER HEAD OF

THE BROOKLYN BALL CLUB.

Brooklyn, New York

Jan. 26th, 1914.

Joseph B. Tinker, Esq.,
    832 Gunderson ave.,
        Oak Park, Ills.

Dear Sir:

        After full consideration of the matter of forwarding you
a contract as a player with the Brooklyn Ball Club, pursuant
to your release and transfer by the Cincinnati Club, to the
Brooklyn Club, and in view of the conversation and understanding had between you and Manager Robinson of the Brooklyn Club as to the compensation to be paid you by way of salary, and you having then insisted upon receiving the sum of
Seventy-five hundred ($7500.) dollars per year, contract to
be for three years, which Mr. Robinson at that time deemed
excessive, but the matter being left open for further consideration, and also referring to the letter forwarded to
you by me as President of this Club, which in part referred

A letter, dated January 26, 1914, from Brooklyn owner Charles Ebbetts to Joe Tinker. It was Ebbetts' hardball stance on Tinker's salary that helped push Tinker to jump to the Federal League, a major signing for the new league. In this letter, written a month after Tinker made the jump, Ebbetts accedes to Tinker's salary request—too late, it turns out. *(From the Federal League lawsuit file at the National Archives)*

Joe Tinker and his wife, Ruby, pictured in 1913. When Tinker left the Reds in the winter of 1913, he wanted to remain somewhere in the Midwest, in part because his wife had health problems. The Reds, instead, ignored his wishes and sold him to Brooklyn. *(Library of Congress)*

# CHAPTER THIRTEEN

# War and Strategy

B ack on April 27, Chifeds manager Joe Tinker showed up for a morning workout at Weeghman Park in a new car, a bright red seven-seater befitting his early success in getting the Federal League off the ground and attracting fans to the North Side park. Call it an ominous sign, but, just eleven days later, while driving in the morning from his home in the nearby suburb of Oak Park to downtown Chicago, on what he described as "skiddy" roads, Tinker tried passing a truck. Only he did not make it. He hit the truck and "the front part of his new buggy was smashed—engine, radiator, lamps and self-starter—and Joe had to get out and hoof it into town."[1] That wasn't the worst of it: Tinker had a meeting set up with an auto insurance agent the next day. His uninsured car wrecked, he canceled the meeting.

His luck on the roadways notwithstanding, Tinker was eminently upbeat about his club's chances to win the Federal League title in the early going, mostly because the team had such a strong pitching staff. Claude Hendrix was the ace, and he would pitch like one—he came through the first month of the season with a 5–2 record, among the best in the league. Ideally, Hendrix would have been the lead in a very good one-two punch at the top of the rotation, with Ad Brennan, who went 14–12 with a 2.39 ERA for the

Phillies the previous season, behind him. Tinker had such belief in his staff that he declared, "If the Chicago Federal pitching staff cannot win the 1914 pennant, I'll be willing to quit baseball. The club is exceptionally strong in the box, and with a month more of practice and in games against strong teams, we should whip together a ball club that will be capable of holding its own against any team in either the National or American League."[2]

Brennan, though, was a bust. He had come down with tonsillitis and, worse, he apparently had a dead arm—which, oddly enough, his doctor linked back to his teeth. Brennan made only 11 starts on the year, and was 5–5. Without Brennan, the Chifeds still managed to keep themselves in the Fed race, thanks in large part to the hot hitting of Art "Home Run" Wilson (who was batting .373 in the first 21 games) and outfielder Al Wickland (.371). The Tinkers, as the papers frequently called the Chifeds, were just 2–5 to start the year on the road, but when they arrived at their new North Side park for a fourteen-game homestand, they went 9–5 and were back in the thick of a tight Federal League pennant chase.

More important, Weeghman Park was becoming a popular place, especially compared to the Cubs' West Side park. Every time the two teams played at home on the same day, the Chifeds brought in the better crowd. On the first weekend in May, there were 1,500 fans on the North Side on Friday, 5,000 on Saturday, and 10,000 on Sunday. Meanwhile, on the West Side, fewer than 9,800 fans showed up for all three weekend games combined. The Cubs were struggling badly, and not only in the stands. The pitching was inconsistent, the chemistry on the team was bad, and the hitting was terrible—according to stats compiled on May 14, the Cubs were batting just .225 as a team. Manager Hank O'Day could not find a decent shortstop. Tinker was two years removed from manning that position for the Cubs, and his successor, Al Bridwell, had jumped to the Federals and was playing for Miner Brown in St. Louis. Red Corriden, a journeyman who was a career .182 hitter before 1914, wound up with the bulk of the action, but he would commit 48 errors (fifth in the N. L.) in just 102 games. A desperate O'Day would even try third baseman Heinie Zimmerman at short, but he committed 10 errors in 15 games, and that experiment quickly ended. Things went awry so quickly for the Cubs that, by May 12, rumors that O'Day would be fired were so rampant that Charles Thomas had to make a public denial.

"The Cubs have not drawn well," N. L. president John Tener acknowledged. "There is no denying the fact that Joe Tinker's club is far more popular in the Windy City than that of Hank O'Day. There are two good reasons for this. Perhaps the Chicago Nationals have made a very disappointing showing so far. ... The West Side fans for many years have had a winner or at least a club very prominent in the race. They cannot brook a loser after many years of success. Then, too, there is a general belief in Chicago that Charles W. Murphy is still interested in the Cubs. No one can get that idea out of people's heads. The selection of Mr. Thomas as president unfortunately has placed that gentleman in a false light. Chicagoans argue that, as Mr. Thomas was a personal friend of Mr. Murphy, the latter must be interested in the Cubs still."[3]

Tinker, though, wasn't quite so popular outside of Chicago, especially where Federal League raids on O. B. rosters were continuing. Even after the Chief Johnson injunction, his former team, Cincinnati, continued to be the target of Federal League rumors as players chafed under the rule of manager Buck Herzog. On Friday, May 8, Cincinnati made a serious mistake when, during a trip to St. Louis, the team secretary booked the Reds at the Buckingham Hotel—which happened to be the same hotel housing the Pittsburgh Federals, in town to play the Terriers. In what was labeled an "executive committee" meeting, Three Finger Brown met with former Reds teammates Tommy Clarke and Rube Benton in the room of persuasive young Pittsburgh manager Rebel Oakes, who had officially replaced Doc Gessler in the manager's spot the previous day. Clarke and Benton told Oakes and Brown that there were seven Reds ready to follow the lead of Johnson and jump if the judge in Johnson's case ruled in favor of the Feds. "Oakes," it was written, "mingled with Herzog's men and painted a lurid picture of all the money behind the new league."[4]

Tinker, though, remained the league's top recruiter. The Feds' new position of using the ten-day clause against Organized Baseball signaled a more aggressive strategy in the pursuit of players, and the chance that Johnson's case would keep him in the Federal League provided some optimism that the league could soon get onto an even footing with the American and National leagues. Tinker was thinking big. The Chifeds would play a series in Baltimore that wrapped up on Saturday, May 23, and would spend Sunday in Washington, D.C., where a game against a semipro club had been arranged. (Baltimore, like many cities on the East Coast, did not allow Sunday baseball.) The game didn't matter much, because for Tinker, the big feature of the day would be the most prized pitcher in all of baseball: the Washington Senators' Walter "Big Train" Johnson.

It can't be overstated just how good Johnson was in 1914. The previous year, when he was only twenty-five, he registered what remains one of the greatest pitching seasons of all time, with a 36–7 record and a 1.14 ERA, finishing 29 of his 36 starts and logging 11 shutouts. He had won the Chalmers award—the MVP award at the time, sponsored by the Chalmers Motor Company. He led the American League in strikeouts for three of the four previous years, posting a record of 119–49 in that span. He was just entering his prime and, always important from the Feds' perspective, he was playing for an organization known to pinch pennies. Johnson was baseball's most valuable player, but he was not being paid like it. Johnson was earning a respectable $10,000 in 1914, but considering Tris Speaker, after his negotiations at the battle of the dock, was making about $20,000 per year, Johnson was undervalued.

Tinker arranged for Johnson to visit the Chifeds hotel after the game on the twenty-fourth. Johnson showed up "in the prize motor car which he won last season, and after talking with the gang for a while, he and Tinker went off and talked secretly."[5] After a conference that lasted more than an hour, Johnson emerged, smiling. He didn't reveal it at the time, but Tinker had made him an audacious offer, telling him that, if he wanted it, the Feds would put a team in Washington, and make him the manager in 1915[6]—though it was doubtful Tinker had the authority to promise the relocation of Federal League teams. Johnson was tight-lipped regarding the meeting, saying only that he and Tinker had not worked out anything definite—Johnson said he was not planning to jump his current contract, which ended when the season was over—but according to the *Washington Post*, "Johnson intimated that the Federals were willing to pay him a salary of nearly $25,000 per year." Tinker told reporters he was not sure whether Johnson would play for his team next year, but that either way, Johnson would be getting a significant raise. Johnson, perhaps unwisely, said, "I have not bound myself to anyone for 1915. I will pitch for the one that gives me the most money."[7]

When Tinker spoke to reporters in New York a few days later, before the Chifeds headed back to Chicago, he was almost arrogant about the Federal League's ability to bring in Johnson because he said, Robert Ward of Brooklyn would be willing to pay him $100,000. By Tinker's logic, it would be a good business investment. Ward would offset Johnson's salary, in part at least, through the good advertising Johnson would bring to Ward's Tip-Top bakeries. Tinker also insisted that the league's ongoing talks with Ty Cobb could bear fruit, too, because players wanted to earn a good living just as much as team owners did. "Walter Johnson will play in with the Federal League next season," he said. "I talked to him for two hours in Washington last Sunday. He frankly stated he was in baseball for the same reason the magnates were: to make money. ... Walter Johnson will be with the Federal League next season for the simple reason that organized baseball hasn't enough money to hold him. Ty Cobb also may be with us. His case is practically the same as Johnson's. Cobb is a sensible man out to earn money, just the same as his employers are."[8]

This kind of chatter was none to pleasing to the magnates of Organized Baseball, who had viewed themselves—and passed the view on to the press and the public—as benevolent stewards of the game who gave the public a much-beloved entertainment and generously granted the players a tidy wage out of their profits. The notion of Ward admitting he was in the game for bakery advertising made him a heretic, and those players who only wanted fat salaries weren't much better. It was all too much for Brooklyn owner Charles Ebbets, who had paid $15,000 for Tinker's rights just five months earlier, only to see him leave Brooklyn in the lurch and now turn against baseball's entire structure by claiming that money was at the root of the game. When Tinker was in town to play Ward's team in Brooklyn, he left behind some unflattering rumors concerning the unhappy state of players on the Superbas.

Ebbets vented to the press: "Tinker is a most dangerous man. He is not content with trying to lure away players under contract to the major leagues. He has tried to show his personal spite toward me by starting tales about my club. Evidently Tinker and certain other Federal League persons wish to make all the capital possible out of cheap advertising. He has admitted that the Federal League backers look upon that venture solely as an advertising medium. Well, that may be all right if they can get away with it. But organized baseball wishes to treat its patrons fairly and to furnish them with the best possible entertainment for their money. ... If I wished to be spiteful I might possibly get back at Tinker. But I am not going to take the trouble, for I do not believe that the Federal League is of sufficient importance. In my mind it is dying on its feet and all the recent noise and bluster is simply a bluff to ballyhoo, if possible, a few more patrons into the parks."[9]

After the Chifeds returned to Chicago from Tinker's tumultuous trip to the East, the city was to be treated to its second North-West-South triple-header, on Sunday, May 31. The atmosphere, though, was considerably different this time around. Both the Cubs and the White Sox had fallen flat in the first month-and-a-half, with identical 17–22 records, good for seventh place in their respective leagues. The Chifeds were 17–17, which, in a balanced Federal League race, put them in second place, five-and-a-half games behind Baltimore. Just how the teams stacked up against each other in popularity in the city was most easily measured on days like this, where attendance let all know where sentiment stood. The Sox brought in 10,000 fans, a low number for a Sunday game but considerably more than the 2,500 who showed for the Cubs on the West Side. That might seem to have created an opening for the Chifeds, who had been neck-and-neck with the South Siders in the first three-way attendance matchup and were the only of the three teams near the top of the standings. But there was disappointment on the North Side too. The game at Weeghman Park drew only 6,000. The three teams combined to draw more than 50,000 fans just three weeks earlier. Now, they brought in a scant 18,500.

One report said, "Chicago's baseball magnates were wondering yesterday where all the fans were hiding. For the second time this season, the three Chicago teams were at home on the same day and although the weather conditions were fine for the national pastime only about two-fifths as many persons turned out as were gathered at the parks three weeks ago."

‡

Tinker's meeting with Johnson, Brown's meeting the Reds, talk about Ty Cobb jumping his contract—all of it was part of the Federal League's scheme to induce a mass number of major leaguers to invoke their ten-day clauses. In every corner of Organized Baseball, rumors circulated about whom the jumpers would be and which teams would be hardest hit. In addition to the reports about the Reds, a large group of Senators besides Walter Johnson were said to be potential jumpers, including first baseman Chick Gandil, pitcher Jim Shaw, and outfielder Clyde Milan, three of the team's best players. Two young Yankee pitchers, Al Schulz and Ray Caldwell, were targets, as was Tinker's former teammate with the Cubs, pitcher Ed Reulbach, now with Brooklyn. Cardinals pitchers Slim Sallee, Pol Perritt, and Dan Griner were among those said to be ready to leave their teams in bunches. Shortly after Tinker's meeting with Johnson, Jim Gilmore proclaimed, "I can name 37 players of the National and American Leagues whose contracts embrace the ten-days' option of release clauses. I can say further that the majority of these men in all probability will be with us before two weeks."[11] For a league that originally would have been happy signing forty big leaguers, the Federals' public aspirations had blossomed. In some corners that was taken as a sign of weakness, that offers such as the one made to Johnson "look like mere efforts to advertise the independent league, and by some are taken as indications the Feds are on their last legs."[12]

Two days later, sitting at Weeghman Park, Tinker received a couple of surprising guests—Joe and Mike Cantillon, who were in town with the Minneapolis Millers, on their way back from a road trip. The Cantillons were, of course, the landlords of the North Side park, and though they were technically members of Organized Baseball and thus at war with the Federal League and Tinker in particular, "the two factions were exceedingly friendly, and although President Gilmore was not present, the Minneapolis magnate sat in his private office, along with Tinker and Secretary Williams and a couple of war scribes, for more than an hour." The parties would not get into the details of their discussion, but it was suggested that, if the Federal League was planning a raid, it would be under instructions not to take any American Association players.[13] It would not be the last time that Mike Cantillon was in contact with the Feds.

For the bulk of the potential jumpers Gilmore claimed, much hinged on the decision to be rendered by Judge Charles Foell in Chicago, who had been mulling the Chief Johnson injunction. Gilmore discussed the ruling as a near-certain victory, and judging by the scramble of teams to remove ten-day clauses from current contracts, the magnates of Organized Baseball agreed. They were wrong. On June 3, Foell came back with his ruling, and on every point brought before him, he sided with the Reds and would not allow Johnson to pitch for any team except Cincinnati. The Feds had been hoping that, at the very least, Foell would rule in their favor about the lack of mutuality in the ten-day clause, but here Foell found that the clause is "contained in practically every baseball contract entered into between the players and the principal clubs of the country during the last 20 years." That included the one Chief Johnson had signed the previous year. Just as they'd done in the Killefer case, the Feds again lost a major case based on some strange legal reasoning—basically, Foell said that because past contracts had always included ten-day clauses, there was no legal right for players to expect mutuality.

This was a hard blow for the new league. The Johnson verdict would be overturned on appeal in July, but by then, the prospect of the early June mass defection had lost momentum. "Scores of players," one report stated, "including a dozen or more stars, were ready to jump to the Federal League at the word that Johnson's case had been decided in favor of the Kansas City Federals, whom he joined after deserting Cincinnati. Contracts, it is said, had already been signed, depending only on the contingency that the pitcher's jump would be held legal."[14]

Gilmore was angry. He slipped from the courthouse down to the Chicago Athletic Association. There, he met with Weeghman and Bill Walker, as well as C. C. Madison of Kansas City, Ed Steininger and Otto Stifel from St. Louis, and league attorney E. E. Gates, to reformulate league strategy.

When they emerged, "their dander was up" and "there were hints of further raiding of the National and American league clubs regardless of the court decision."[15] And why not? Having already sunk so much into the league, their only choices were, as Stanley Milliken wrote, "Either to quit right now, stand the big loss, which might run as high as a million, or dig into their purses, yank out another million or two and start a general raid on organized baseball."[16] They chose another million or two.

The Feds kept the pressure on Walter Johnson, the superstar who had, thus far, given them the most serious audience. While the Senators were in New York on a road trip, representatives of the Tip-Tops intercepted Johnson and he agreed to go by car to Homewood, the New Rochelle estate of Robert Ward, who was trying to sell him on jumping to the new league now rather than next year. After a doubleheader with the Yankees on the very night of the Chief Johnson ruling, Federal League officials met Walter Johnson at the Waldorf-Astoria and presented him with a three-year contract for 1915–17. It was reported that he got as far as "Wal-" when he stopped and decided to think it over. While rumors spread that the deal was worth $100,000—$25,000 per year plus a $25,000 bonus—*Sporting Life* reported, "the contract calls for three years and a salary of $13,000 (annually), not $33,333 as has been reported." The Brooklyn Feds, the story said, "have the half-signed contract in their office."[17] Washington manager Clark Griffith made a counteroffer to Johnson of five years at $10,000 per year, but Johnson continued to make no commitments.

Similarly, Walter Ward, son of the Brooklyn owner, had dinner with Athletics second baseman Eddie Collins in Chicago, and made the same pitch he'd made to Johnson. In mid-June, Collins "tells us that Walter Ward yesterday raised that offer if he, Collins, would join the Brooklyn Feds. Just what figure Ward made him he would not say, but he declared the offer was for three years and that the salary would be guaranteed. As to his future action, he declared he wouldn't jump his present contract which expires next fall."[18] Collins likely had reason not to give out salary numbers because, as with overblown reports about Johnson's offer, in reality, the salary probably was not the $100,000 that was being reported.

The indication of both Collins and Johnson that they would not jump their current contracts but would consider it when those contracts expired line up with another mantra the Federal League seemed to take on after the Chief Johnson ruling—think ahead. Rather than straight contract-jumping in 1914, the Feds wanted to line up players for 1915, even in the middle of June. One player said that "there were six major-league ballplayers who had already signed Federal League contracts for next year; that their money was in the bank and drawing interest and that at least 25 more were ready to fall in line."[19] The *Chicago Daily News* reported that one of those would be White Sox outfielder Ray Demmitt, who would sign a two-year contract to play for the Federal League's Buffalo team after the season. "Snatching players from the National and American leagues and signing them to future contracts has been going on quietly for months," the paper noted.[20]

The South Siders had another problem besides Demmitt, though. On June 15, though the ten-day clause had been held as binding by Judge Foell, it was reported that five major leaguers would serve ten-days' notice to their teams and join the Federal League immediately. Among the five were three Reds—Tom Clarke, Rube Benton, and Red Ames—who would potentially add to the growing list of Tinker's former players making the leap. Benton and Ames were slated to bolster Tinker's pitching staff on the North Side, which would be a happy turn of events for him, because his vaunted pitching staff had been a disappointment. The five players were to be part of a group Jim Gilmore was again billing as a massive set of jumpers, this time touting a list of forty players. "Let 'em jump," Tinker said. "The more the merrier, but what I need is pitching. When I see a few pitchers from the other side who look good to me, I will grab them and then look out for this North Side bunch."[21]

Also among the five was a struggling pitcher for the Yankees, Al Schulz, and, on the opposite end of the talent spectrum, star first baseman Hal Chase of the White Sox, known as one of the greatest fielders of his position in the game, and one of its shadiest characters. That Chase would jump wasn't a surprise. Back in March, he had thought to be a cinch to join the Federal League and had come close enough to agreeing to a deal with the Feds that he was late showing up at White Sox training camp. But at the time Weeghman was trying to maintain healthy relations with the Cubs and Sox, and, the *Tribune* reported, "The determination of President Weeghman of the Chifeds to keep hands off the White Sox and Cubs is believed to be one of the reasons why Chase remains in organized base-ball."[22] By the start of the season, with the pursuit of Larry Cheney and other West Siders, that policy had changed, at least for the Cubs. Now, rumors were rampant that the Feds were going after Comiskey's men—in addition to Demmitt, infielder Lena Blackburne, and outfielder Ping Bodie were reportedly planning to sign contracts with the outlaws for 1915.

Given Comiskey's popularity in Chicago, this was dangerous ground. Not only Weeghman, but Gilmore, too, had been in favor of leaving Comiskey's men alone. That was off now. Chase, it was said, "has been intensely dissat-isfied with the conditions on the South Side, and he was looking about for an opportunity to better himself."[23] Before he had been traded from the Yankees to the White Sox, Chase would later say, his salary had been cut from $6,000 to $3,000, and that was the source of his dissatisfaction.[24] But the opportunity to better himself came with a jump in pay to $5,000 from Buffalo, where he would join friend and one-time business partner Dick Carroll, the Buffeds' business manager. And so Chase—as he told it—walked into Comiskey's office and handed the team owner his ten-day notice. All he'd have to do was to bide his time.

Just after Comiskey received Chase's notice, he huddled up with Ban Johnson and Red Sox owner Joseph Lannin to discuss the next move. Comiskey still couldn't be sure that Chase was really going to jump—of the five players that were named as ready to leave for the Feds, only Schulz actually went through with it, while Ames, Benton, and Clarke remained with the Reds. If Chase did go, there would be another injunction, as with Chief Johnson and others. The Chase situation was accompanied by the usual media bluster between Johnson and Jim Gilmore, with Gilmore this time going so far as to say that Organized Baseball's business amounted to "peonage" and served to "enslave" players. But through all of that, Gilmore did have a moment of clarity about what was going on in baseball. "We cannot try our lawsuits in the press," he said, "and the public is uninterested in our quarrels."[25]

# CHAPTER FOURTEEN

# Lazy Days

On Saturday, June 20, Hal Chase was at Comiskey Park on the South Side, manning first base for the White Sox. He went 0-for-3 with a walk in a 5–2 win over Red Sox ace Smoky Joe Wood. The next day, his locker was cleaned out. Rather than his usual two-block jaunt from his residence at the Warner Hotel over to the Sox's park, Chase went north to Sheffield and Addison. He was no longer a member of the White Sox, as he saw things, and by chance, his new team—the Buffalo Federals—were in town to play at Weeghman Park. Chase arrived just after lunch, made his greetings, and was measured up for a uniform. He got in a few minutes of practice before the start of the game, and only a few of the 10,000 fans at the park recognized him. That changed, though, as the announcer moved from section to section around the park, using a megaphone to inform fans that Chase would be playing first base in place of Joe Agler. "Each section in turn gave loud cheers," the *Tribune* reported. "When Hal went to bat the first time, he nearly stopped the show. The whole crowd seemed to join in the applause and it was continued for fully a minute, until Hal acknowledged it with an appreciative touch of the cap."[1]

It was no accident that Chase made his debut on a Sunday—the courts were closed, so even though Comiskey had knowledge that Chase would be jumping, he couldn't file an injunction to keep him from playing. The Buffeds played in Chicago again on Monday, but by then, Chase was already in Buffalo, hoping to stay one step ahead of the courts. His first home game would come on Thursday, and "Hal Chase Day" was greatly advertised around the city. In the meantime, the Federals had to keep him out of sight of Organized Baseball's agents, because if he could be located, he could be served papers. He was met at the train station in Buffalo and taken across the Canadian border to Niagara-on-the-Lake, where he and his wife "spent several days sojourning at the Queen's Hotel and enjoying the beautiful scenery." On the day before his Buffalo debut, he was taken across the river to Grand Island, and then to the outskirts of Buffalo. Once Buffeds officials snuck him into the park (a rumor that Chase was dressed in women's clothing to dodge O. B. agents was denied), Chase was hidden in a toolhouse. Antsy fans had no inkling of Chase's presence until it was his turn to bat, at which time, the toolhouse door opened, Chase emerged, and "the stands burst into a roar of approval."[2]

Of course, while Chase had been hiding out in Canada, Charles Comiskey was on a train from Chicago to Buffalo, accompanied by Ban Johnson's secretary, Robert McRoy, and attorney Ellis Kinkead. Having signed the indemnity bond for Chase, Comiskey was seated in the stands when, after the first inning (to aid the Chase surprise, the visiting Pittsburgh club agreed to let Buffalo bat first), Chase made his way to the bench. As expected, he was stopped and handed a court order dictating that he was not to play for Buffalo, which he accepted with a smile. He changed out of his uniform, which now had just one game and one inning's worth of use, and went to his hotel.

Chase's case would be up to a judge now, but Comiskey knew that the string of injunctions and the focus on salaries were dragging the game down. Because his team had gone largely untouched by the Feds, he mostly had stayed silent on the new league. Now that he had been dragged into it, he showed some wisdom on the situation. Surely, the Sox-Chifeds-Cubs tripleheader of May 31, which failed to draw even 20,000 fans total, was an eye-opener in a baseball-mad town like Chicago. "It is all due to contract-jumping and the demoralized condition of the players," Comiskey said.

"There is no use trying to hide that state of affairs. The public sees the true condition of the game even more quickly than the players. It has been the players, aided and abetted by club owners and their agents who have brought baseball to the condition prevailing at the present time. If there is room for three leagues, well and good. The gate receipts will tell the story. The players have a right to get more money if they can, but not at the expense of their conscience in jumping their contracts. It is not so much a question of losing money as it is of keeping up the standard of the game. If that is lowered, the public will desert it."[3]

The public was already deserting it. Across baseball, the quality of the game was flagging, and it wasn't difficult to figure out why. The Federal League was using the ten-day clause as a weapon to nullify O. B. contracts, and in response, owners had been plucking the clause out of player contracts (when he jumped to Buffalo, Chase was the only White Sox player to still have a ten-day clause). Most players were now on guaranteed contracts for the first time in their careers, and removal of the fear of being released meant that, suddenly, they didn't have to try all that hard. Comiskey would later say that the ten-day clause was "one which enforces on the part of the player the highest order of skill and effort of which he may be capable, and insures to the baseball going public a guarantee that the contestant will give to each and every game their best and most skillful effort in their attempt to play the game to win."[4] Without it, the public had no such guarantee.

Stories about player laxity appeared regularly, like one out of Pittsburgh that quoted a manager as saying, "I know that my men are not keeping in shape, but I don't want to see it." The same story claimed a Forbes Field patron had suspicions about the efforts of an unnamed team and staked out a local bar, where, "his surmise was true to the letter. Four-fifths of this suspected team crooked elbows before going to their hotel." It also suggested that New York Giants Red Murray and Larry Doyle had been keeping company with Federal League agents and could jump, adding that Murray "didn't train a lick this Spring, isn't in shape and perhaps won't be this season." It showed. Murray had hit .277 in 143 games and .267 in 147 games the two previous years, but hit just .223 in 86 games in 1914. Doyle, too, waned, hitting .260, his worst average since his rookie year.[5]

Even Tris Speaker, with his huge new guaranteed contract, was a disappointment—he was batting .283 at the end of June. (He would rally to hit .338 on the year.) When the Red Sox came to Chicago in late June having won nine of their twelve previous games, they promptly lost four of their next five because, as one writer put it, "in that hot-bed of Federal League activity several of [manager Bill] Carrigan's best ball players forgot about the game in contemplation of the wonderfully alluring offers made them by the scouts of the new league. The relations between President [Joe] Lannin and one or two of his stars became somewhat strained."[6]

The case of Reds third baseman Bert Niehoff, a promising young player and one of the many former charges of Tinker's to come close to joining the Federals before the 1914 season, was not uncommon. On June 20, Niehoff gave Reds owner Garry Herrmann ten days' notice, and he was reportedly set to join the Chifeds. "Well, the blow is falling now," Tinker said.[7] But when Tinker left his team in St. Louis to see Niehoff play against the Cubs, Reds manager Buck Herzog benched Niehoff because "he refused to allow a 'Federal Leaguer' to play on his team."[8] Herzog had Niehoff back in the lineup the next day, and the results were not appealing—Niehoff was 0-for-4, with an error and a botched play that allowed a run to score. The out-of-sorts Reds were swept in their four-game series on the West Side. After watching Niehoff's follies, Tinker pulled the Chifed offer[9] and Niehoff fell into a slump, hitting .197 from June 25-August 13. He was benched again, in favor of light-hitting utility man Fritz von Kolnitz. "The batting of Niehoff has been uncertain and his hitting slump has made him a bit wobbly in the field," a dispatch from Cincinnati read. "[Niehoff] has been more or less of a mercurial player this season. It took him quite a while to start, and then he was assailed by the Federal temptation, but he resisted that and got back to his stride."[10] He quickly lost that stride again, however.

As Comiskey suggested, the fans saw the true condition of the game—players were out of shape, they were not going at full speed, and they were distracted by the temptation of the Federal League. Gilmore's repeated promises of dozens of players jumping in a massive Federal League raid grew tiresome, especially when those raids, in reality, produced so few new players for the league. On July 1, Tinker himself conceded, "There has been too much brass band publicity already" when it came to the trumpeting of a planned defection of major leaguers to the Feds. Of course, he said that even as he was predicting twenty to twenty-five players would jump "by tomorrow night."[11] Again, when "tomorrow night" arrived, no jump materialized.

Backlash against players was increasing. Chicago reporter I.E. Sanborn wrote that the action of players chasing more money from the Feds could be likened to fixing games. "We don't wish anybody any hard luck," Sanborn wrote, "but cannot resist expressing the belief that it would be a good thing for baseball if all the men who consider a contract a joke were enjoined permanently from engaging in the game anywhere. It's only a stop in the public's mind from accepting a sum of money to break one's word to taking the coin for throwing a ball game, don't you know."[12] An editorial in the *Philadelphia Record* read, "The talk of fabulous salaries is having the effect of making some of the stars dissatisfied with ordinary bank president's pay, with the result that they are turning a listening ear to the voice of the charmer. The fact that it may be only talk does not lessen the damage any, since it is affecting the play. Ball players who are flirting with $35,000 offers cannot be expected to give their whole attention to a game of ball, and it does not take a crowd long to discover this fact. Nothing kills interest in the [game] more effectively than careless play, and this the club owners are being made to realize."[13]

‡

If Chicago was, indeed, such a hotbed of Federal League activity that opponents became distracted by the offers of the league's agents, by the beginning of July, the Cubs and White Sox finally were taking advantage of the situation. Under the headline, "These Be Fat Days for Chicago Fans," Sanborn wrote, "Baseball interest has been looking up decidedly hereabouts."[14] The White Sox, despite the injunction to keep him with the team, actually played better without Chase and his dissatisfaction. Veteran pitcher Ed Walsh was in the midst of a comeback year and, one report noted, "It is now an open secret that he was on the outs with Hal Chase and would not exert himself to his utmost so long as Chase played the initial sack. The correspondents traveling with the White Sox say there is more of the old-time fighting spirit to be seen on the Sox now than in any former year since [1906]."[15] On June 19, the White Sox were 24–31 and in sixth place, ten games out of first place. They won sixteen of their next eighteen games, climbing as high as second in the American League standings.

The Cubs surged at the same time. They were in sixth place, too, on June 18, seven games out of first, but they won fourteen of their next sixteen, also getting themselves into second place. Tinker's team did both the Sox and Cubs one better by winning eleven out of thirteen games in late June and early July, including a set of three wins in four games over league-leading Indianapolis. That performance pushed the Chifeds past the Hoofeds, earning first place in the Federal League. The run of luck for the three Chicago teams came at an opportune time, because for the third time of the 1914 season, there were games scheduled at the North, West, and South Side parks, and they would happen on the Sunday of the Fourth of July weekend, the height of baseball attendance in a typical season. The first two tripleheaders had seen the Chifeds show well at Weeghman Park, essentially tying the White Sox the first time around in early May and finishing well ahead of the Cubs in late May. But this time, things were different. With the ever-popular Walsh on the mound, the White Sox drew between 13,000 and 15,000. The Cubs had 8,000 fans and, with their fortunes having turned around, the *Tribune* reported that, "it seems Chicago's fans have forgotten their hated for the West Side club since it has battled its way close to the top. ... Fully 8,000 rooters attended and screamed with delight."[16] On the North Side, though, there was disappointment. The Chifeds were in first place but the novelty of the Federal League was wearing off. The game brought in only about 5,000 fans.

This wasn't necessarily cause for Organized Baseball to celebrate. Though the Chifeds were trounced at the gate on July 5, the fact remained that, on a huge holiday weekend with all three teams surging to the top of their leagues, the teams failed to bring in 30,000 fans. Remember, the first three-way matchup of the Cubs, Sox, and Chifeds drew more than 50,000 fans. It was becoming obvious that the battle of the turnstiles wasn't only a battle of Federal League teams vs Organized Baseball teams. As fans grew more and more put off by the legal battles and salary wars that dominated the headlines, it became a matter of fans simply losing interest in the game and refusing to patronize it. "There was not much satisfaction in the showing, however, for any of the rivals," Sanborn wrote, "for the total crowd at the three parks was not equal to the attendances that either White Sox or Cubs have drawn in past big days."[17]

One of the very reasons the Federal League came into existence was that Weeghman felt he could knock the Cubs off their perch with fans in the city. After his initial success, though, things were faltering. As far back as May, Weeghman was having financial worries and was reportedly borrowing money. Ban Johnson had managed to place a mole, posing as a landscaper, within the Chifeds organization, and had been getting inside information on the state of the team through him. Charles Murphy, who knew Weeghman well and had been around the team going back to the groundbreaking at the North Side park in March, told the planted landscaper that Weeghman was "getting more crazy every day," and that "if he don't quit spending money he will go broke."[18] By July, with the Chifeds slipping behind the Cubs in popularity and more empty seats in his new North Side park, Weeghman was surely going a little crazier.

But Chicago was the least of the Federal League's problems. By one estimate, the league was losing $10,000 every day, and would lose $1 million on the season.[19] When the Federal League had its stormy meeting at the Hotel LaSalle in January—when Weeghman nearly walked away—it had been decided that a reserve fund of $200,000 should be established. The Feds had obviously already blown through that, and that was without the cost of signing up a big-name star. Kansas City, with its small and antiquated ball park, was especially in trouble. By mid-May, the team was playing to crowds that averaged about 400 fans.[20] When a flash flood of the nearby Turkey Creek wiped out the team's playing field, the Packers had no choice but to play the final month of their season playing on the road—bad news considering that the team's initial capitalization of $50,000 was spent by early August and there was a question of whether the Packers could make payroll. Buffalo was handicapped by the fact that the State of New

York did not allow Sunday games, and the Buffeds typically drew "1,200 to 2,400 on week days and about 4,500 on Saturdays."

In Brooklyn, where $275,000 had been spent on rebuilding the Dodgers' old stadium at Washington Park, attendance was so poor that at the end of June, the team slashed its prices to minor league levels. On the day before Gilmore was announcing the intention of the Federal League to sign Eddie Collins, Walter Johnson, and Ty Cobb the following season, a story appeared on the news wires reporting, "The most serious blow that has befallen the Federal League's claim to major ranking developed on the inside when the Ward brothers of Brooklyn announced a cut to minor league prices for the rest of the season. Beginning Wednesday, the Tip-Tops will play 25 cent baseball at the New Washington park." Part of the Federal League's pitch to fans was that it was a legitimate third major league, on par with the American and National leagues. Slashing prices undermined that claim.

No team, though, was having a worse time of it than Three Finger Brown's Terrapins in St. Louis, who had started fast but quickly sank to eighth place. Worse, no one was showing up—in part because the N. L.'s Cardinals and the A. L.'s Browns, long the doormats of their respective leagues, were actually having good seasons, and in part because there was just no appetite for a third league in a small city like St. Louis. The Chifeds played a four-game series in St. Louis that wrapped up with a Sunday game on June 28, and one report reminded readers that poor attendance wasn't just a problem for the home team—the road team lost out on its cut of the receipts, too: "Yesterday being Sunday, the Mound City fans swarmed to the ball park in numbers that barely passed the 200 mark. Week day attendances averaged close to 100. It can be seen easily that the Tinx as well as the Terriers dropped a nice bunch of money playing the series."[22] Even when the Terriers acquired Reds outfielder Armando Marsans, his debut drew only about 500 fans. It was so bad in St. Louis that Gilmore made a trip just to prod Otto Stifel into getting more fans to the park. Gilmore "seemed to think the local magnates are to blame. He gave reporters the impression that he had talked quite sharply with them about it. Just how they took their call down from the man who got them into their present predicament is unknown, but one reporter said that Mr. Stifel, the chief local backer of the Feds, seemed "dazed."[23]

Brown was said to be "disgusted" by the state of his team.[24] He had been easygoing with his team in the early part of the year, but now he was forced by ownership to institute tough "blue laws" that would cut down on gambling and force players to be in bed by 11 PM under the threat of a fine. All the while, his players tuned him out and performed in front of thousands of empty seats, while rumors percolated to the effect that Cubs catcher Roger Bresnahan, former manager of the Cardinals, was in talks to replace Brown. Bresnahan stayed put, but by August, Brown was out, replaced by another big name from the Chicago baseball scene—Fielder Jones, president of the Northwestern League and the manager of the 1906 champion White Sox, whom Comiskey had tried to coax back to his team for the last three years. He turned down Comiskey, but accepted a post with the Feds.

The Federal League did get some other pieces of good news. Though the verdict came back against them in the appeal of the Killefer case—the unclean hands conundrum remained—the injunctions against Chief Johnson and Hal Chase were lifted in late July, as judges in those cases found that the ten-day clause's lack of mutuality was against the law. It was a hollow victory, though. Late July was too late to make the kind of big-league raid that would bring in a wave of new fans, and besides that, fans had already begun to shun baseball in general, and the Feds in particular. Gilmore assured the press that the Federal League would play the entire season despite the sputtering crowds. He did not mention that several teams would only be able to do so with an influx of cash.

Back in May, Brooklyn owner Robert Ward was quoted as saying, "The Federal League is in the field to stay. Certainly, if baseball survives, we will survive. A great deal of fun has been poked at the drawing cards of some of our towns. Well, just remember this: There is such a fraternal feeling among the Federal League colleagues that if anybody needs assistance he will not have to beg for it. We will stand together from start to finish."[25] He couldn't have known then just how much "fraternal feeling" the weak teams in his league would need, and he couldn't have known that it would mostly come from his pocket. But as attendance sagged, Ward was called on for help, and, in fact, he gave $38,000 to keep Kansas City from going under altogether. In all, Ward would wind up sinking $1 million into the Federal League.

# CHAPTER FIFTEEN

# Stretch Run, 1914

Promised raids that fizzled, lax play, and rampant commercialism were some reasons the Federal League lost fans as the 1914 season went on. But perhaps the most significant reason was that the quality of play simply wasn't up to snuff. Whether the Feds constituted a legitimate major league was—and to an extent still is—a matter of debate, but the failure to induce star players to jump, and the legal wrangles that weighed down those players who did jump, hurt public perception of the league. Beyond that perception was the reality that green minor leaguers and washed-up veterans who were not of star caliber were putting up oddly stellar performances. That was certainly the case on the North Side.

Coming into the year, Tinker felt he had the kind of pitching staff that should dominate the league, headed by Claude Hendrix and Ad Brennan. But with Brennan's struggles and injuries, Tinker scrambled and turned to a pair of spitballers from the Chicago area, Roseland's Max Fiske and Forest Park's Erv Lange. Fiske was a holdover from Chicago's 1913 entry into the Federal League and was, frankly, lucky to even be alive. The previous March, he had been working a job in the Pullman car factory when an electrical junction box fell on his head, putting him "in a hospital wavering between life and death. Surgeons administered seventeen shots of serum of antitoxin while combating blood poisoning of the head."[1]

Fiske emerged from the hospital in June, had three weeks of rest, and was pitching again the next month.

Lange was, at one time, a White Sox signee, having pitched for the semipro team in Rogers Park on the North Side. He made his mark in the circuit in 1910 when he beat Gunther Park, usually Chicago's best semipro outfit in that era, five straight times, then struck out fifteen batters in a seventeen-inning game against Jimmy Callahan's Logan Squares. When the White Sox tapped him, though, he did not want to report to a minor league assignment in Dubuque, Iowa, so he continued to knock around with the semipros until Tinker gave him a shot before the season and was impressed.[2]

It's questionable whether Lange or Fiske, then, were of even decent minor-league quality, let alone major-leaguers. But when Tinker was forced to give them a chance, each performed well, giving the North Siders a workable staff behind Hendrix. Lange was the more reliable option, and by early August, he ranked among the Federal League's top pitchers in winning percentage, at 10–5. Fiske held his own, too, and was 9–4 at the end of July. With the Chifeds hitting better than expected, they surged to a three-and-a-half-game lead in the standings on July 30, and looked poised to run away with what had been a bunched-up race. But Tinker, who turned thirty-four in July, was dealing with multiple injuries, having suffered from tonsillitis in May and breaking a rib which punctured his lung later in the season. He wasn't himself at shortstop. The Chifeds also had injuries to their best hitter, Dutch Zwilling, and best defensive outfielder, Max Flack. The absences were piling up and the Chifeds lost three out of four games against Pittsburgh in late July and early August, followed by two losses in three games in Baltimore, pulling the Chifeds back into a tie with Baltimore and allowing Brooklyn (one-and-a-half games behind) and Indianapolis (three-and-a-half) into the pennant picture.

Starting on August 8, though, the Chifeds were settling in for a long home engagement on the North Side, not hitting the road again until the twenty-sixth. They started that stretch with a doubleheader sweep of Brooklyn that moved them back into sole possession of first place. With a day off on Sunday, Weeghman brought his team south to his hometown of Richmond, Indiana, for an exhibition—one that would show that the

Chifeds still had some comically bush league features. It rained most of the morning, but there was a break and the game started. Soon after, the rain picked up again, but the umpire refused to call the game. By the fourth inning, third baseman Harry Fritz took his position clutching an umbrella. Richmond didn't get a hit until the fifth inning, when Tinker joined Fritz under the umbrella and a ground ball bounced through the shortstop hole. Finally, after six innings, Tinker refused to send his men back onto the field. By the time Weeghman and Bill Walker fetched their car, it was "stuck in the mud and they had to walk half a mile in water and mud ankle deep. It was a sorry party that reached the hotel hours later."[3] Hard to imagine, say, the New York Giants in that predicament.

The Chifeds faced Brooklyn in a doubleheader two days later, and managed a bittersweet split. In the first game, Tom Seaton bested Hendrix—if things had gone as planned, Seaton would have been a member of the Chifeds because he had been recruited by Tinker and was to play alongside his friend and Phillies teammate Brennan. But Brennan stayed in Chicago and Seaton was induced to join Brooklyn, a decision Tinker would regret. While Brennan's dead arm had been useless all season, Seaton wound up going 25–14 for the Tip-Tops. Worse yet, two other pitchers Tinker had signed but allowed to go to other clubs in order to ensure even roster composition in the Federal League—Cy Falkenberg of Indianapolis and Russ Ford of Buffalo—combined to go 46–22 in 1914.

But Tinker's annoyance at his pitching situation was soothed some by the arrival of a new pitcher, Rankin Johnson, who was with the Boston Red Sox to start the year but was traded in late July to Cleveland. When he talked with owner Charles Somers, Johnson asked that he be granted a contract for 1915 and '16. Somers wasn't about to hand a two-year extension to a twenty-six-year-old rookie who had gone 3–9 with the Red Sox that year. When Johnson met with Jim Gilmore, Hal Chase, and Dick Carroll in Cleveland, then, he was ready to join the Feds—the players with whom he was traded, catcher Ben Egan and pitcher Fritz Coumbe, were tempted as well, but stayed in Cleveland. With Tinker desperate for another quality arm, Johnson was delivered to Chicago in early August. He was brilliant in winning his debut game for the Chifeds and, in the second half of the doubleheader against the Tip-Tops that had begun with Seaton's victory, Rankin came through with a 5–3 win that kept the Chifeds a game-and-a-half in the lead. Johnson's arrival was perfectly timed because it was obvious that Lange and Fiske—semipro bushers who had never played a full season, never dealt with the travel and wear-and-tear of a full major league schedule—were fading. After their fast starts, Fiske would finish on a 3–6 skid and Lange would be worse, at 2–6.

Now that the team was back playing at home, Weeghman did his best to keep the crowds coming to his new ballpark. He attempted to trade for Mordecai Brown after Fielder Jones took over in St. Louis, which would have surely boosted late-season crowds, but Jones instead sent him to Brooklyn. But then, Weeghman had already tried "Mordecai Brown Day" at his park. After that, he designated a "day" for just about every entity imaginable. Every Friday was Ladies' Day on the North Side, and there were days dedicated to secretary Charles Williams, to Jones when he brought St. Louis to town, to local hero Max Fiske, to German-Americans, to the YMCA, to the Elks, and to the National Union. Weeghman even devised a day honoring bowlers when Falkenberg, a native Chicagoan and, apparently, a big bowler, was visiting with the Hoosiers and was feted by local lovers of bowling. In August, there was a Masonic Day that drew 8,000 fans—3,000 of whom were Masons—who were greeted by a speech from one of the group's most prominent members in the city, William Hale Thompson. Despite those efforts—and despite the first-place fight—crowds on the North Side continued to register in the 5,000 range.

That was a disappointment, especially as the White Sox and Cubs, following their midseason surges, sank back in the standings. The White Sox embarked on a sixteen-game road trip in early July that started with three straight wins, getting them within two-and-a-half games of the A. L.-leading Athletics. But they went 3–10 on the rest of the trip, fell to sixth place, and were irrelevant by late July. The Cubs hung around longer, but they, too, were undone by a sixteen-game road trip, one that lasted into mid-August and saw the Cubs go 4–12. Rumors of player trouble with manager Hank O'Day, rumors that players would be jumping to the Feds, rumors that O'Day would be fired, and rumors that star infielder Heinie

Zimmerman would be traded all lingered and weighed on the team. "There is no doubt the Cubs this year are a rather spiritless lot," I. E. Sanborn wrote. "Whether or not that is Hank O'Day's fault no one can tell. There are a lot of other teams playing listless baseball this year and it is not all the fault of the managers. Too many of the players have no incentive whatever to exert themselves to the limit this season or even keep themselves in condition. So many of them are signed up to ironclad contracts that they know they can't get an increase in salary by working their heads off to win, nor can their salaries be cut if they loaf on their jobs. ... It is largely a case of each man for himself on that team."[5]

But then, it was a tough few months all around for those connected to the Cubs, especially the famed infield of their championship teams. Second baseman John Evers, playing his first season outside Chicago, left the Braves in early August to return to his home in Troy, New York, where his three-year-old daughter, Helen, was sick with scarlet fever. She died shortly thereafter, and there was some question whether Evers would play again. "Evers is just now suffering from the shock of a terrible affliction and is wrung with grief," N. L. president John Tener said. "Give him time to recover."[6] Just ten days after Helen Evers's funeral, the third baseman for those Cubs dynasty teams, Harry Steinfeldt—whose last name didn't quite fit with the Tinker-to-Evers-to-Chance poetry—died at age thirty-six. "It has often been said," one article claimed "that Steinfeldt's health broke shortly after being released by Manager Chance in 1910." Steinfeldt played briefly for the Boston Rustlers in 1911—they would become the Boston Braves in 1912—and was with the minor league Louisville Colonels in 1912, but was never the same. In 1913, rather sadly, he would go out every day to watch the Reds, donning a uniform to practice with his old teammates Tinker and Three-Finger Brown, though he was no longer in any shape to play. He was "only a shell of the Harry Steinfeldt of old."[7]

Those tragedies made the problems of Frank Chance seem minor in comparison. After leaving the Cubs in his fiery dispute with Charles Murphy, things hadn't worked out for Chance in New York, and by the middle of September, complaining about the level of talent he was being given and with his team hopelessly out of the race in seventh place, Chance offered his resignation. It was accepted, though the owners of the Yankees did not want to pay Chance for the final year of his contract in 1915. While Chance was addressing the media, he got into a shouting match with owner Frank Farrell and "Big Bill" Devery, the former police chief of New York who also had a partial interest in the team. Devery nearly punched Chance, but reporters intervened. Finally, Chance got into his car, left the team behind, and embarked on an "overland motor journey from Manhattan Island to his own vine and orange tree in California." He stayed for a few days in Chicago, but vowed that he was out of baseball forever.[8]

Tinker's troubles—with his pitching staff, with his health, with attendance at the North Side park—were relatively palatable. Still, when the Chifeds opened a crucial series against Indianapolis on September 1, with the two teams tied for first place, only 2,000 fans showed up. They saw Falkenberg in top form, shutting out the North Siders, and the following day, the Chifeds were shut out again by Indianapolis, this time with Earl Moseley on the mound. When Tinker committed three errors in the third game of the series, it led to a 5–4 loss that put Chicago a full three games behind the Hoosiers. But the team rallied to win the final home game of the series, then won two of three (with one tie) when the teams shifted to Indianapolis for a series. The net result of what started off as a disaster in the back-to-back series was just a loss of one game in the standings, the Chifeds in a close second place.

They would regain first place thanks to Buffalo. On September 11, the Chifeds suffered their worst defeat of the year, a 12–0 debacle played while battling the frigid winds off Lake Ontario. In the game, it looked like Buffalo was playing "against the Goodland, Morris or Princeton Yellow Hammers instead of a prospective pennant winning team in the Federal League. The Tinx could not hit a lick. They could not field and they dropped flies and messed things up generally."[8] But the Chifeds swept a doubleheader the next day, then returned home for a Sunday doubleheader with the Bisons. On Charles Williams Day—and on the final three-way attendance matchup of the Chicago teams—the Chifeds drew 8,000 (to just 7,000 for the White Sox, easily outdrawing the hapless Cubs) and won both games, giving them four wins in two days and a hold on first place.

Tinker's men continued to battle Indianapolis in the standings through their September road trip, going 14–8 (which included the Sunday sweep of Buffalo, played in Chicago because New York did not allow Sunday baseball), carrying a two-and-a-half-game lead in the pennant race, before they returned to Indianapolis for one more game on September 30. After that, the Chifeds would go home and close the season with seven games against two of the worst teams in the league, St. Louis and the well-traveled Kansas City Packers. In the game against the Hoofeds—a makeup of a game that ended in a tie three weeks earlier—the Chifeds saw Falkenberg, who was getting to be invincible against the North Siders. Falkenberg had started the month with a shutout of Chicago, and he closed the month in the same fashion, beating Rankin Johnson, 3–0, in what the *Tribune* called "one of the best games of the season." The win cut Chicago's lead to a game-and-a-half.

Losing to Indianapolis to end the trip was a disappointment, but the seven-game homestretch that would close the season started with a disappointment too—on October 1, another Ladies' Day, only 2,000 fans were at the North Side to see Tinker's first-place team. One of them happened to be Frank Chance, who watched Mike Prendergast pitch the club to a 2-1 win and told Weeghman he thought the Chifeds could beat his Yankees, which was likely a slight on the Yankees as much as a compliment to the Chifeds. Tinker got another strong pitching performance in the second game of the series from Hendrix, who breezed through the Terriers, allowing just two hits and striking out seven. But in the finale, one of Tinker's decisions cost the team badly. Back in the beginning of September, with Rankin Johnson having bolstered the staff, Tinker let veteran pitcher Doc Watson go, sending him to St. Louis for cash. Watson got his revenge on October 4, pitching the Terriers to a 1–0 win and beating Johnson as a bonus. With Indianapolis sweeping a doubleheader, Chicago's lead was only a half-game.

Prendergast was slated to pitch the Chifeds' next game, the opener of the final series against Kansas City, and he found himself in trouble early. Tinker, knowing his team needed this game, called on Fiske to relieve him. Fiske would be using the "emery ball," a freak pitch in the vein of a spitball, on this day. Rather than rubbing the ball up with saliva, a pitcher would slide the side of the ball against a strip of emery in his glove, scuffing it

and causing a more dramatic break than a spitter. Falkenberg and Russ
Ford—two of the top pitchers in the Federal League—had pioneered the
pitch and it had spread through much of the American League until Ban
Johnson outlawed it in September. The National and Federal leagues would
later do the same. "How the piece of emery paper figured can be told in
one sentence," Irving Vaughan wrote. "In the third, with the bags loaded
and one gone, Max Fisk [sic], accompanied by the emery, rushed to the
hill to supplant Mike Prendergast, retired the next two batters without a
run resulting and from then to finish allowed only two harmless singles,
only one hostile reaching second base."[9] The Chifeds won, 2–0, maintaining
their lead over Indianapolis.

Things would be different the following day, though. Slated for a doubleheader against the Packers, Tinker put his best pitcher, Hendrix, against K.C.
manager George Stovall's best, lefthander Gene Packard, Tinker's former
player with the Reds. Hendrix would go 29–10 on the season and Packard
would wind up 20–14. They pitched like two of the best in the league,
Hendrix holding Kansas City to seven hits, while Packard took advantage
of a lineup that had struggled to hit lefties, holding the Chifeds to five hits
and securing a 1–0 win. The second game took a farcical turn, not the kind
of sidelight one would expect during a matchup that would settle a league
championship. Tinker attempted to come back with Fiske and his emery ball
in the game, but Fiske was not nearly as effective and was replaced by Lange
in the third inning. After the seventh inning, with the Chifeds trailing, 5–3,
the umpires called the game because of darkness. Those in the small crowd
of 3,000 were outraged, including one "robust woman bug who has been a
steady customer of the park." She was angry enough to wait for the umpires
and when they tried to sneak out "although built for comfort rather than
speed 'Mrs. Irritation' dashed a block after the retreating umpires at almost
ten second speed. … The excited shouting of the woman attracted a crowd
which joined in denouncing the umps. The arbiters escaped only when the
'L' station was reached."[10]

That, essentially, marked the end of the first baseball season at the North
Side park—a doubleheader sweep followed by a large woman chasing two
umpires up Addison Avenue to the "El" station. The Chifeds would play one

more time, beating Kansas City, 8–3, on October 8, but with Indianapolis closing the season on an eight-game winning streak, the Hoosiers were the Federal League champions. Weeghman had offered a challenge to the White Sox and Cubs, pitting his team against the winner of the city championship in a seven-game series. He didn't receive any response and claimed that would make the Chifeds city champs by default. Of course, Rube Foster offered to have his Negro League Giants play Weeghman's team, but Weeghman said, "I told him that the Tinx could not play such a series with his team."[11]

Weeghman didn't want to face Foster's club for the same reason that the White Sox and Cubs didn't want to face the Chifeds, and the same reason the magnates of O. B. did not want the winner of the World Series between the Athletics and the Giants to play Indianapolis: because they might lose. It's impossible to tell how strong Foster's Giants were at the time, but the cases of Lange and Fiske, two of the team's top pitchers, give some indication of the overall weakness of Federal League rosters in 1914—if two semipro pitchers could be credible contributors on a pennant contender, the overall quality of the league was dubious. Lange was with Chicago in spring training the following year but never appeared in another Federal League (or minor league) game. Fiske held out for a raise in 1915 and was dumped by the Chifeds altogether. He was back to pitching for Roseland's semipro outfit the following summer.

As the Chifeds' final game was unfolding, Weeghman was in the press box of his North Side park, a little wistful. "I never thought I'd be sitting here watching 'em wind up the season," he said. "In the first place, I didn't think they would ever finish the park in time for us to start."[12]

# CHAPTER SIXTEEN

# Peace Foiled

When Mike and Joe Cantillon stopped by to speak with Joe Tinker at Weeghman Park in late May, the *Tribune* speculated that the discussion had centered on keeping the Federal League from acquiring American Association players. That might have been a topic, though if it was, it had little real-world effect—just two months later, when the Reds were sending infielder Johnny Rawlings to the Cantillons' Minneapolis team, Kansas City manager George Stovall stepped in and signed Rawlings to a contract with the Packers. It's more likely that, in stopping by the North Side, the Cantillons had something bigger on their minds. Weeghman's North Side park had worked out nicely, much as they and Charles Havenor had figured it would years earlier, and while the fight between the Federal League and Organized Baseball was being waged on the major league level, it was the minor leagues that were suffering most. The suspension of roster limits, a measure to keep players sent to the minors from jumping to the Federal League, forced big league teams to carry on their rosters players who would normally star on minor league teams. Teams that attempted to run the Federal League gauntlet by sending a player down—like the Reds and Millers tried to do with Rawlings—found themselves losing out altogether when the player jumped his contract.

Major league teams counted on the revenue generated by selling players to the minors, and minor league teams counted on those players to anchor their lineups, but in 1914, those transactions were stifled. One estimate, from the *Chicago Examiner*, figured that "taking the lists of the American, National and Federal League clubs, we checked off exactly 61 players who are now on the payrolls of the 24 clubs who beyond doubt would be back in the minors were it not for the coming of the Federal League. The condition is an astounding one. It means that the clubs are paying out nearly $20,000 a month in salaries for players they cannot use and do not need. Examine the conditions more fully; they are keeping 61 really good players away from the minor leagues that need good ball players."[1]

Ed Barrow, president of the International League—the I.L., based mostly in the East, and the American Association in the Midwest were the two best minor league operations, given a designation of Class AA—declared that every team in his league would lose money in 1914 and that it was unlikely any of the hundreds of teams under the umbrella of Organized Baseball would make money. This was one of the conditions that the Federal Leaguers had hoped to create, delivering enough pain to the minor leagues that they would abandon O. B. and force a top-to-bottom restructuring of the game, with the Federals as a third major league. One Chicago writer recalled that back in the winter of 1913, "Joe Tinker of the Chicago Federals boasted … over a glass of wine at the Waldorf-Astoria that the Federal League would put all the minor leagues out of business."[2]

But, Barrow said, every team in his league had been worth $50,000-$250,000 before the appearance of the Federal League and that his owners would be willing to wait and see whether the outlaws collapsed, after which time, his teams would regain their value. "Why are we hanging on? Why are the minor leagues hanging on? Why is the Federal League hanging on? The answer is hope of a peaceable settlement to the present situation in baseball, which will bring back the old profitable days."[3] This was the case all over baseball at the end of the 1914 season. Teams had suffered. But they hadn't quite suffered to the breaking point. The leagues were willing to hang on because the belief remained that the old profitable days would return.

As bad as the Federal League had been for business in the American Association, there was also an opportunity for the Cantillons, who had more connections on both sides of the war, and a bigger stake in peace, than any other owners. They were landlords of Federal League's most valuable grounds, friends of Tinker and Weeghman, owners of a prominent O. B. team, and had, themselves, once dreamed of the very North Side invasion that the Chifeds had carried out successfully. The Cantillons wanted to see the war end, like everyone in baseball, but wanted to craft a solution that guaranteed a team would occupy Weeghman Park—and, if there was a way to boost the A.A. and their own profits along the way, all the better. With that in mind, in the summer of 1914, Mike Cantillon and Garry Herrmann, owner of the Reds and chairman of the National Commission, began a dialogue. The result was that Cantillon met with Weeghman and Gilmore in Chicago and on September 4, reported to Herrmann that a deal could be worked out—one that would settle the war and, conveniently, reorganize the high minor leagues.

Under the proposal, Brooklyn and Pittsburgh's Federal League entries would be replaced by International League teams, the Fed franchises in Baltimore and Buffalo would amalgamate with the International League teams in those cities, as would the American Association teams in Kansas City and Indianapolis. Weeghman would get an American Association team for his North Side park in Chicago, and the St. Louis Federals would be bought out. Either the I.L. or the A.A. would take the Federal League name (a point of pride for the Feds) and, significantly, there would be an end to the draft, the system which allowed major league teams to pick off the best minor league players each year. Further, the newly reconstituted A.A. and I.L. teams would operate under the National Agreement but would not be members of the National Association. That sounds like a semantic change but was actually asking O. B. for a huge concession: It would mean the two Class AA leagues would operate under Organized Baseball's rules, but they would maintain some independence and, though they might not quite be a major league, they would not be a minor league, either.

Weeghman was suspicious of Cantillon's authority, and he should have been, because Cantillon hadn't been expressly granted the right to speak on behalf of O. B. Herrmann, for that matter, later said in a deposition that he wasn't sure about Cantillon's ability to speak for the Feds as a whole. But because he had a foot in each camp, Cantillon did so anyway, telling Herrmann he was speaking for the Federal League and telling Weeghman that he was speaking on behalf of O. B. (Later, an argument in the press would break out over which side initiated peace talks—both claimed that they were not responsible for starting the talks, and they weren't necessarily lying, because Cantillon misrepresented his authority.) The plan put forth to Herrmann was one that could be seen as beneficial to Federal League owners, but would most definitely benefit Cantillon: The two high minor leagues would expand and have a path toward becoming major league, the American Association would get a team in Chicago, Cantillon would have a secure tenant on his land and, as a side benefit, the draft would be eliminated. But the plan had little hope of success with major league magnates. Herrmann's fellow owners didn't feel they needed to give up that much just to placate an obviously struggling Federal League, which was teetering in several of its cities.[4]

Herrmann had not given up on settling the Federal League problem, though, and Cantillon continued to play intermediary. Just before the World Series between the Philadelphia Athletics and the Boston Braves began on October 9, Cantillon asked Herrmann to meet with Weeghman and other Federal League officials at the New York office of Brooklyn owner Robert Ward after the series was over. When the Braves were finished sweeping Philadelphia on October 13, Herrmann boarded a train to New York and checked in at the Waldorf-Astoria. When Weeghman called Herrmann's room the next day to ensure that the meeting was on, Herrmann suggested they meet sooner, one-on-one. Here, Herrmann brought up the scenario proposed by Cantillon and was surprised to learn that Weeghman wasn't interested in talking about the draft or minor league issues. Instead, Weeghman offered another proposal: Ward would pull out of the Federal League if he could purchase the Yankees, and Weeghman would also pull out if he could buy the Cubs.[5]

Herrmann was noncommittal, but this was definitely promising. Instead of a wholesale remake of baseball's structure, as proposed by Cantillon, all that would be required would the sale of the Cubs, a declining franchise owned by an aloof Cincinnatian with no interest in baseball, to Weeghman, a popular Chicagoan who happened to have a brand new park. The same could be said of New York. The owners of the Yankees, Frank Farrell and Big Bill Devery, were none too popular themselves, and did not have nearly the bankroll that Ward boasted. Herrmann wanted to explore this notion. He suggested Weeghman start by contacting Cubs owner Charles Taft. Weeghman did just that and learned that Taft still was looking to sell. The following week, Weeghman was in Chicago, preparing to go to New York for the Federal League's meeting on October 23. He got a telegram from Cincinnati, asking if he would stop to see Taft. Weeghman arrived early in the morning, and Taft "let Mr. Weeghman know that he was tired of the team and, as always, was willing to sell—at his price. This is less in figures than that which floored the Connery syndicate last spring, but it is big enough, when improvements necessary are taken into considera- tion, to approximate $1,000,000."[6] The price Taft had given Connery was $875,000, and the "improvements" that would drive the price to $1 million were for the Cubs' stadium on the West Side. But Weeghman didn't have the problem of requiring improvements. He made clear that the Cubs would not be on the West Side if he got hold of them. "If in the final arrangement we should get the club I regard as a fixture in Chicago, it will not play at West Side Park," Weeghman said. "My park in the North End is a better plant and in a better part of the city."[7] Weeghman came away from the Cincinnati meeting with what he thought was a short-term option on the team (though Taft would later deny offering an option).

Amid it all, Weeghman was on edge. At the Feds' meeting at the Biltmore Hotel in New York, he spotted the *Sun*'s Joe Vila, who had become Weeghman's greatest antagonist in recent months. Vila was well-connected to the magnates of Organized Baseball and had spent much of the year lampooning the Federal League in his paper and in *The Sporting News*— poking fun at Weeghman's fast-food background, his favored moniker was the "Lunch Room League," but he would also derisively call it the "Ham and Eggs Circuit" and the "Fritters League." According to one report, on seeing Vila, Weeghman called to him and "with no gentle force seized him by the lapel of the coat." Said Weeghman: "You are either subsidized by Organized Baseball or you are the damnedest liar in the world!"[8]

Vila, none too pleased about the attack, wrote: "Weeghman didn't make much of a hit here with newspaper men. He was peevish and hot tempered. He has much to learn as a base ball promoter. His present trouble seems to be an inability to believe that a writer who differs with him is on the square. Weeghman evidently doesn't understand that every man has a right to his opinion. He seems to think that a hostile critic is guided by pecuniary influences. If he expects to get along in the role of magnate, he'd better reach the conclusion pretty quickly that many base ball reporters, unlike waiters, do not receive tips."[9]

‡

Publicly, Federal League president Jim Gilmore continued to make loud threats about player raids and the possible relocation of franchises into major league cities. Philadelphia was mentioned, as were Boston, Washington, Cincinnati, Detroit, and, most seriously, New York (where one far-fetched story had it that legendary Giants manager John McGraw would take over). Gilmore promised, "If within a month, I do not hand Ban Johnson, Garry Herrmann and Governor Tener four distinct blows that will make them quake then I quit."[10] Coming out of the October meeting in New York, the league announced a "war fund" of $100,000 "in an effort to impress upon organized baseball that they wanted peace at their own terms or not at all."[11]

Privately, though, the talks between Weeghman and Herrmann continued. They met at the Congress Hotel in Chicago on October 31, and here, it was becoming clearer that settling the matter of the Federal League would be more complicated than simply giving the Cubs to Weeghman and allowing a team in the East to be purchased by Ward. Weeghman now asked if three or four major league teams could be bought—he and Herrmann discussed Phil Ball, who owned the St. Louis team with Otto Stifel and wanted to buy the Cardinals from the Brittons. Weeghman, obviously, wasn't quite ready to abandon the Federal League without a more comprehensive solution that took care of his fellow Fed owners. Part of the reason for that may have been given out by Walter Ward, secretary of the Brooklyn club, who said that the Federal League held all the leases on all the parks in the league "to forestall treachery."[12] If Weeghman abandoned the Federal League to buy the Cubs and move them to the North Side, he would have to have the lease on the park, and he could not get the lease unless the Federal League dissolved. And it wouldn't dissolve if the peace deal did not include those owners wealthy enough to block his departure.

By the time Herrmann left Chicago on November 1, newspapers were already heralding the coming of baseball peace. The following day, a story appeared under the headline "Peace Pact is Approved by Moguls," which stated, "Peace was declared at the meeting which was held under cover but only after organized ball agreed to make several concessions in favor of the third circuit, according to a tip from the inside."[13] But the tip was wrong. While Herrmann and Weeghman might have ironed out the framework for peace, with the Wards, Ball, and Weeghman getting major league clubs and the other Federal League teams to be bought out or given arrangements in minor leagues, the fact remained that Weeghman and Herrmann were just talking as individuals. There were twenty-two other ownership entities in three leagues, plus the affected minor leagues, that would have to go along with whatever agreement Weeghman and Herrmann made.

As details of Weeghman's discussions with Herrmann leaked out, so did objections and obstacles. The Wards getting the Yankees was a problematic proposition, first of all, because Ban Johnson remained steadfastly opposed to Federal League men in the American League. Complicating it further was that the Yankees' home at the time was the Polo Grounds, which was controlled by Giants owner Harry Hempstead—and Hempstead said that if the Wards got the Yankees, they'd no longer be welcome at his park. Herrmann had been told by Weeghman that Phil Ball had already worked out a deal to buy the Cardinals, but when Hermann spoke to Schuyler Britton about the negotiations, Herrmann was surprised to find that "this has been most emphatically denied by Mr. Britton. He stated he did not know Mr. Ball, and never met him in his life."[14]

Objections and obstacles came from the Federal League side too. Gilmore didn't believe that Herrmann had the power to act on behalf of O.

B. and he refused to participate in talks unless they involved fellow league presidents Ban Johnson and John Tener. Pittsburgh Federal League owner Edward Gwinner—one of the wealthier Fed magnates, who was notably not mentioned as a future major league owner—was annoyed by the Weeghman-Herrmann confabs. "I do not know what Weeghman is doing," Gwinner said. "But if he is trying to arrange peace between the Federal League and Organized Baseball, he must be acting on his own initiative. I am certain that our league never has given him the right to make or receive overtures looking to a cessation of the war now in progress."[15]

Against this backdrop, the American League held a meeting in Chicago in early November. The object of the meeting was to formulate a plan for handling the minor leagues, which were holding their meeting in Omaha three days later, but peace talks continued to rule the day. Among the attendees at the meeting, it was reported, was "Archie" Archambault, the Milwaukee businessman and brother-in-law of the Cantillons, who had only recently transferred a three-tenths share of the North Side grounds to Mike Cantillon for $1.[16] Archambault was "gumshoeing about town hobnob-bing with [Ban] Johnson's forces, with Tom Chivington, president of the American Association and with Messrs. Weeghman and Gilmore of the Fed organization." When asked by a reporter, Weeghman professed ignorance about Archambault's dealings. So did Cleveland owner Charles Somers, who stopped by Chivington's office while Archmbault was present.[17]

But Archambault did have some business with Somers—the following day, November 6, Archambault asked to see Somers in the lobby of the Congress Hotel. There, he arranged for Weeghman to have dinner with Somers at the Blackstone Hotel. Somers was having financial problems, and not only owned Cleveland, but had four minor league clubs, too, including Toledo in the American Association. It was known that he was the one American League owner who would go against Ban Johnson's war-at-all-costs edict and accept peace, which had led to a tense meeting between Somers and Johnson in Cleveland in late September.[18] At dinner that night, Weeghman told Somers "he could in fifteen minutes bring all those interested in the Federal League to terms which, in his opinion, would be acceptable to so-called Organized Baseball."[19] Weeghman very much overstated his ability to bring about that peace. There were too many disparate interests involved. On the Monday after the A. L. meetings, Weeghman and Herrmann met again, this time with Ward and Buffalo owner William Robertson. Much like Baltimore, the city of Buffalo had been cast aside during the expansion of the American League in 1901, and the psychological wound of being reduced to minor league status was still raw. Robertson thought there should be a major league club in Buffalo, another condition for peace that came as a surprise to Herrmann. The major leagues could find room for Weeghman and possibly the Wards. Maybe even Ball, too. But Buffalo as a major-league city? Not a chance.

Making peace even less tenable was the surprising action taken by the minor leagues as a whole when their meeting got underway on November 10. Some leagues had been rumored to be willing to align with the Feds, and one report had five of the biggest minor circuits—the A.A., I.L., Pacific Coast, Southern, Western, and Northwestern—approaching the upcoming meeting in a "rebellious mood."[20] But after receiving financial assurances from Herrmann and Ban Johnson, the minor leagues as a whole pledged universal fealty to Organized Baseball. Pressure from the minors had been one of the most important drivers of a deal with the Feds, something Cantillon had tried to expose. Now, with the minors staying loyal to O. B., that pressure was gone. Making peace got all the more difficult.

‡

Even the one element of peace that appeared easy—Weeghman's purchase of the Cubs from Taft—turned out to be a spectacular fiasco. Despite the setbacks among other owners, Herrmann and Weeghman kept up their discussions and met again on November 12 in Chicago after the minor league meetings. Already, word was circulating that Weeghman was poised to buy the Cubs, to the point that the *Chicago Herald* very embarrassingly printed a story declaring that the deal was finished, and ran a photo of Weeghman with the caption "Welcome and Good Luck!" that further read, "The change in ownership seems to promise an end to the factional strife that has almost wrecked the Cubs on several occasions. It is possible now that a manager will last out a season, that players who make good will be rewarded instead of canned and that their game will be played in a park that is not a disgrace to the sport."[21]

Strange to consider now, but there was considerable outrage over the plan to sell the team to Weeghman and move it to the North Side. The Cubs were a West Side institution and had no business on the North Side, where they would be out of place and underappreciated by the locals. The *Chicago Daily News* took a poll of readers looking for reaction to the potential move of the Cubs and printed readers' responses. "Last season, the Chicago Feds were fighting for a pennant all the season yet could not draw except on special days," one letter read. "There are more real fans on the West Side than the North Side will produce in 10 years." Another pointed out (very truly as anyone who has watched an April game on the North Side knows), "In the early spring season the cold winds from the lake do not reach the West Side park, whereas the North Side park being so near the lake it is a question of great doubt if you could induce a handful of fans to sit in the North Side stands. It would be folly to shift."[22]

The papers were getting ahead of themselves—no deal was completed. Even the *Herald* story that declared Weeghman the Cubs' new owner quoted National Commission secretary Joseph Flanner saying, "There are several small details to be arranged and nothing will be announced until December 1." One of those details was mentioned later in the same story. Back in March, John T. Connery had stated that one of the hardships for a new owner of the team would be the expiration of the lease on the West Side Grounds, slated for three years later. Now, though, Weeghman was asked about a story saying that the lease on the Cubs park had been extended, and would run for eighty-eight years. Weeghman said he thought the story was "bunk."[23] He was partly right. It wasn't eighty-eight years. Charles Thomas would later say under oath that the lease had eighty years yet to run, at $12,000 per year, bumping up to $15,000 per year and then to $18,000.[24]

The owner of that lease? Well, Charles Webb Murphy, of course, in conjunction with the wife of Charles Taft. Undoubtedly, as a way to guard against the potential move of the Cubs out of the West Side, Murphy had quietly extended the team's lease. When Flanner said that there were small details to be worked out, he should have known better than to consider Murphy a small detail.

After his meeting with Herrmann on the twelfth, Weeghman was supposed to arrange to see Taft in Cincinnati. He had already asked that the deadline on the option for the Cubs be extended twice and he needed another extension—the Federal League was meeting again on the twenty-eighth, and Weeghman needed to confer with his fellow owners before he bought the Cubs. He sent a telegram to Herrmann to ask that Taft extend the deadline, and Hermann responded that he should ask Taft directly. Meanwhile, Murphy was already heading to Cincinnati to talk with Taft. Murphy had leverage. When he was bought out in February, Taft reportedly had only made a payment of $75,000 to Murphy, the rest of the stock remaining in Murphy's hands. That meant Murphy still had more than $400,000 worth of Cubs shares, and unless he was given a lump cash sum as a buyout, he still had veto power over a deal with Weeghman.

There was some question, too, about whether Weeghman could pull together the financing to make the deal. Herrmann would later say Weeghman had been unable to pull together $150,000, but Weeghman denounced that as an insult. Still, he had already spent considerably on the Federal League, and as part of the payment to Taft, he was said to be offering half the new North Side park at a value of $400,000, plus $150,000 in cash for 50 percent of the Cubs stock. That means Taft, who turned down $770,000 from Connery for the Cubs because he wanted $875,000, was being asked to take $350,000 for half the team a year later. But even that arrangement was problematic because Weeghman could not prove that the park was worth $400,000 and among baseball men, the estimated value was $250,000.[25] In addition, *The Sporting News* reported, "Mr. Weeghman had an option on the Cubs and was anxious to place his base ball park at a good figure in payment to the Cubs owners. On investigation, however, it is said that it was found that a mortgage is sitting quietly on the park, which is something hard to get over."[26] Weeghman disputed this, claiming the park and his baseball holdings were worth $412,000, when the salary already advanced to players was factored in.[27]

It was all academic, anyway. Murphy had already gotten to Taft in Cincinnati and convinced him not to sell, arguing that the Cubs should remain a West Side team. When Murphy arrived back in Chicago on the train from Cincinnati on November 18, he was triumphant. Murphy, out of the limelight for eight months, now had no trouble admitting that, though he was allegedly bought out months earlier because he had proven such an embarrassment to the game, he was still very much the owner of the Cubs and the West Side Grounds. In fact, he played up the loyalty to the very neighborhood that had so reviled him as part of the reason he got Taft to squelch the deal. "Charley Weeghman has no option on the Cubs, either verbal or written, and never has had," Murphy said. "It is true he has talked with Mr. Taft a couple of times recently, once in New York and another time in Cincinnati, but that is far from constituting an option. Weeghman has, for a long time no doubt, wanted to be a big-league magnate but that ambition cannot very well be achieved. The Cubs will remain on the West Side, where they belong, and where they have been loyally supported. I told Mr. Taft it would be suicidal to take the Cubs from the West Side. ... The West Side constitutes nearly two-thirds of the population of Chicago and how silly it would be for the Cubs to leave that section."[28]

In *The Sporting News*, a dispatch from Chicago reads rather strange now, given the modern fan's easy association of the Cubs with the North Side and the North-South rivalry that separates Cubs and Sox fans. But it essentially repeated Murphy's claim of fealty to the West Side: "Murphy's logic was convincing and unanswerable. The greatest rivalry in base ball in a single city, that of the South and West Sides, was to be destroyed perchance, to make room for an angel of the third league organization. The Cubs of the West Side were to be a catspaw to be shoved about and finally lose their identity in order to bring peace in baseball. ... Then Murphy reviewed to Taft the fact that the West Side of Chicago, the most populous district in the Western Hemisphere outside New York City, was to be sacrificed to make way for the ambition of one man, Charles Weeghman, the archenemy of the Cubs."[29]

Weeghman was crestfallen. In talking to the press, he emphasized that Murphy was clearly still very much in control of the Cubs, the one small comfort that he could take from the way events transpired. It was Murphy's intense unpopularity that had been the basis of Chicago's Federal League experiment, after all, and the more he remained connected to the Cubs, the better it was for the Chifeds. Weeghman's assertion was boosted by a *Chicago Herald* story that pointed out that Murphy maintained a shadowy influence throughout the National League—he also held stock in the Philadelphia Phillies and held the lease on their park. In both Philadelphia and Chicago, Murphy had agreed to the sale of stock but still had not been fully paid and held notes against the teams. It certainly looked like Murphy, supposedly booted from the National League, actually controlled one quarter of it. "For a man who is 'out of baseball' Mr. Murphy seems to be nearly as active in the sport as some men who are known to be definitely, not to say deeply, 'in' the game," the story declared.[30]

Weeghman had maintained a cordial and even friendly relationship with Murphy, a North Side neighbor and sometime business associate of his over the years. That appeared to be off. Weeghman suggested that Murphy had gone to Cincinnati and "succeeded in poisoning Mr. Taft's mind."[31] As for the allegation that he had never had an option to buy the Cubs, Weeghman said, "I had always been led to believe that Mr. Taft owned the club and when he granted me two options, one verbally and the other in a telegram, I considered his word was as good as mine. I have worked my hardest to bring about peace and if I have failed, I am indeed sorry. I don't care to discuss Murphy further. He is a neighbor of mine on Sheridan Road, and I happen to own a valuable bulldog which I should hate to have poisoned."[32]

For a couple of weeks, at least, there had been a lull in the baseball war, a break from player raids and rhetoric and insults. Now, though, Weeghman was suggesting the quasi-retired president of the Cubs might kill his dog. Weeghman sent a telegram to Herrmann on the eighteenth, saying he planned to talk to Taft. That was the last telegram Herrmann would get from Weeghman in 1914. The peace talks were off. "It means war to the end between the Federal League and Organized Baseball," Weeghman said.

# CHAPTER SEVENTEEN

# "I Have Just Signed Walter"

There was a moment, just after 4 PM on December 3, 1914, at which it seemed that all of the struggles Charley Weeghman had undergone in the previous year—buying into the Federal League, building the new park on the North Side, losing the Bill Killefer lawsuit, the war with Organized Baseball, missing out on the Federal League pennant in the final week of the season, the failure of his peace talks with Herrmann, the personal insults he endured along the way—had proven worthwhile. That's because, at that moment, sitting in his office where he had been cooped up all afternoon with his partner, Bill Walker, plus Chifeds shareholders Al Plamondon, Adolph Schuettler, and Charles William (not the team secretary), Weeghman received a long-distance telephone call from manager Joe Tinker in Coffeyville, Kansas. "I have just signed Walter," Tinker said, "and he is tickled that he is out of the American League. I am starting right back to Chicago and will be there tomorrow."[1]

There was much rejoicing in the Otis Building. Walter, of course, was Washington's Walter Johnson and his signing, the *Daily News* reasoned, "cracked the backbone of American League opposition." Weeghman beamed as he stepped out to inform the press that Johnson would be pitching at Weeghman Park in 1915. This gave the Chifeds a staff that would be headed by Johnson, followed by the Federal League's 1914 wins leader, Claude Hendrix, and another newly signed jumper, Indians righthander, Rip Hagerman. If Rankin Johnson could build on his strong finish to the '14 season, and if Ad Brennan's dead arm revived, the Chifeds would not only have the best pitching crew in the Federal League, they could, arguably, have the best group of flingers in all of baseball. Tinker, in blustery Federal League fashion, had said that sort of thing about his pitching staff before the 1914 season, but surely he knew at the time it was a bluff. Now he could say it and actually mean it.

The Federal League had been seriously working on getting Johnson as far back as May, when Johnson visited Tinker in Washington and announced he would pitch for the team that paid him the most. He had nearly signed with Robert Ward's TipTops in June before losing his nerve. At the end of October, St. Louis manager Fielder Jones was given orders by Terriers owner Phil Ball to "get Johnson at any cost," and to that end, Jones met with Johnson to make a three-year, $60,000 offer. Johnson still was hesitant to leave Washington and had enough loyalty to Washington manager Clark Griffith to honor the promise he had made that he would not sign a Federal League contract without first giving Griffith the chance to make a counteroffer. Johnson felt as though Griffith would come through for him with a raise that would keep him in a Senators uniform. Ball had seen how players had leveraged the Federal League for their own gains over the past year and soon decided he didn't want to be manipulated into helping Johnson get a raise to stay in the A. L. and pulled the $60,000 offer in early November. At the Federal League meeting on November 28, Ball granted Weeghman the right to pursue Johnson.

Weeghman sent Johnson a letter thereafter, and his timing could not have been better. Johnson had let Griffith know about the $20,000 per year offer from St. Louis and figured that deal set the bar for their negotiation. Griffith had been discussing a three-year deal at $16,000 per year with Johnson but those discussions took a turn before a formal offer was made. After Ball pulled his offer to Johnson, Jim Gilmore told the press that the Federal League would not be paying any more big salaries but would rather focus on building up its rank and file players. When word of Ball nixing his offer to Johnson got back in Washington, Senators owner Ben Minor was smug. He knew Johnson wasn't getting $20,000 per year, and that cut out all the leverage Johnson thought he had.[2]

As November wore on, Johnson had already sent two letters to Griffith without a reply. He was annoyed. Finally, in a letter dated November 28, Johnson heard from Washington owner Ben Minor, who was also a lawyer. Because of that, in Johnson's estimation, Minor was "no doubt accustomed to being somewhat decisive in his correspondence." Minor's letter bluntly stated that Washington couldn't meet Johnson's demand for $16,000 per year and the best offer the team would make would be $12,500 for his choice of one, two, or three years. If Johnson refused that, he could play at $10,000 for the year, as his 1914 contract stipulated. Griffith, it seemed to Johnson, had abandoned him and left the real negotiation to the tough-talking Minor. "I had just turned down an offer for $20,000 and had a previous offer from Washington for $16,000 and a good hope of getting $18,000," Johnson said. "So, in my situation, coming so suddenly and unexpectedly, the letter made me sore, and I resented it."[3]

Johnson didn't think he was being treated fairly, and it was that sense of fairness that guided him. He had always been a likeable guy and had a good relationship with Griffith. During the World Series back on October 9, in the café at the Majestic Hotel in Philadelphia, he had had breakfast with Griffith and the two had discussed the contract situation. When the conversation was over, Johnson spoke with some members of the Braves seated nearby, and they asked him what would be done about the contract. "I haven't done anything yet," Johnson told the players. "We have just been having a little farewell talk on the subject and I have told Griffith just where I stand. I'd like to remain with Griffith, but it is only natural for me to want to play where I can get the most money. And Griffith told me not five minutes ago that he didn't blame me for feeling that way."[4]

That was important to Johnson, and it was a way of looking at his situation he repeated often—he was merely out to make the most money he could at his job, as any employee would do. But he was also aware that the fans in Washington hadn't taken kindly to the declaration he had made in May, that he'd pitch for whomever paid him the most money, and his relationship with the D.C. faithful had grown strained. He had gotten a taste of that firsthand back on September 8, when the Philadelphia Athletics knocked six straight hits off Johnson in the fourth inning of a loss in the nitecap of a doubleheader that the *Post* dubbed "the worst inning that Johnson has ever experienced."[5] Philadelphia would get two more hits after Johnson was removed from the game, setting a record with eight straight hits. What was remarkable about the inning, though, was that Washington fans turned on Johnson, cheering as each Philadelphia batter hit safely off of him.[6] He knew he was in bad with the locals and that their collective disdain was the price for chasing personal riches.

That's why Johnson had hoped he could wrap things up with Washington without much fuss, which seemed to be Griffith's intention too. When Johnson got the lawyerly letter from Minor, it was obvious it wouldn't be that simple. He wasn't feeling much loyalty to his old team and it was at that moment, miraculously, that Weeghman contacted Johnson. When Tinker showed up in Johnson's hometown of Coffeyville days later, Johnson met him at the train station, took him back to his sprawling farm nearby, and talked about a contract. It was only twenty minutes later that Tinker and Johnson were shaking hands on a new two-year deal that would pay Johnson $17,500 per year. Tinker handed Johnson a check for $6,000 as an advance payment.

Johnson would play in Chicago, and, at last, the Federal League would have their headliner. The news hit baseball like a bombshell. The American League reacted harshly. Ban Johnson declared that, in fact, the Senators had little use for Johnson and were planning on getting rid of him anyway—a laughable face-saving statement that some reporters still lapped up and repeated. "He became a dead one down there the minute he announced, in the middle of last season, that he would go where the most money was offered and that after the Washington fans had given him loving cups full of coin, an automobile and many other favors," the A. L. leader said. "Gratitude, well, his latest action looks like it."[7]

Griffith was outraged, and also played up the angle of ingratitude. Griffith's outlook was disingenuous, though, especially if, just two months earlier at breakfast, he had told Johnson it was reasonable to seek the biggest payout. Griffith and the Senators had bungled the Johnson situation, especially with Minor's letter, and now Griffith attempted to make Johnson look like the villain to the local fans. "We paid Johnson an exorbitant salary of $12,000 and, to show you the caliber of fellow, he turned down my offer of $16,000 and accepted one of $17,000 with Chicago," Griffith said. "What he received for signing I do not know. Like most star players, he is money mad and has no sense of gratitude."[8] Griffith failed to mention that Washington's last offer was not actually $16,000, it was $12,500, and that Minor had suggested he could make it $10,000 or go find another job.

Johnson wasn't the ideal Federal League jumper, most of whom were either blindly mercenary or had suffered some bad treatment at the hands of Organized Ball and could weather media and fan criticism for vengeance's sake. Hal Chase, for example, was the Feds' kind of guy. Johnson, though, was too thin-skinned. The criticism got to him almost immediately. On December 11, he wrote a bitter and ill-advised letter to the *Washington Post*. In it, he said, "I have been reading all the good things the newspapers and fans have been saying about me lately, but that doesn't make much difference—a ball player has to take so much any way. When you are going good everything is lovely, but when you are not, people can find all kinds of things to say about you. Several newspapers, rather sporting writers, have hit me hard for jumping and not knowing where I will land. I can say one thing for them, I could buy them and their whole newspaper for a lot less than I am getting with the Feds."[9] It's never a good idea, in the heat of a PR battle, to suggest one could buy and sell the entity that is central to that battle. But the stress was getting to Johnson. Griffith would later say Johnson lost fifteen pounds in the days after signing with the Federal League.

For Organized Baseball, there was an issue at play that went beyond Johnson. He was by far the biggest star to sign a contract with the Federal League, and though he was quickly losing prestige back in Washington, it appeared he was on the vanguard of a new willingness by players to take consideration of the outlaw league and follow through by actually signing a contract. As writer Stanley Milliken noted, "His jumping will have a moral effect on every baseball player in the country. The fact that he, the king of all pitchers and the most talked of man in baseball, has signed a Federal League contract, will be an incentive for others to follow suit. There is no question that there are many players in both the American and National leagues, to say nothing of the minors, who were waiting for just such a move."[10]

Early December proved to be a satisfying time for the Federals. Pitcher Ray Caldwell, who had left the Yankees late in the year and appeared on the bench with the Buffalo Federals in September, officially signed on December 1. Baltimore's Harry Goldman slipped over to Gettysburg, Pennsylvania, and on December 2, signed star Athletics pitcher Eddie Plank, following that by landing his fellow Athletics pitcher Chief Bender—manager Connie Mack of the A. L. champion Athletics had, surprisingly, asked waivers on both Plank and Bender, paving the way for them to jump to the Feds. Ward's Tip-Tops locked up Giants pitcher Rube Marquard and also signed infielder Lee Magee (the same Magee who Three Finger Brown said would never play in the Federal League after he spurned the league at the battle of the dock). That group came in addition to a haul of players that the Feds had signed near the end of the 1914 season. Pitcher Pol Perritt and catcher Ivey Wingo were induced to leave the penny-pinching Cardinals, and slugger Ed Konetchy—after a miserable year in Pittsburgh—signed on with the Feds, too. Reds infielder Marty Berghammer, Brooklyn outfielder Jack Dalton and pitcher Frank Allen, and Red Sox pitcher Hugh Bedient were among the group too.

The players in this new bunch of Federals were not (to use a favored putdown of the time) pikers. The previous winter, the Federal Leaguers got too late a start on naming managers and putting together rosters to attract much legitimate major league talent. That wasn't the case with this batch of players. Beyond Johnson's obvious stardom, the Feds had managed to get four players who had already made good in the big leagues and were twenty-five years old or younger—Bedient (a 20-game winner as a rookie in 1912) and Perritt (16-13, 2.36 ERA in 1914) had shown they were quality major league pitchers, while Magee (.284 with 36 steals) and Wingo (.300) had three years' experience and were coming off of solid years. Marquard and Konetchy simply had bad years in 1914 but were still accomplished players in their prime.

In the wake of the failed Weeghman-Herrmann peace negotiations, the Federal League hit back, and hit back hard—especially Weeghman and Tinker. Spring training was a little more than three months away and Opening Day would come shortly thereafter. Walter Johnson already could be penciled in for the starting pitching duties for the Chifeds on that day.

‡

Shortly after the signing of the Big Train and the wave of players that accompanied him to the Feds, Ban Johnson brought up a point that boiled down to some simple math—eventually, the Federal League would have to dole out paychecks to their new stars. Some harsh reality would follow. "Let them go on signing ball players," Johnson said. "It may be easy to sign a bunch of stars, but the trouble is the salaries come due regularly and the Federals may have some bills yet to pay." Johnson predicted that when the Federal League was done sending out paychecks, they "wouldn't have enough left for cigar money."[11]

That wasn't the usual Johnson bombast. Coming out of 1914, the economics of the game, for the first time in about a decade, were universally poor. Exact figures on how much teams lost are impossible to come by and most of the numbers that can be dug up are anecdotal. Some things can be said for certain, though, such as that the National League managed a better year than the American League, primarily because the N. L. staged a compelling race that saw the Braves come from last place on July 18 to blow away the field and finish first, sweeping the World Series. The fact that the Red Sox allowed the champion Braves to use Fenway Park (which opened in 1912) helped drive attendance, pushing the Braves from what was a $70,000 deficit at midseason to a $75,000 profit. The Giants, in first place for the bulk of the summer, made $125,000, and the league as a whole reportedly made $115,000 in profit. The Cubs managed a profit of $50,000, which wasn't bad relative to the rest of the league and was impressive considering how miserable a season they'd had, but the intake was well below the six-figure payouts the team usually reaped.[12]

In the American League, the net profit was reportedly $58,000, particularly disappointing considering the Red Sox and White Sox alone had taken in $75,000 and $70,000 respectively. According to a conversation he'd had with an A. L. magnate, Weeghman claimed that the league-champion Athletics had made only $25,000 and that ten of the sixteen teams in the majors (the Giants, Cubs, Braves, Red Sox, White Sox, and Athletics being the exceptions) lost money.[13] If the numbers for the A's, Red Sox, and White Sox are accurate, then the other five teams in the A. L. lost an average of more than $22,000 each. It was reported that Cleveland lost $50,000—little wonder that the team's owner, Charles Somers, was strongly for peace with the Federal League. The same can be said when weighing the profits of the Braves, Cubs, and Giants in the N. L. The other five teams would have lost an average of $27,000.

The Feds suffered much bigger losses, though. Weeghman's club was said to have come in with a profit, but as a whole, the Federal League reportedly lost $176,000.[14] That figure was well below the estimates that some O. B. magnates fed the press, which ranged from $500,000 to $900,000 in losses—even without including the expenses each team incurred to build their parks. It was reported that Brooklyn lost $60,000, Kansas City lost $60,000,[15] and the Pittsburgh Federals lost $100,000.[16] Those numbers are rough estimates and might be inaccurate, but the point that the Feds had lost significant money was inarguable. Also in bad shape were the two big minor leagues—the American Association lost $90,000 and the International League got crushed for $150,000.[17]

The Federal Leaguers were easy scapegoats for the attendance drop, and rightly so. It wasn't just that the Feds siphoned off fans, it was that fans everywhere seemed to stop caring about baseball enough to attend games. Federal League raids had diluted the talent pool, put too much focus on the financial aspect of the game, and killed the interest of fans tired of reading about injunctions and appeals. This was evident in Chicago most of all. Charley Weeghman claimed that, in its first year, the North Side park drew 321,000 fans. Taking that as true—it was most definitely inflated—then the Chifeds, Cubs, and Sox combined to attract 992,000 fans in 1914. In 1913, the Cubs and Sox alone had an attendance of about 1,063,000. In 1912, it was 1,116,000. Baseball fans crossed the turnstiles for the Cubs and White Sox at least one million times in Chicago in every season since 1904, the infancy of the American League.[18] It is counterintuitive, but the numbers are stark: adding Weeghman's Feds to the North Side actually *decreased* total baseball attendance in Chicago. The advent of the Federal League had made baseball less popular, everywhere, even cities that didn't have a third-league team. The Athletics won the American League yet suffered an attendance drop of almost 40 percent in 1914. Washington is a good example, too, because Walter Johnson's personal stardom had long driven attendance for that team. In 1912, the Nationals drew 351,000 fans, and drew 326,000 in 1913. In 1914, with Johnson having alienated the locals, Washington suffered a 25 percent drop, to an attendance of just 244,000.

The Federal League wasn't the only reason for the drop-off. Observers of the time cited the U.S. involvement in the Mexican Revolution, which created a sensation across the country and dominated the newspapers, pushing baseball off the front pages. That might have had something to do with the drop in baseball interest, but the economy was likely a much bigger factor. There was a recession in 1914, and though it was relatively brief, it had an impact on the kind of everyday fans who would typically populate baseball's stands. According to the National Bureau of Economic Research, estimated unemployment in the U.S. leapt from 4.4 percent in 1913 to 8.0 percent in 1914, and would rise to 9.7 percent in 1915. For nonfarm payrolls—employment in the cities, where major league baseball teams operated—the unemployment rates were much worse, 11.9 percent in '14 and 14.3 percent in '15.[19]

Chicago felt the sting of the recession as badly as any city. In the newspapers of the day, joblessness was a chief topic. Even for the employed, the shaky labor market was cause for alarm, reason to economize and cut out frivolous spending—baseball, for example. In the winter before the '14 baseball season, the *Chicago Daily News* referred to "Chicago's army of unemployed men, forced out of work by the tightening of the labor market," and predicted more joblessness to come, quoting one unemployed man as saying, "What you going to do when there ain't no jobs? We're getting let out by the hundreds all over the country."[20] A year later, the Chicago municipal markets commission issued a report estimating that the city would be home to 129,000 "employable unemployed" men in the first three months of 1915, and that their combined lost wages in those months would be $18 million.[21] That's a staggering number in a city of 2.5 million people just fourteen years removed from the turn of the century.

Unemployment was stubborn in 1914 and would remain so in 1915, especially as the Great War in Europe—which began in August of 1914—deepened and drew in more of the world. The Federal League wasn't only fighting Organized Baseball for its survival. It was fighting much larger economic factors, a hammering of the disposable incomes in all major cities. For all of the Federal League's missteps, perhaps its greatest was purely poor timing. Even Walter Johnson couldn't change that.

# CHAPTER EIGHTEEN

# Showdown in Judge Landis's Court

Weeghman would never get to find out just what Johnson might have done for him on the North Side and the Feds would never find out whether he would finally turn the tide in favor of the third league. After learning of Johnson's signing, Clark Griffith set into motion a two-pronged plan, much as other major league teams had done with players who signed with the Federal League. First he would start legal proceedings, figuring the threat of an injunction would provide a scare to the players. On December 4, after reading about Johnson's signing in the newspaper, Griffith sent Weeghman a telegram formally warning him that Johnson was the property of Washington because of the reserve clause in his contract. Further, he informed Weeghman by telegram that if Johnson pitched for the Chifeds, Weeghman would be "prosecuted for conspiracy in tampering with a player already held by contract." Griffith stated that "Johnson will have to return to my ball club. I don't care if he is in bad with the fans here. I don't care if he doesn't draw more than two fans to the games. ... Walter can't get off my club by the method he is apparently using. He's the property of the Washington club and will remain here."[1]

Griffith also had another, more personal plan for Johnson—this, again, was a common approach by O. B., which had certainly used injunctions to stop players from joining Federal League teams, but also, as in the case of Bill Killefer and others, used direct appeals to sway them back after jumping. Griffith first got Pirates manager Fred Clarke, who owned a farm in Kansas about ninety miles west of Johnson's, to pay Johnson a visit and talk with him. Clarke explained that the reserve clause meant his rights belonged to Washington, and asked that Johnson at least meet with Griffith. Johnson was agreeable, telling Clarke he would always meet with Griffith because he had no trouble with him. Griffith contacted Johnson and asked that they meet in Kansas City.

Meanwhile, the American League had a plan too. If Walter Johnson was to be pitching for Weeghman on the North Side, then Comiskey had better fortify his South Siders or he would run the risk of further losing out at the gate. Comiskey had a fine pitching staff but badly needed offense. With Connie Mack dismantling his team in Philadelphia, Ban Johnson saw an opportunity to help. He had tried to arrange a deal that would send Eddie Collins, Mack's star infielder, to the Yankees in order to facilitate the sale of the team, which Johnson wanted to get out of Frank Farrell's hands. But when that failed, Johnson instead joined up with Comiskey, figuring Collins—who had hit .344 the previous year and had led the league in runs three straight seasons—was the ideal counterbalance to the Walter Johnson signing. It would be no minor feat. On December 8, Comiskey paid a reported $50,000 for Collins, a record price for a player by a whopping margin. Just the previous winter, remember, the record had been set with the $25,000 Ebbets was to give the Reds for Tinker. Upon acquiring Collins, Comiskey said, "I am tired of paying a lot of good money for players who have been no earthly good to my club and therefore decided to go the limit and turn over a large sum for a player who will make the White Sox a sure pennant contender."[2]

But the signing of Collins did not mean that the A. L. was giving up on Johnson. On December 18, Johnson and his wife went north to Kansas City. When he was spotted by newspapermen, he explained they had come to do some Christmas shopping and nothing more. His wife did, in fact, slip off to shop, but Johnson stayed in his hotel room, with

Griffith avoiding notice and meeting him secretly. It was later reported that both Johnson and Griffith had with them their own teams of lawyers, but Johnson himself later said, "There were no lawyers there. But Griffith himself showed me where he thought I had not done right by him and by my old club. ... He said he didn't deserve any such treatment from me, as he had always done well by me. I cannot tell here all the arguments he used, but I will say he convinced me that I ought to have remained with Washington and ought to return even then."[3]

Johnson now wrestled with the moral dilemma of having to either break his relationship with Griffith or break his contract with Weeghman. Throughout the ordeal, Johnson comes off as fairly malleable and sentimental, as though the last person to talk to him in an argument would be the one whose side he would take. And while Tinker had his say first, getting Johnson to sign on with the Feds, Griffith got the last word. "Whichever way I turned I was wrong," Johnson said. "I had unwittingly got myself into a position where I had to choose between two evils. Either was bad, but I had to decide for myself which was the least of the two. And I did decide that question to the best of my ability. ... I did not treat the Federal League right. I broke my contract with them. But I broke it only because I was convinced that by not doing so, I would be doing an even greater injury to Washington."[4] Thus Johnson chose to sign with Griffith, for three years, at the $12,500 salary that had offended him when Minor offered it in his letter. Johnson now had two contracts on his hands.

There was also a matter of the $6,000 bonus Johnson had gotten from Tinker. A story out of Coffeyville reported that Johnson paid it back "with the money obtained from the sale of a herd of steer,"[5] but the writer Shirley Povich gave a different account, saying that after Griffith got Johnson to agree to sign with Washington, he called the American League office looking for help in repaying the bonus. Ban Johnson at first refused and passed Griffith off to Comiskey, who also refused. Until, that is, Griffith asked him, "Well, then, how would you like to see Walter Johnson playing for the Chicago Feds next season and drawing all those fans away from White Sox Park?"

To which Comiskey, after a pause, eventually replied, "You'll have my check in the morning, Griff."[6]

When the announcement came from Kansas City that Johnson was going back to Washington, Weeghman was incredulous. It was like the Killefer experience all over again—except that Killefer, at least, came out with a raise from the Phillies. Johnson had somehow leveraged the Federal League into a worse deal, going from an offer of $16,000 per year from Washington in the summer to $12,500 six months later. Weeghman expected that getting Johnson on the mound for the 1915 season would require a legal fight but he did not expect that Johnson would simply hop back to Organized Baseball, without so much as a phone call. "I won't believe the story," Weeghman said, "until I hear it from him."[7] Gilmore desperately tried to change Johnson's mind and asked Johnson to come to Chicago and bring his two contracts so that they could be examined by three impartial lawyers who would determine their legality. On December 23, however, Johnson mailed the bonus money back to Weeghman. Three days later, Weeghman received a registered letter, took one look at the return address—"Coffeyville, Kan."—surely got a little queasy, and "told the mail-carrier there was nothing doing and that he could cart the letter back to the post office and return it to Coffeyville."[8]

That wasn't the only bad news for the Feds. The momentum of early December quickly gave out. After the signing of pitcher Rube Marquard by Brooklyn, the Giants protested that he was under contract already for 1915 and 1916—not just through the reserve clause, but through an existing deal signed the previous summer with no ten-day clause. That seemed impossible to Ward because Marquard had signed an affidavit stating he was in no way under contract with the Giants. Alas, Marquard had lied. Ward attempted to contact Giants owner Harry Hempstead to see that Marquard did, in fact, have a Giants contract. But, on December 11, Hempstead said he wouldn't deign to reply to Ward and was instead considering legal action. He was cynical about Ward's intentions, especially when Ward very publicly voided his contract with Marquard, as though it had been an act of good grace on his part. "In this matter the Brooklyn Club and the Federal League were engaged in a mere effort to advertise," Hempstead would later say of Ward. "The writer makes a great pretence [sic] of virtue over an act of common business honesty (or was it not rather common business discretion?)."[9]

Meanwhile, Ray Caldwell, who had actually appeared on the Buffalo bench in September after butting heads with New York manager Frank

Chance, was wavering on his commitment to the Federal League. With the Yankees changing ownership and bringing in new manager Bill Donovan, Caldwell was willing to be talked into returning to Organized Baseball—he was considered the Yankees' best pitcher, having gone 18–9 with a 1.94 ERA the previous season, and when he was offered a raise from $4,500 per year to $8,000 for four years, Caldwell rejoined the Yankees. Third baseman Jimmy Austin, too, would later go back on his Federal League contract and return to the Browns, and another of Tinker's signees—pitcher Rip Hagerman—changed his mind and stuck with the Indians. Other players who had been disgruntled with their teams or managers were lured back through trades. Catcher Ivey Wingo, who had signed with the Feds mostly because he wanted out of St. Louis, was coaxed back to the big leagues after he was granted a trade to Cincinnati. Pitcher Pol Perritt, who also wanted out of St. Louis, would later go back on his contract, too, when he was traded from the Cardinals to the Giants.

But nothing stung quite like the loss of Walter Johnson. Weeghman was gloomy but vowed that the Federal League would go on. There was no choice really. His negotiations with Herrmann had gone nowhere and he was embittered by the experience. Now there was this. "I have always favored peace," Weeghman said, "but I want to tell you honestly that there never yet has been the slightest chance of a peace pact being signed. All the peace stuff just before the Omaha meeting was tommyrot. We are prepared to fight for our own terms, not Organized Ball's. ... There is more than one millionaire in our circuit. As I said, we have more than $3 million invested. Now, can you picture, in your wildest dreams, us quitting?"[10]

‡

If Weeghman and friends were not going to quit, it was clear that they, at least, would need yet another a new strategy. They hadn't gotten a clear ruling on the legality of the reserve clause and any progress made on exposing the lack of mutuality in the ten-day clause had been erased by teams removing such clauses from their contracts. The Feds had plenty of trouble signing up new players at all, and a significant percentage of the ones they did sign either were legally prevented from playing or simply disregarded their Federal League contracts and were brought back to Organized Baseball with a raise or a trade. The "unclean hands" label that had been hung on them during the Killefer trial made their prospects of defending the validity of their own contracts murky, at best, and the fact that the series of lawsuits from the previous summer had not brought decisive rulings, meant that another series of injunctions was on the horizon for the players who had just signed. That meant more legal bills and more money spent on salaries for players who could be legally barred from playing. Already, Gilmore claimed, the league had $50,000 invested in advance payments on the 1915 season. What the Federal League needed was a definitive, overarching legal ruling to protect their rights. They thought they knew just the man to deliver that ruling—Chicago Federal Judge Kenesaw Mountain Landis.

Tough and direct, with a square jaw and intimidating gruffness, Landis had, at the time, established himself as one of America's best-known jurists—and was known as an avowed baseball fan, a lover of the old Cubs dynasty, and a friend to White Sox owner Charles Comiskey. He had been appointed to the bench in 1905 by Teddy Roosevelt, who saw Landis as a like-minded progressive Republican. After earning a reputation for his pragmatism and anti-trust credentials with his decisions in several rail-road cases, Landis presided over the antitrust case of John D. Rockefeller's Standard Oil, the largest oil refiner in the world. When the jury in that case found that Standard Oil was guilty on 1,462 counts, Landis calculated a maximum penalty of $20,000 per count and came up with a record fine of $29,240,000. The fine would be overturned on appeal, but Landis's willing-ness to come down on unfair practices by big business made him a hero for many, and in the wake of the trial he was "the most talked of person in America."[11]

In the wake of the Walter Johnson defection, the Federal League had few options. It was decided that the only way the league could succeed would be to take a high-risk gamble, and on January 5, the Feds shocked the baseball world by filing a lawsuit in Landis's court, alleging (as Chicago congressman Thomas Gallagher had done three years earlier) that baseball was an illegal trust. At the time, even beyond Landis's courtroom, there had been much momentum for trust-busting in the U.S., and just three months earlier,

Congress passed the Clayton Act, which tightened regulations on anti-competitive behavior. The hope was that such momentum, with Landis's background as a defender of the underdog, would work to their benefit, and that the new league finally would be allowed to conduct business on a level footing with the American and National leagues. The ninety-two-page lawsuit listed twenty-one defendants—the sixteen major league teams, National Commission members Ban Johnson, Garry Herrmann, and John Tener, plus the American and National leagues as wholes—and created a stir around the country. One dispatch from Chicago read, "The suit, it is said, threatens the entire fabric of organized baseball, carrying not only the possibility that the intricate organization be declared illegal and that the interleague agreements be dissolved, but that the 10,000 ball players in major and minor leagues be declared free agents."[12]

The Federals had entered eleven prayers for relief, among which were:

- That the National Commission's rules and the National Agreement be declared illegal and that all twenty-one defendants be declared a "combination, conspiracy and monopoly" that violates antitrust law. Further, the Feds asked that all contracts agreed to under those rules be voided.

- That the defendants had conspired to destroy the Federal League's business by making false claims about the finances of the league and by threatening players with a blacklist. The Federal League further sought damages for the injury caused by O. B.

- That all cases enjoining Federal League players from performing for their teams be dropped and that the defendants not be allowed to file further injunctions.

- That Landis issue temporary injunctions to put aside the pending legal fights involving players like Chief Johnson, Hal Chase, and Armando Marsans.

The scope of what the Federal League was requesting in the lawsuit was enormous. It wasn't merely a matter of asking to be left alone and not have their contracts breached. If the Feds were to get everything they wanted, then the entire structure of baseball would be torn down and every player, from Ty Cobb, Walter Johnson, and Tris Speaker down to any teenage signee of a Class D club, would have his contract voided and be declared a free agent, able to sign with whomever paid him most. The suit compared the plight of players to "peonage," and the basis for that notion was strong—players coming up from the minor leagues had virtually no rights to choose where they would wind up. If you lived in St. Louis and wanted to play there but were drafted by Boston, you had to go to Boston. And if Boston sold you to Toledo, you either went to Toledo or nowhere at all. That was the system established by the National Agreement between the American and National leagues twelve years earlier, and the Federals were asking Landis to call it unfair and dismantle it. It was a tall order, but the Feds had been backed into a corner and were desperate. "Why should we worry?" Weeghman asked. "We have nothing to lose."[13]

The Federals filed a series of affidavits on January 12, mostly designed to highlight two facts for Landis: First, that players had signed contracts with the reserve clause and ten-day clause over their own objections because they felt that had no other choice; and, second, that the magnates of Organized Baseball held players in shockingly low regard. The deposition that drew the most comment came from Mordecai Brown, who, in addition to telling of his ill treatment by Charles Murphy and the Cubs in 1912, also recalled the story of Minneapolis manager Joe Cantillon trading "a professional player for a bull dog, that the fact of said trade is common knowledge among baseball players." Brown also claimed that Cubs manager Roger Bresnahan, when he was in St. Louis, traded a pitcher to a minor league team for a bird dog.[14] An affidavit was filed for Joe Tinker, too, in which he detailed the erratic behavior of Reds owner Garry Herrmann and Brooklyn owner Charles Ebbets in determining his fate back in the winter of 1913, just before he signed with the Federal League.

While there was little doubt that players were not granted the rights of others in the labor market, the wider question for the Federal League remained and was put to Tinker after a Federal League strategy meeting in Indianapolis on January 7 when a reporter asked: "What are you going to do with this suit, Joe, break up professional baseball?"

Tinker's answer was revealing. The Feds may have been asking for a wholesale teardown of baseball's structure, but they had only asked for an extreme with the expectation that the final ruling would yield something more moderate: "I should say not. All we are trying to do is give it a good house cleaning and when we have eradicated the 'business men,' put in nothing but sportsmen. Baseball is a game for sportsmen, and we propose to have nothing but sportsmen in it. We are tired of having it run by two men … Ban Johnson and Garry Herrmann. And believe me, I know. I was in Cincinnati one year, but long enough to learn who runs the game."[15]

‡

When Organized Baseball responded with its affidavits on January 17, the crux of their defense seemed clear: "If we are such a repulsive monopoly, why do the Federal Leaguers so badly want to be like us?"

The longest affidavit was that given by Garry Herrmann, and he detailed the negotiations he had with Weeghman the previous October and November, which had ended with Murphy pushing Charles Taft to pull the Cubs off the market. In Herrmann's deposition, he showed that the baseball war would have ended if Weeghman had been allowed to buy the Cubs and if Robert Ward had been allowed to buy the Yankees. This was a point directed at the public more than a legal point—by saying Weeghman and Ward wanted into major league baseball, the impression was left that they were hypocrites to now say that the group they so badly hoped to join was, in fact, an evil trust. It also allowed O. B. to paint the entire lawsuit as an act of vengeance taken by Weeghman and Ward, and with a judge like Landis, who was known for gauging public opinion when making his decisions, this was a wise tack to take. As Chicago's George Robbins wrote, "To understand the full force of this manifest inconsistency one must go back several weeks ago when certain magnates of the Federal League sought to become club owners in the major leagues. Did these gentlemen contemplate entering a circle of conspirators, porch climbers and undesirables operating a bunko game? The Federal League has also sought recognition among this band of alleged conspirators."[16]

To further that defense, O. B. also presented the Federal League rules and a Federal League contract—which was nearly the same as an O. B. contract, containing both the reserve clause and the ten-day rule. Not only did Federal League owners want entry into the major leagues, but they ran their league in much the same way that the defendants ran theirs. As Tigers president Frank Navin, who was also a lawyer, said, "The Federals have done everything we have done and more. They took a number of our players, some of whom were under tight contracts, and we did not try to take any of theirs. If we are trying to monopolize the ability of the men in our employ are they not doing the same with the men in the Federal League? What difference is there between their contract and ours? If we have offended, they have offended as greatly and more."[17]

By the time the trial started, Chicago had been abuzz for days, as baseball dignitaries and well-known lawyers flocked to the city. On the morning of January 20, the *Tribune* ran an article that began with the listing of line-ups, as in a box score, with the headline "Organized Ball and Feds in Big Legal 'Game' Today." In Landis's courtroom on the sixth floor of the Federal Building in the Loop, National Commissioners Herrmann, Ban Johnson, and John Tener were present, as were at least eight big league magnates. Recently deposed Cubs manager Hank O'Day was on hand, as was his replacement, Roger Bresnahan (who had been flirting with the Federals for months). Managers Fielder Jones and Jimmy Callahan were also in the crowd, as well as current Sox manager Clarence Rowland and, of course, Joe Tinker. Even Walter Johnson, the catalyst for the case, appeared. There were seats for 200 observers, but about 600 crammed into the courtroom and another 1,000 were turned away.[18] When the hearing began, one jokester shouted, "Hey boy, gimme a bag of peanuts!" Landis was not amused, and warned that any repeat of such outbursts would result in the courtroom being cleared of spectators.[19]

Over four days, Landis listened to the arguments of the lawyers on both sides. In his opening, Federal League attorney Keene Addington attacked the reserve rule, calling the contracts of O. B. a "sham." He highlighted the case of Brown's release by the Cubs—Brown was a favorite of Landis, and Addington surely was encouraged when Landis asked him to repeat Brown's story. But the next day, Landis interrupted Addington and raised a key point: He wasn't sure that he had jurisdiction in the case because a Federal court could only hear a case like this if it involved interstate commerce, and though baseball as a whole required interstate travel, each individual team operated its business in its own state. O. B. attorney George Pepper seized on the jurisdiction question, pointing out that part of the Clayton Act specifically said that labor could not be counted as commerce. He cited a case involving the Metropolitan Opera, in which it was determined that the labors of the performers were not considered a commodity of commerce.

Pepper was a legal star, described as "silver-tongued," and when he had the floor after Addington's opening attack "in a very few minutes [he] had every one in the room giving his undivided attention. With a few remarks, he turned the tide." Pepper curried favor by lamenting the treatment of Brown, and though he was from Philadelphia, he made a statement that was all too Chicagoan—he blamed Charles Murphy and called Brown's dismissal an anomaly. He also pointed out that players like Brown had been made stars and become wealthy off of baseball. "I do not believe I would have treated an old war horse like Mordecai Brown the way he was treated, but I ask that the answers of the defendants to the allegations of the players be read carefully," Pepper said. "The latter omitted to tell their life story, how they were brought from the minors and of the progressively larger salaries they received."[20]

Throughout the hearing, other than raising the question of whether he had jurisdiction over the case, Landis gave little indication of his leanings in the case. On the third day of arguments, Pepper paused and leaned into Landis, saying, "I love baseball." Landis shot back quickly: "We'll have to keep love and affection out of this one, I think, but I want both sides to know that he who strikes a blow at baseball strikes a blow at a national institution."[21] That was the crux of the matter for Landis. He was capable of putting aside his love of the game in order to make a fair decision. He surely recognized the unfairness of the reserve rule, at the very least. But if he were to find that baseball was operated as a trust, he would tear down an organization that was beloved throughout the country, not just by him personally. Breaking up baseball would be a lot different than breaking up railroad monopolies and fining oil barons like John D. Rockefeller.

On the final day of the trial, Landis decided he had heard enough. He knew the ins and outs of the game and understood each side's argument. But what he didn't know was the answer to the same question Tinker had been asked by the reporter in Indianapolis—was he expected to break up professional baseball? He was blunt when directing questions to Federal League attorney E. E. Gates: "The time has come when I should ask you gentlemen just what you want me to do. Do you want me to stop the teams from going on spring training trips? Do you want me to break up the clubs or, what do you want me to do? ... Do you realize that a decision in this case may tear down the very foundations of this game, so loved by thousands, and do you realize that the decision must also seriously affect both parties?"[22]

Gates explained that "what the Feds wanted was that organized baseball be restrained from dragging the players already signed by the Feds for 1915 into court, thus depriving the public the right to see those players."[23] But that only covered the temporary injunctions and a small part of what the Federal League's entire antitrust case had been about. Landis was in a difficult position. Baseball had the trappings of a monopoly. But he didn't want to be the judge who handed the game that label.

# CHAPTER NINETEEN

# The 1915 Season Begins

At 6:30 PM on March 4, 1915, local dignitaries made their way to the Rienzi restaurant and cabaret at Clark and Diversey on Chicago's North Side, where they were greeted by rows of torches giving off "red fire" to lend the place a celebratory glow. Inside, the dining room was overseen by a giant whale, assembled just for the occasion. The guests of honor would be Charley Weeghman and Joe Tinker, and the whale had only recently taken on some meaning to them—just one month earlier, as the result of a contest seeking team nicknames to replace the decidedly uninspired "Chifeds," Weeghman decided his new team would be called the "Whales" because the moniker "carried a suggestion of athletic prowess and power and at the same time was absolutely unique as a nickname for a ball team."[1] Now, at the Rienzi, the Whales were to be given a banquet that would send them off to Shreveport for spring training and "was intended to convey the impression to President Weeghman and his team that the Whales were solid with the North Siders."[2]

There were more than a dozen prominent judges on hand and more than 700 revelers in general, including league president Jim Gilmore and Weeghman's partner, Bill Walker. Four hours' worth of speeches and plenty of libations (as one account noted, "water was scarce") kept the atmosphere raucous all the way to 1 AM. The guests were entertained by the Oxford Quartet, who serenaded them with improvised songs, like this one to the tune of "Tipperary":

We are the Whalers, some swimmers, some sailors,
And we sail on the baseball side!
Weeghman and Walker, and Gilmore the talker,
Give the O. B. crowd a slide!
Bound now for Shreveport
And come back to old Chi—
We'll keep way up in the running,
Ban J.'s due for downing
When he sees our pennant fly!

By the time it was over, "the fans voted it one of the greatest baseball festivals ever held in the city."[3]

For Weeghman, Gilmore, and the Feds in general, a night of debauchery probably was welcome. In the weeks following the hearings in front of Landis, rumors repeatedly cropped up that the judge would be making some sort of announcement as to his decision soon. But Landis himself remained silent, not even offering a ruling on the preliminary aspects of what the Feds were seeking. Weeghman had threatened an injunction for Walter Johnson should he ever pitch for Washington, and Gilmore had threatened the same for the other players who had jumped to the Feds and then flopped back to O. B. They were hollow threats, though. Some Federal League owners might have had the money to wage a legal war for the players they'd signed and lost, but no one really had the stomach to pursue every case the way that teams in the American and National leagues had done. It would be a waste, too, to start new court proceedings when Landis could make a decision at any point.

Besides, the Feds had their own internal legal problems brewing. In February, Gilmore had succeeded in that aspect of his job he performed best: He persuaded a very wealthy man to invest in his league. This time, it was Oklahoma oil man Harry Sinclair, who was brought along by former

Eastern League (now the International) president Pat Powers. This was a huge coup for Gilmore because Organized Baseball had been after Sinclair too—he had once turned down the opportunity to buy the Cardinals for $500,000, had another chance to take the Braves for $600,000, and had been rumored to be interested in the Phillies and Athletics.[4] Sinclair was the ideal owner for the third league. He was only thirty-eight, willing to take a risk on the outlaws, and wealthier than any other owner in the Federal League, with a net worth said to be (most likely exaggerated) $25 million.[5] That granted the Federal League a new source of wealth it badly needed after the bruising 1914 campaign.

At a secret meeting at the Blackstone Hotel in Chicago on February 4, Powers, on behalf of Sinclair, agreed to take the Kansas City franchise and move it east to Newark, putting a Federal League team within the New York market, with designs on moving to the Bronx the following season. Gilmore assumed he had the power to conduct the transaction because the Kansas City club was, basically, broke—in fact, Gilmore claimed the team owed the league $38,000. Sinclair put a down payment on the team and he and Powers purchased a spot for a park in Harrison, New Jersey. But the Packers wouldn't go easily. They got an injunction to prevent the move to Newark and sued the Federal League. The lawsuit landed in the Chicago court of Judge Jesse Baldwin and on March 15, Baldwin announced he would give his decision in a few days, but in doing so, gave a strong indication that he didn't think the league had a right to forfeit the Kansas City franchise. Gilmore, as Baldwin was discussing his postponed decision, leaned over to a friend and whispered, "We're beaten."[6] The Feds were left to gather back at Weeghman's office and, as they'd so often had to do in their short term of existence, hammer out a plan B.

The next solution wasn't at all satisfying, though it had been discussed for more than a month. The Feds would give Sinclair control of Indianapolis, which was also on untenable financial ground and lacked the wherewithal to raise more capital. On March 19, having failed to get control of the Packers, the league demanded that Indianapolis give up its franchise and allow Sinclair and Powers to move it to Newark. The team's directors tried to take the same tack as Kansas City, threatening to sue, but the situation was different—the

Hoosiers had massive debts and though they had hoped to raise money over the winter, by February, "the financial activity of the Indianapolis magnates [had] apparently ceased."[7] The Hoofeds could not be saved. By the end of March, a deal was worked out through which the Federal League paid Indianapolis's stockholders $76,500, effectively releasing them from all debts, allowing Sinclair and Powers to take hold of the club.

The entire ordeal, though, made the Federal League look like something of a joke. The debts of the Hoosiers were a particular embarrassment, given that they were two-time defending league champs. But there was more. After Kansas City was sold to Sinclair, the team left for spring training under the impression that they were now bound for Newark. At their camp in Marshall, Texas, players who had been forced to spend all of September playing on the road because a flash flood wiped out their bush league stadium "heard that there was a chance that they would have to go back to that pleasant Kansas City, they sent word to Pat Powers that they would mutiny."[8] Brooklyn owner Robert Ward, whose willingness to help the league's other franchises had allowed Kansas City and Indianapolis to finish the 1914 season and keep the league together in the first place, was not happy to watch Sinclair be awarded the league champions. Ward sought to pilfer Indianapolis's two best players, outfielder Benny Kauff and pitcher Cy Falkenberg, as a reward for his generosity, and his fight over the players with Sinclair and Powers went public (a deal was eventually reached whereby Ward got Kauff). With so much confusion at the top, when the leaders of the league met at the Biltmore Hotel in New York on March 27, they still had not finalized a schedule with the season set to open in about two weeks, and would not finally do so until three days before the season began. The Feds in 1915 were just as disorganized as they'd been the previous spring.

‡

Despite those embarrassments, getting Sinclair in the fold was a needed boost. Ward and Weeghman had been dubbed the Federal League "angels" because they'd kept the league afloat, but, as the *Tribune* stated in February, "Reports in the past were that the Wards, owners of the Brookfeds, and

Weeghman of Chicago have had to lend financial aid to some of the clubs in the league ... Recent reports were that they have tired of putting up for others."[9] Weeghman, once the fulcrum of the entire Federal League experiment, perhaps was feeling the financial strain of the European war abroad and rising unemployment at home on his restaurant business, which was no longer growing with the pace it had in the early part of the decade. Back in August of 1914, Weeghman made a major investment in a 1,000-square-foot space at the new Webster Building on Van Buren and LaSalle in the Loop, committing to a $200,000 lease in a spot that required $25,000 in improvements. It was reported that the restaurant was Weeghman's twelfth in the downtown district[10] and newspaper records show it was the last storefront he would buy while an owner in the Federal League. That is not a coincidence—Weeghman would later say he lost $3 million on the Feds alone, and if world economic troubles were affecting his restaurants' revenues, Federal League expenditures were draining him. Weeghman would have been much more cost-conscious entering 1915 than he had been in 1914.

At least it could be said that Weeghman and the Feds were not alone in facing another long struggle in 1915. According to its annual report released in March, the National Commission opened 1915 with a balance of $1,480.07 in its bank account. That was down from $27,709.01 the previous year and $46,906.70 in 1913, and the loss could entirely be blamed on legal fees required to fight the Federal League.[11] In an attempt at economic retrenchment, both the A. L. and N. L. cut down on the length of their training camp and reinstituted roster limits, which had been suspended in 1914 to prevent demoted players from jumping to the Feds. The National League had voted to accept a stringent twenty-one-player rule, but the A. L., voting later, returned rosters to the normal twenty-five-player limit (much to the annoyance of N. L. magnates who were told that the A. L. would also go to twenty-one ).

The Rienzi party for the Whales was a respite in what was a spring packed with gloom around baseball. Even Jim Gilmore, usually so spunky in his pugilistic stance toward Organized Baseball, sounded a somber note about the state of the game:

"It is a shame that the lawyers and the players are getting all of the money. The promoters have little but experience for their pains. Peace and readjustment is bound to come in time and the sooner the better for all concerned. Mind you, the Federal League is in the field to fight until it gains its point. … I do not attempt to claim that the Federal League has been a financial success everywhere. The backers of the various clubs do not expect to reap financial harvests at the start. They were content from the start to await the readjustment of the game, which they are bound to force.

"But getting back to the folly of this prolonged war. There are many players in our league and in the National and American Leagues, too, who are at best only a heavy burden to their employers. Their services cannot be dispensed with because they have been able to take advantage of chaotic conditions to extract iron bound contracts at salaries far beyond their real worth. The rank injustice to the promoters lies in the fact that these men are utterly indifferent about their moral obligations to those who pay salaries. … These unfortunate conditions may not be alleviated while the rival forces of baseball are at each other's throats. That is why I declare further continuation of the fight is a shameful waste of time and money."[12]

There was, at least, some hope on this front, however minor, and it started with the man who was the biggest obstacle to peace in the game and who had become Gilmore's mortal enemy—Ban Johnson. Throughout the winter, rumors had percolated that Johnson had grown tired of having his friend Herrmann serve as the National Commission chairman because he felt he had been too soft on the Federals and that the negotiations with Weeghman for the Cubs gave the third league a greater sense of their worth than was warranted. Taking the speculation further, there was even talk of the National Commission, and the A. L.-N. L. bond, dissolving altogether. One story "had it that President Ban Johnson of the American League was on the war path, seeking the scalp of an Indian chief whose wigwam is in Cincinnati and who sometimes goes by the name of Garry Herrmann. That war would follow in the ranks of Organized Base Ball was one of the dire predictions during the week."[13]

But the *New York Sun's* Joe Vila reported that, though Johnson had, as late as February 15, "opposed a conference of any kind with one or more representatives of the Federal League," he had, in fact, arranged to meet with Ward in March. During the secret meeting, Johnson sought to prove to Ward "how the third major-league scheme was impossible," by detailing how difficult it would be to drum up enough interest to maintain profitability, city-by-city. "Ward was a patient listener," Vila wrote, "and at times, so the story goes, he was free to admit that something should be done to settle the long-drawn-out controversy." The two ended the meeting amicably, and said they hoped to meet again.[14]

Johnson also held a less secret meeting with St. Louis owner Phil Ball on the Saturday night before the season was to open in April. The meeting was arranged by Taylor Spink, editor of St. Louis-based *The Sporting News*, at McTeague's Café, a popular place among baseball men.[15] While rumors almost immediately sprang up that Johnson was arranging for Ball to purchase the Cardinals, Johnson insisted that the conversation was not about business. But when the two met again a couple of weeks later in St. Louis and then in Chicago on April 22 for the White Sox home opener, peace rumors flourished, with Ward, Ball, and Weeghman to be brought into Organized Baseball. Johnson, though, flatly denied such talk. "That story about a peace conference between the Federal Leaguers and representatives of Organized Baseball is one fine joke," he said. "It is true that I talked with Mr. Ball here this week. Our subject of conversation did not relate to peace, however. We are good friends and the whole peace yarn seems to have been spun around the fact that our paths crossed and we had a friendly conversation."[16]

The fact that Johnson so much as acknowledged the existence of Ward and Ball, though, was progress. Perhaps if he had done so months earlier, peace could have been assured before the 1915 season started. As it was, the rumors that emerged that spring did not materialize, and, for all three leagues, the season would go on as planned.

‡

The Whales departed Chicago for spring training on March 6, with spaces kept for Walter Johnson and the more recent flopper Rip Hagerman, their spots reserved more in the name of grim ceremony than in any real hope that either would actually report. Tinker did have some good news, though, when old friend Three Finger Brown joined up with the Whales in February, his contract having been bought by the league when Brooklyn decided it didn't want him and could not trade him. Overall, though, Tinker was "downcast" and said, "All I am anxious for now is to get down to Shreveport. I don't think there will be any more desertions, although, the way the players flop nowadays, it is hard to tell how many players one has from one day to another."[17] The scene in Shreveport wasn't all that comforting, though. In 1914, spring training had been had been a struggle for Tinker because of the rain, but when the Whales arrived this year, they "found that an overcoat was almost as great a comfort as it had been in Chicago. The air wasn't the sort to make a fellow yearn for baseball. The sizzle of the steam radiator sounded good."[18]

With the exception of a handful of merely chilly days, the cold in Shreveport was the rule. That was true across the South, and for most teams in all three leagues, spring training proved a bust—Ban Johnson even went so far as to propose abolishing the trips altogether, saying, "I am going to suggest to the club owners … that hereafter all players be compelled to report in condition or to play one or two weeks before the season opens. These training trips are getting to be a joke."[19] On days that were not too cold, Tinker had a hard time finding competition, as games against the collegians from Centenary were listless routs and the Whales spent most of their time playing intrasquad scrimmages. As the team prepared to leave on April 2, reporter James Crusinberry wrote, "The southern climate has been something of a 'frost' this spring, and as far as balmy breezes are concerned the Chicagoans might have done as well at Weeghman Park."[20]

While the players were shivering in Shreveport, though, Weeghman Park was undergoing some renovations. The park had been forced into an awkward layout in its first year because there were two brick houses in left field that could not be torn down before the field was set up. Now, though, those buildings had been torn down, which allowed the left-field fence to be pushed back by 25 feet, to 340 feet down the line. Beyond the fence in left, a new set of bleachers was erected, able to seat 3,000 fans, and the right-field bleachers—which held half as many spectators—were torn out altogether, at a total cost of $17,000. The field itself was laid out like a diamond and the centerfield corner was pushed back fifty-six feet, punctuated by a new electronic scoreboard. Weeghman wasn't investing in new restaurants, but he was putting money into the ballpark. "President Weeghman has spared no expense in fixing up his beautiful park," it was reported, "and the management of the Cubs and Sox will have to hurry some to keep up with the procession."[21]

After the trek back from Shreveport, Tinker ordered his players to the park for a morning practice on April 9, the day before the opener against Fielder Jones's St. Louis club. The practice drew 2,000 fans. The players gawked at the changes made to the field. Particularly dismayed was outfielder Dutch Zwilling, who had led the Federal League with 16 homers the previous year. When Zwilling, a left-handed hitter, saw the room left by the removal of the right-field bleachers, he said, "That may rob me of a few home runs."[22] Catcher Art Wilson, who had caused a stir in the home opener the previous season by clouting two homers, was still confident. He wagered a new hat that he would hit one over the left-field fence the next day.[23]

There was, also, a new face among the Whales—righthanded pitcher George McConnell, nicknamed "Slats" because he stood 6-3 and weighed 190 pounds. McConnell was hardly Walter Johnson. He was thirty-seven years old and had pitched two full seasons for the Yankees, in '12 and '13, compiling a 12–27 record in those years. The Cubs brought him up briefly in 1914 but he pitched just one game. That was good enough to earn McConnell a look at Cubs training camp in Tampa that spring, but the team had enough pitching and decided to send McConnell back down to Kansas City of the American Association. After Gilmore declared that the Federal League didn't want McConnell, a telegram from Buffalo manager Larry Schlafly urging him to get McConnell changed his mind. Tinker got in touch with a friend with the Cubs and decided McConnell was worth signing.

For Cubs president Charles Thomas, a longtime friend of Weeghman's, this was a violation of a verbal agreement he had with Weeghman that they would not tamper with each other's players. Thomas sent a stern letter to Weeghman, seeking $3,000 in financial restitution for McConnell, writing, "I would have just as much right, at least morally, to go and take one of your lunchrooms."[24] Weeghman was livid—the Cubs obviously did not want McConnell and the pitcher was, in Weeghman's mind, a free agent. Besides, after the way the peace negotiations with Herrmann the previous winter had wound up, Weeghman wasn't feeling a particular need to stick to the gentlemen's agreements of 1914. "Organized Baseball men made a fool of me last fall in their efforts to bring peace back to the game," he said. "They had me running all over the country, when all the time they were stacking the cards against me. I had kept off the players of the two rival clubs in Chicago, but the bars are down now. ... As for McConnell, Thomas can whistle for him. He will not get him back and neither will I reimburse him, because I don't owe him anything."[25]

Watching McConnell throw in practice, Tinker was impressed enough to consider using him as his Opening Day starter, especially with Claude Hendrix having returned from Shreveport with a sore shoulder. Ultimately, though, Tinker went with Hendrix to open and Jones picked Eddie Plank ahead of Bob Groom and Dave Davenport, which surely gave Tinker a pang of regret—Plank was one of the few late–1914 signees of the Federal League who actually stuck with the league, and the Whales probably would have wound up with Plank, who would win 21 games in 1915, had they not fruitlessly pursued Walter Johnson. Tinker made another decision that raised some eyebrows. He would not be on the field during the game. At thirty-four and having dealt with a litany of injuries the previous year, Tinker handed his shortstop post to nineteen-year-old Jimmy Smith and would play only occasionally in the upcoming year. It was nothing formal, but Tinker was essentially retiring as a player.

On April 10, the Whales did something few would have thought possible back in the winter of 1913, or, heck, even for much of 1914: They opened the 1915 Federal League season. There was the usual 300-automobile parade from Grant Park that preceded the game, and despite rain into the afternoon, it was well attended. When the players themselves arrived at the park, fans got their first look at the new Whales uniforms, which were white, with blue-and-white socks and blue hats, their jerseys bearing a large blue "C" on the left breast, with a whale in the center. The players were met by blaring brass bands and cabaret dancers, while the crowd also prepared for another debut—that of Mayor William Hale Thompson, who had been elected for the first time just four days earlier and, true to his "Big Bill" persona, he showed up wearing a large cowboy hat, which he doffed when given a loud ovation. Thompson, a known sportsman and a lefty, had agreed to throw out the first pitch and "took off his hat and pulled up his sleeves and threw the first ball over the plate with his left hand. Of course, it split the pan."[26]

Once the game got started, Plank's famed curveball was every bit as effective as Hendrix's spitter, as the two kept the game scoreless through four innings. The Terriers scratched out one run in the fifth inning and might have had another in the inning if they hadn't botched a squeeze play with a runner on third. Plank kept the Whales off the scoreboard through seven. In the eighth, though, with runners on first and third, Plank must have had a disturbing flashback—he was facing Whales outfielder Les Mann, who had beaten Plank in Game 2 of the previous year's World Series when Mann, then with the Braves, knocked an RBI single in the ninth inning for the only run of the game. Mann got the better of Bender again, hitting a single off the shins of shortstop Ernie Johnson, opening the way for a three-run rally that gave the Whales a 3–1 win. There wasn't quite as much fanfare as there had been for the 1914 opener, but still, the *Tribune* reported, "Seldom has Chicago seen the baseball season ushered in with more frills than attended the affairs."[27]

# CHAPTER TWENTY

# The Cubs, the Whales, and the Future of Chicago Baseball

For the Whales, maybe the only disappointment on Opening Day was in the stands. Rather than the predicted crowd of 25,000, attendance estimates ranged from 16,000 to 20,000. Poor weather had seemed to follow the Whales up from the South and now it was hurting the gate receipts on Opening Day. It hurt worse on the following day, a Sunday in which a sellout was expected, when rain forced the game to be postponed altogether. The finale on Monday against St. Louis was called off, too, and a series that should have brought in more than 50,000 fans instead attracted about a third of that. In fact, of the Whales' first twenty-four home games, eleven were rained out, including an entire three-game series against Newark in late May. The weather bureau reported that in May it rained in Chicago for twenty-three out of the first twenty-eight days, which was said to be a record. For Jim Gilmore, this was no issue—he had been saying all along that 1915 was set up to be a disaster. "Why should we become disheartened?" he said. "The weather condition and hard times are things that cannot be offset. In my opinion, the present baseball season will be the most disastrous ever experienced in the history of the national pastime, and while the poor attendance throughout the league has served to put a crimp in our receipts we are satisfied."[1]

Elsewhere around Federal League, attendance continued to be a problem. For the newest team—Sinclair's Newark Peppers—there was a massive showing for Opening Day, with about 26,000 in reported attendance. Interest in the team quickly faded, though, and when Brooklyn visited the Peppers later that week, there were reportedly just 550 fans on hand.[2] By midseason, attendance was so bad that Powers and Sinclair already were threatening to move the franchise. Kansas City, too, had a good opening crowd, with 10,000 fans, and 18,000 showed for the Terrapins in Baltimore. But enthusiasm petered out and bad weather was hampering the game everywhere. "May, with unusually cold or wet weather, to May 23, caused 18 postponements in the National League, 16 postponements in the American League, and 20 postponements in the Federal League, thus giving the sport a blow for which good weather for a mouth or more cannot atone," *Sporting Life* reported on May 30. Later in the season, Weeghman would estimate that the gate receipts lost at his park in rainouts on Saturdays and Sundays tallied $83,638,[3] and *The Sporting News* would report that "Attendance here in Chicago for the Federals is about 50 percent of what it was last year, and this city no longer is a 'stronghold' of the Gilmore circuit, except by comparison with the cities that are not drawing at all."[4]

It didn't help that one of Weeghman's Whales-related pet projects backfired badly. For the 1915 season, Weeghman had arranged to give away passes to the North Side park for patrons of his restaurants, based on a lottery system. It was a success, though Weeghman was lampooned for the scheme. "Surely the eminent Weeghman … didn't believe when he started his lottery that he would escape unnoticed and doesn't this beanery trick prove conclusively that the whole Lunch Room venture is a sham?" wrote Federal League nemesis Joe Vila. "The exposure of the allotment of beanery season tickets has caused a big laugh here, and incidentally it has opened the eyes of persons who were inclined, for a while, to regard the Lunch Room League with some favor. The scheme is so cheap and shoddy that it is surprising how the eminent Weeghman could have pulled such a terrible bone."[5] Worse, though, it was deemed that the whole plot was illegal. There was a crackdown in the city on gambling in all forms, including lotteries, and on May 25, Chicago police made a sweep of downtown restaurants and cafes, making seven arrests—including Albert Smith, the manager of Weeghman's restaurant at 180 W. Adams.[6]

As the season got underway, the team under the most pressure to show well at the gate in 1915 was the Cubs. This was a strange turn, of course, because until recently, the West Siders had been the biggest money-maker in baseball. The presence of Weeghman's team on the North Side surely had cut into attendance but the team was still paying for the antics of Charles Murphy and the continued impression that Murphy was still running the team that had truly wiped out the Cubs' popularity. Those negatives might have been neutralized, though, had the Cubs been able to maintain the dominance of the National League they'd shown for much of the previous decade. If there was a simple way for the Cubs to lure back their lost patrons and begin returning big profits again, it was winning.

In the offseason, though, the Cubs' repeated efforts to improve the club fell short. While Weeghman nearly landed Walter Johnson and Comiskey did get Eddie Collins, Thomas had come up empty all winter in his attempts to bolster the team, which needed a right-handed hitting outfielder to go with lefties Cy Williams and Frank Schulte, and—in a disappointing twist for the club that once employed Tinker and Evers—much better middle infielders. Back in February, Thomas went to the National League meeting armed with $30,000, with Reds infielder Heinie Groh said to be their target, but returned empty-handed. Still, the Cubs had a good pitching staff and showed promise at the plate. One writer who traveled with the team in spring training reported, "The Cubs have hit better, harder, longer, oftener than any West Side team that has toured the South for years."[7]

The most important change, then, would come with manager Roger Bresnahan—who, when he managed the Cardinals in 1912, had been accused by Charles Murphy of helping fix the National League race for the Giants and who had nearly joined the Federal League six months earlier. The recruiting of Bresnahan actually began the previous July, when he showed signs of dissatisfaction playing for Hank O'Day, who favored Jimmy Archer as his catcher. St. Louis's Ed Steininger and Phil Ball offered Bresnahan

$12,000 per year plus a $5,000 bonus and a $25,000 stake in the team, but Bresnahan remained wary of the third league and stuck with the Cubs, despite his unhappiness there.[8] The Feds tried again in the fall, when Robert Ward wanted Bresnahan to manage Brooklyn. In October, Bresnahan met with Gilmore in Chicago and named his terms: a jaw-dropping $50,000, three-year contract. Ward was, to Bresnahan's surprise, amenable, offering him a contract at a meeting in New York. Bresnahan said he would think it over. According to Bresnahan, he simply turned the offer down, but Ward said he had asked Bresnahan to produce his Chicago contract, and when Bresnahan failed to do so, Ward withdrew the offer. Bresnahan continued to flirt with the Federal Leaguers, and said that after meeting Ward again in Chicago, "I met Mr. Gilmore and Mr. Weeghman on several different occasions, and they both told me they thought I was very foolish for not going to Brooklyn."[9] Bresnahan was using the Federal League as a bargaining chip with the Cubs, because in November, when Murphy announced Weeghman wouldn't be buying the club, he also announced Bresnahan would be the team's new manager, replacing O'Day.

Bresnahan knew that turning around the Cubs would be a difficult job. As talented as they were, the team was pocked with bad attitudes, and none had been more of a problem than that of infielder Heine Zimmerman. A flamboyant and strong-willed slugger from the Bronx, Zimmerman was prone to loafing and fighting, and his ability to erode team chemistry outweighed his playing prowess. Many hoped the settlement of Zimmerman's personal affairs would help. In 1912, he had married seventeen-year-old Helene Chasar, but the marriage quickly deteriorated and in January 1915, she had sued for alimony, alleging that Zimmerman had sent her and their daughter no support. When an arrangement was made to have $10 a week during the season and $20 in the offseason sent to his wife, it was expected that Zimmerman would be more productive because he wouldn't worry over his often scattered finances. Even with a $7,200 salary, Zimmerman was frequently broke. "He saw so many fascinating neckties in haberdashers' windows that he could not resist the temptation to buy them as long as the money held out," one writer noted. "Now Zim will instruct his 'banker' to pay his wife her alimony first, then will spend the rest on neckwear and his worries will be over. Watch Zim play a lot better baseball this year than he did last."[10]

Bresnahan was a product of the John McGraw managerial school—tough and direct, McGraw was well known for taking on talented problem players and getting them to produce for the team. Though Bresnahan and Zimmerman had gotten into a fistfight on the bench during a game in Brooklyn when both were players during the previous August, Bresnahan thought he could get through to Zimmerman as the manager and that relationship would be the key to the season. It wasn't just Zimmerman, of course. The entire Cub team had been listless and uninspired under O'Day in 1914. Bresnahan vowed to change that. "We are going against the enemy with a united front," Bresnahan said. "There is no dissension in our ranks and every man on the club has told me I will get his very best. The players do not look on me as a driver at all, but as a player who has not forgotten that he was and is a player simply because in the fortunes of war he was elevated to the managerial rank."[11]

If the Cubs were going to realistically fend off the challenge of Weeghman's Whales and return the West Side to its former glory, they would need to wipe clean the stains left by the dissolution of the Tinker-Evers-Chance dynasty and start fresh, with Bresnahan as the second coming of Chance, a good team behind him and—drumroll, please—a new West Side park. Murphy had promised and not delivered a new park for years but in 1915, Thomas announced that Charles Taft was planning on starting work on new grounds in the fall. An item in *The Sporting News* noted, "Owner Taft and his baseball adviser Charles Webb Murphy refused to fall in line with other magnates who owned expensive plants until they became convinced that Roger Bresnahan might develop another pennant championship." If Bresnahan could win, there would be a new park on the West Side.

Despite what was going on with the baseball war, the perception was that Chicago's baseball landscape had the potential to be forever reshaped by Bresnahan and his Cubs in 1915. George Robbins wrote: "With Bresnahan on the West Side the question relative to his ultimate success and popularity as the successor to [Frank] Chance is problematical. Chicago is the Federal League stronghold and even the popularity of so good a fellow as Roger probably never will be able to restore the lost prestige of the Cubs in Chicago unless the Feds blow up. ... Sentiment is a mighty big factor in the success of baseball, as much as some magnates and many ball players have tried to kill it in recent maneuvers. The best thing that the owners of the Cubs could do in Chicago is to build a new park and with Bresnahan and a mighty good ball team as its principal assets, try to rebuild its winning fortunes in this city—build up a new sentiment and a new following to take the place of the old guard that rooted and cheered Chance and his warriors nearly a decade ago."[13]

‡

The early returns for Bresnahan and the Cubs were very promising. After a 5–6 start, they won seven straight, and when they embarked on a three-week trip to the East, they were just a half-game behind Philadelphia for first place. Bresnahan told his players that if they returned from the trip in first place, he would buy them all hats. The Cubs moved into first thanks to a four-game sweep in Boston, and when they played Cincinnati on May 29, the last day of the trip, they knew the hats were on the line. "The players have a deep suspicion that the Dook [Bresnahan] will make good on the hats if they beat Cincinnati today," Billy Birch wrote in the *Herald*. "As the players are woefully shy of summer straws, you can bet Cincinnati is going to have a tough time between the hours of 3 and 6 today."[13] Indeed, pitcher Bert Humphries was able to hold off the Reds despite allowing ten hits and the Cubs won 3–1, running their first-place record to 21–14.

It wasn't just the Cubs that were bolstering Chicago baseball, though. The White Sox, too, had gotten off to a bad start—they opened with eight straight road games and returned home 2–6—but had rallied, winning seven in a row in late April and topping that in May with a nine-game winning streak. The White Sox had gotten stellar pitching from second-year righthander Red Faber, who was off to a 9–2 start, and nearly as good a showing from Joe Benz, who had led the league with 19 losses in 1914 but was 5–0 by the end of May. Led by outfielder Jack Fournier, who was hitting .376, the offense was humming and their 199 runs in the first 37 games were easily the most in the American League. They were 25–12, with a two-game lead over the Tigers in the American League, at that point.

And there were the Whales. Tinker had his club in first place in early May, but a rough trip to the East (they went 5–7) knocked them back in the standings. They played better when they returned home, but it had been difficult to get into a rhythm with the repeated rainouts the team suffered. The Whales were 21–14 and just a half-game behind Pittsburgh on May 24, but with the Sox and Cubs on top of their leagues—even in May, there were already references to 1906, when the Cubs and White Sox met in the World Series for what remains the only time in history—Weeghman's club could not translate its success into turnstile clicks. "The Feds have been more popular in Chicago than any other city in the third league owing to the popularity of Charley Weeghman, a real sportsman, but the Feds cannot hope to hold the attention of Chicago fans with both major league teams in the pennant fight," *The Sporting News* pointed out. "Even the Cubs are bound to find new favor, while as for the Sox—well, this is an American League stronghold, win or lose, and winning there is nothing to it but, 'Oh, you White Sox.'"[14]

On May 30, the Sox, Whales, and Cubs—as they had done on the previous Memorial Day weekend—played simultaneously, on what was a seasonable, fifty-eight-degree afternoon. Proportionally, the division of fandom in the city was still running about the same as it had in 1914. The White Sox, hosting the struggling Indians, drew 16,000 fans. The Cubs, with the Cardinals in town, brought in 6,500. The Whales had a doubleheader against Kansas City, which was only a game-and-a-half behind Chicago in the Federal League standings, and drew about 8,500 to the North Side.[15] But as any modern-day North Sider knows, the proximity to Lake Michigan means that a fifty-eight-degree day in Chicago doesn't necessarily mean a pleasant few hours at Clark and Addison, and the Whales' crowd "was considerable of a surprise, for everybody except the fortunate folks in the sun boxes just shivered and chattered through the two combats."[16]

The Whales' attendance edge over the Cubs took a hit, though, when the West Siders surged in June, seizing control of the National League race as the White Sox pushed their lead in the A. L. to as many as six games. The highlight of the month came on June 24, with Zimmerman returning to uniform for the first time in more than a week, having sat out because of a knee injury. Zimmerman didn't start the game, but after the Cubs blew a 10–9 lead to the Cardinals in the ninth inning at the West Side park, he inserted himself as a pinch-hitter without waiting for the call from Bresnahan. The score at the time was 13–11 and Zimmerman rocketed a line drive to right field to bring in two runs for a double, tying the game. He advanced to third on a groundout, then shocked fans and players on both sides by rushing to the plate on a steal of home, bad knee and all, giving the Cubs a 14–13 victory in what the *Herald* called, "The Greatest Game of the Year."

Alas, it was all short-lived for Bresnahan and the Cubs. Four days after Zimmerman's heroics, the Cubs were in Cincinnati, and, when Zimmerman hit a slow roller to Buck Herzog, he pulled up and stopped running—the kind of half-hearted effort that had long infuriated any manager with Zimmerman on the roster. In the dugout, Bresnahan told Zimmerman, "That will cost you $100 and you are out of the game." Zimmerman went after Bresnahan, assailing him with foul language, before he was finally pulled away. "I am tired of seeing Cub players taking life easy when I am in there fighting every inch of the way," Bresnahan said. "We should be ten games in the lead now, for in the last five defeats … I can show you where indifferent playing on the part of certain Cubs has cost us the games. I know Zimmerman is a great player, but he must do as I say or get out of the game. I have been his best friend and if he throws me down, he will regret it."[17]

Zimmerman was apologetic the following day and promised to return to his best behavior but during the Cubs next game, he got into an argument with umpire Bill Klem and was ejected. On the train ride home from Cincinnati on June 30, his Cubs teammates confronted Zimmerman, warning him that he was costing the team a shot at the pennant and "This force formed a flying wedge and assaulted the big fellow so viciously and with such unanimity, also with such feeling, that it is said Heinie came near weeping, he felt so bad for his actions. … Zim capitulated and promised to be good. 'If I get kicked out again I'll make a present of $5 to each member of the club,' said Heinie, after hearing the forceful, but at times tearful, appeal of his desperate mates."[18]

While Zimmerman was melting down and eroding the chances of Bresnahan becoming Peerless Leader II, Tinker's Whales surged. The outfield of Dutch Zwilling, Max Flack, and new Federal Leaguer Les Mann carried the offense, and though recruit shortstop Jimmy Smith showed he was not up to the challenge of replacing Tinker for a full season, the Whales had enough hitting and got surprising performances out of his two over-age pitchers—Slats McConnell, at thirty-seven, would go 25–10 on the year, leading the league in wins, and Three Finger Brown was resurgent on the North Side, going 17–8 with an ERA of 2.08. Rather than getting into fights with his own players, Tinker was uniting his crew by fighting the opposition. On June 26 in Brooklyn, Tinker received a one-game suspension when he and the Tip-Tops' Hap Myers came to blows after Tinker tagged Myers too hard for his liking on a play at second base. At that, "Myers landed the first punch and the Whales closed in on the scrappers, bearing Myers to the turf."[19] The Whales won the game, part of a six-game winning streak that moved them within two-and-a-half games of first place.

The Cubs had returned to their usual unlikeable state and the Whales were on a roll, but for Weeghman it wasn't helping much at the gate. The Whales returned from their road trip on July 2, a Friday, and there was some hope that the North Siders could bring together a strong Fourth of July weekend crowd, with Pittsburgh in town. Opening on a Saturday, though, didn't do much to boost the crowd, as the Whales attracted 5,000 fans. Over on the West Side, the Cubs' game against the Reds drew 10,000, a sure sign that the Feds were losing ground in their Chicago stronghold. Fourth of July might have been a savior, but again, Weeghman could not catch a break—there were heavy rains on the morning of the Fourth, and though Weeghman had a crew of workers fixing up the field as soon as the rain stopped and delayed the start of the game by a half-hour, only 3,000 fans made their way to Clark and Addison. With a doubleheader on July 5, the Whales drew 8,000 fans. The Cubs had about twice as many, though, on the West Side.

Weeks later, on July 24, Chicago suffered the worst disaster in the city's history, when a steamship named the Eastland set out to Lake Michigan carrying more than 2,500 passengers, far too many for a ship of its size. The boat was scheduled to take employees of the Western Electric Company across the lake to Michigan City, Indiana, for a picnic, but it never made it that far. Top-heavy with overcrowded passengers, the boat wobbled along the Chicago River and capsized, killing 844 people. The Whales canceled their game the following day as the city observed a day of mourning. Weeghman, in a gesture of goodwill, dedicated July 29 as Eastland Sufferers' Day on the North Side and set a goal of raising $10,000 to be donated to victims' families. But, naturally, it rained for much of the twenty-ninth, and though the Whales still tried to put on their game, only 3,000 fans showed up.

The attendance problem was overwhelming the Feds. When the Whales were in Brooklyn back on June 28, the Tip-Tops had done something unique: They threw open the gates and declared it "Fans' Day," allowing 10,000 rooters in for free. The purpose was to accustom fans with the new Fourth Avenue subway, which made getting to Washington Park much easier, in hopes that they'd patronize the park more regularly afterward. Jim Gilmore was on hand, with W.E. Robertson of Buffalo, as well as Harry Sinclair, Pat Powers, and Robert Ward. Brooklyn had a difficult time attracting fans from the beginning, and the success of Fans' Day started the Feds on a new path to attract fans—make it cheaper. When Weeghman returned from the trip, he instituted a policy which declared that one day per week, schoolchildren would be admitted free. In August, Newark dropped its twenty-five-cent bleacher tickets to ten cents. Brooklyn did the same, and the ten-cent bleacher prices spread throughout the league. On August 10, Weeghman announced that his new pricing for games starting August 22 would be: 3,000 bleacher seats for ten cents; 5,000 pavilion seats for twenty-five cents; 10,000 grandstand seats at fifty cents and 4,500 box seats at $1.[20]

Charging a dime for admittance wasn't exactly a show of strength, and the Federals were again lampooned for getting minor league prices for what they claimed was major league baseball. That wasn't really the point, however. From the beginning, Gilmore said that 1915 would be a painful year in baseball, but with the Feds losing the attendance war decidedly, even in Chicago, the league needed to figure out how to inflict some form of pain on Organized Baseball—they were counting on that pain to force O. B. into a settlement of the war in the off-season. Every fan the Federals attracted at a measly ten cents meant less profit, but it also meant keeping those fans from going to see O. B. games. It smacked of desperation, for sure. But the Feds were, in fact, desperate.

# CHAPTER TWENTY-ONE

# A Champion on the North Side

It could not have been a good sign for the Federal League when, on July 16, a Friday, the White Sox packed nearly 30,000 fans into Comiskey Park to see one of the franchise's great heroes—pitcher Ed Walsh—take the mound in his continuing comeback attempt. Seven years earlier, Walsh had posted one of the greatest seasons a pitcher has ever had, when he went 40–15 with a 1.42 ERA, hurling 42 complete games in 49 starts, and walking only 56 batters in 464 innings. It was the second consecutive year that Walsh topped 400 innings, and the workload eventually caught up with him, because by 1913, at age thirty-two, Walsh was effectively finished as a pitcher. Getting him back on the mound in July, though, was a big boost for a White Sox team that was beginning to slide in the standings. When Walsh downed the Athletics, 6–2, fans rushed onto the field and "lifting Walsh to their shoulders, carried him proudly to the Sox bench, where for many minutes Walsh was unable to escape the scores of admirers who pressed from every side to shake his hand."[1] It wasn't the size or enthusiasm of the crowd over Walsh's performance that should have worried the Federals, though. What was troubling was that among the first to shake Walsh's hand was Judge Kenesaw Mountain Landis, who had been a regular at White Sox games that spring.

Since the sides had finished filing depositions before the season started, there was a rumor that cropped up suggesting the Landis would soon issue a decision in the Federals' landmark case just about every week. Those rumors most likely emanated from Federal League sources because the league had so much riding on whatever Landis said—even if he didn't completely tear down the structure of baseball, it seemed that he might at least rule on the more immediate issues and that maybe the Federals could get the injunctions lifted on the players who had been barred from the league by lower courts, or that, maybe, players who had signed and flopped like Walter Johnson, Ivey Wingo, and Pol Perritt would be forced to play for the third league.

Landis remained silent, though, and in light of the peace moves made by Ban Johnson, Charles Comiskey, and Phil Ball early in the spring, it was becoming clearer that Landis was stalling in hopes of letting the two sides come to their own agreement. Even when he was asked, in July, to rule on the injunction preventing Armando Marsans from playing, Landis simply said that his decision would come soon, but offered no inkling as to how he was leaning or when, exactly, "soon" would come. "Judge Landis has had the time to read and inwardly digest the voluminous testimony in that now famous baseball anti-trust suit ten times over, and yet a decision is withheld or delayed," one New York reporter wrote. "It is not fair to assume, perhaps, that it is being withheld or delayed for the purpose of giving the warring factions a chance to reach some agreement, and yet the feeling seems to be growing that such is the case. ... Constant rumors of peace talk, and equally constant denials, lend credence to this feeling."[2] In an interview in Chicago, Landis strongly denied suggesting to either the Federals or to magnates of Organized Baseball that he was prepared to make a decision or that the two sides should compromise. The following year, Landis would admit that he stalled. "After taking counsel with my own judgment, I decided that the court had the right, or at least the discretion, to postpone decision in the case and this was done."[3]

The Feds were hinged to a Landis decision, but for the magnates of O. B., more important was to find a way to return the game to profitability, something that had become exponentially more difficult in the face of the exorbitant contracts that the Federal League had forced teams to enter into with players who did not warrant such paydays. With ten-day clauses having been removed from 1915 contracts and, in some cases, expensive deals running through 1916 and even 1917 on the books, many teams were facing a wave of red ink. In the midst of that reality, Garry Herrmann of the Reds gave out a solemn interview in which he speculated that team owners would have to approach players to renegotiate their contracts downward or run the risk of folding franchises altogether. Asked why a player would agree to such an arrangement, Herrmann said, "Do you not think that if a player were confronted with the alternative of taking less money or seeing his ball club quit business he would appreciate the seriousness of the situation and accept a cut in salary? There is positively no feeling against the player in this matter. It is a business proposition. Men who are operating losing baseball plants can't go on like this forever."[4]

Jim Gilmore, naturally, spoke up to agree, but Herrmann was roundly chided by Ban Johnson, Charles Comiskey, and other owners. If Herrmann's Reds were losing money, the sentiment went, that was Herrmann's own fault and in no way should major league teams be seeking to cut salaries during the season. That would be merely showing weakness in front of the Federal League and give them undue leverage when it came to the possibility of a peace settlement. "If Garry is kicking because of poor business it must be because the management has been bad," Johnson said. "Herrmann should cheer up. The American League is not making any holler. Herrmann was wrong in giving out that interview."[5] But on the Saturday after making his statement about player salaries, Herrmann's troubles were evident—with the Cubs in town on a weekend day, the game drew only 1,500 fans.

That is why another tactic emerged out of Cincinnati the following month, one that had more backing from other teams. The magnates, it was reported, thought it would be worthwhile to challenge the legal validity of the gaudy contracts players held if those players were not performing up to the level the contract warranted. The player would, under the plan, be given ten days to improve his performance, and if he failed to do so, would be released and his contract voided. The report said that two Reds players were to be the initial targets for this approach, and one would be pitcher Red Ames, who had been part of the mass of Reds who were prepared to jump to the Federal League in June of 1914 before being lured back to Cincinnati with a generous contract. Ames was awful to start 1915 and was just 1–4 when the story about the Reds' plan broke. In the end, Ames was not released, but was, instead, sold to St. Louis on July 24, and after having gone 2–4 with a 4.50 ERA in Cincinnati, he bounced back to go 9–3 with a 2.46 ERA down the stretch for the Cardinals. But the fact that Organized Baseball was considering releasing the very players they'd fought so hard to keep from jumping in 1914 was a reflection of how the Federal League threat had waned. "Incidentally," the story out of Cincinnati went, "the talk of testing the contracts indicates that all fear of the Federals is past—that Gilmore's organization is regarded as a dead fish in the pond. There wouldn't even be talk of dropping any players if the Feds were considered still dangerous."[6]

No matter how bad things might have been for the Federal Leaguers, Gilmore understood perception mattered far more than reality, and the perception that he had going for him was that the richest magnates in his league had enough money to wait out the magnates of O. B. and force a settlement. He made several loud announcements in an attempt to portray his league as not only financially strong but boldly planning to move into more direct competition with major league teams. At the end of June, Gilmore huddled up in New York with representatives from all eight teams and announced that not only would the league be back again in 1916, it would most definitely have a team in New York, as it had threatened several times over the past year. As if to emphasize the point, Gilmore also announced that the Federal League headquarters would be moved, on August 1, from the Loop in Chicago to a New York office at 42$^{nd}$ and Broadway. Gilmore also said there was a chance the league would move into Boston too, despite the fact that the very popular Red Sox had just opened Fenway Park and the Braves were to open a new 45,000-seat facility in August. Harry Sinclair confirmed that, at the meeting in New York, the Federal League had put together a war chest of $1 million to back those moves and that a Federal League financial committee had been established, which essentially amounted to the five wealthy Fed owners (Sinclair, Phil Ball, Weeghman, Robert Ward, and Ed Gwinner) plotting what to do about the languishing franchises in Baltimore, Buffalo, and Kansas City. Gilmore probably wasn't overstating the $1 million fund—it would be later shown that Ward had put up almost $200,000 for the league on August 15.[7]

Gilmore also could not resist one of his favorite fallbacks—the promise of an impending player raid. While one story held that the Feds came out of a meeting vowing to attack the minor leagues, Gilmore's press agent put out a story, which was ridiculed, saying they "will make a bid for some of the stars of the game. Four players were mentioned, Tyrus Cobb, Eddie Collins, J. Franklin Baker and Grover Cleveland Alexander. The Federals, as usual, tack on a humorous paragraph. This one reads: 'Price is no object to our league. We want these players at any cost.' … One might suppose that if the promoters of the Fed venture had any business sense they would realize by this time that their bombastic tales of capturing stars from the majors have proven boomerangs and done them more harm than good."[8]

‡

There would be, however, one final legitimate player battle between the Federal League and Organized Baseball, and it would center around one of the most eccentric characters in the game—outfielder "Shoeless" Joe Jackson. By the summer of 1915 just about every player in the major leagues had been locked into an ironclad deal that the Federals could not legally violate. But Jackson played for Cleveland and after more than a year of baseball war, owner Charley Somers was nearly broke. Though Ban Johnson and Somers had a heated exchange the previous year, Johnson (with Charles Comiskey) tried to come to Somers's aid, feeling some sense of loyalty because, in more prosperous times fifteen years earlier, Somers had bankrolled Comiskey and most of the fledgling American League in its fight to ascend to major league status opposite the National League. Already, Comiskey had purchased outfielder Nemo Leibold off Somers for $8,000 and there was a rumor he would pay Somers $20,000 for shortstop Ray Chapman.

But Jackson was Cleveland's best talent. He had a .327 average in 1915, but still, Cleveland was perfectly willing to move him, and not only because Somers was broke. Jackson was something of a head case. He had been late

in reporting for spring training in Atlanta, instead "appearing in small thea-
tres in the South with a woman as a partner. ... Jackson says he can make as
much money on the stage as he can in baseball, but he fears that his drawing
power will stop the moment he gets out of the national game." After he
arrived in camp, a deputy had been dispatched to find Jackson and bring
him back to his hometown of Greenville, South Carolina, on a personal
charge lodged by his wife. Jackson got into an argument with the deputy
and when the deputy attempted to handcuff him, Jackson punched him.[9]
Then, on July 7, Jackson was in Cleveland taking an afternoon drive with
his wife and her sister, when something went wrong with his car's engine.
Rather than pulling over, Jackson had his wife take the wheel and stepped
out onto the running board while the car was in motion at full speed. Of
course, "neither noticed the approach of a heavy truck and Joe was side-
swiped off the running board. One leg and his left arm were badly bruised
and a dozen or more cuts were inflicted, enough to cause him to go to a
hospital." Jackson was out for a week.[10]

On August 9, while the Whales were in Brooklyn and the Indians were
in New York, Jackson met with Tinker at the Somerset Hotel in New York,
where the Whales were staying. There, Jackson told Tinker that Somers
hadn't paid him in weeks and, according to Weeghman, "begged [Tinker]
to sign him to a Chicago contract."[11] Tinker was very interested in the
possibility—the Federals had approached Jackson several times over the
course of the last year and a half, and before the season, he claimed they had
made an offer of $15,000 per year for three years, which he turned down.
But Tinker told Jackson he needed to investigate the situation, to make
sure that Jackson had not been paid. If the claim turned out to be true, the
Federals could have the legal grounds to regard Jackson as a free agent.

On August 14, after a Saturday doubleheader in Baltimore, Tinker
received a telegram at the Hotel Emerson from Jackson and left immediately, keeping his mission a secret—in the *Chicago Herald* two days later,
it was reported that Tinker "dashed to his room and that was the last seen
of him by any of the players or Secretary Williams. The boss of the Whales
did not even stop to partake of his evening meal. It is known, however, that
he took an early train. That much was learned from the taxicab driver who

hustled him to the station. He could have gone to Philadelphia or Boston, and there is a rumor afloat that he will return with a star from organized baseball, and the rumor appears to be well founded."[12] Tinker was, instead, heading to Cleveland. He was going to see to it that Shoeless Joe Jackson would play on Chicago's North Side.

Tinker later admitted to making a key mistake, though. On Sunday, he showed up for the game in Cleveland, well-dressed and easily spotted by Jackson, who repeatedly waved to Tinker during the game. That also meant that several of Jackson's teammates also saw Tinker, and informed Cleveland manager Lee Fohl. Tinker expected to leave straight from the game and take Jackson on the train back to Baltimore, but Jackson's teammates were told to watch him and accused him of the obvious—that he was about to desert for the Feds. His plan to go with Jackson right from the game foiled, Tinker instead went to Jackson's apartment, but already the Indians were onto him. Cleveland team secretary Bill Blackwood was there and Blackwood informed Jackson that if he did sign with the Federals, he would be hit with an injunction and would not allowed to play. Still, Tinker was under the impression that Jackson would make it to the train station on his own and come with him to Baltimore, but there was one other detail Tinker could not contend with—Jackson's wife, who "was averse to leaving Cleveland from the start."[13] Jackson never showed up at the train station.

With the disaster of losing Jackson to Tinker averted, Somers instead put Jackson on the trade market, and Comiskey sent secretary Harry Grabiner with the instructions to "Go to Cleveland, watch the bidding for Jackson, raise the highest one made by any club until they all drop out." On August 20, when it was reported that Washington's Clark Griffith would get Jackson for $20,000 and two players, Comiskey and Grabiner raised the stakes, offering three young players and what was reported as somewhere between $15,000–$25,000.[14] Somers accepted. Ban Johnson was livid at Tinker for trying to sign Jackson, threatening a lawsuit. But for Comiskey, the North Siders' interference had worked out well for the South Siders—again. The previous winter, Ban Johnson had helped Comiskey acquire Eddie Collins from the Athletics as a way to offset

Tinker's signing of Walter Johnson. Now he had both Collins and Jackson, two of the best offensive players in the game.[15] Two years later, when the White Sox would win the World Series, Jackson and Collins would be the team's top two run scorers.

‡

Having, again, come oh-so-close to bringing a legitimate major league star to the North Side, but having again come up empty, Tinker was left to return to his club and figure out how to come out on top of a Federal League race that was, for much of the year, a five-team mess. It would only become more of a mess for the Whales down the stretch, too, as the team would make up all those April and May rainouts with doubleheaders in August and September. After returning to Baltimore without Jackson, Tinker's team was still in first place, but four other clubs—Pittsburgh, Newark, Kansas City, and St. Louis were within three-and-a-half games of the lead. The race was so volatile that the Whales came into their August 20 game against Buffalo in a tie for first. But after losing that one and being swept the next day in a doubleheader, Chicago had suddenly dropped to fourth, in the space of a little more than twenty-four hours. Things looked particularly grim for the Whales when, on August 31, they were swept in a doubleheader by first-place Pittsburgh, falling five games out of the Federal League lead.

The slump of the North Siders appeared to be a wasted opportunity for the Federal League. The early giddiness about a possible Cubs-Sox 1906 World Series redux faded in the depths of the summer, as the White Sox's pitching depth failed to hold up behind Red Faber and Jim Scott (Ed Walsh's comeback was short-lived, as he made only three starts) and Jackson had a hard time getting into rhythm with his new team, batting .272 for the Sox. On the West Side, Zimmerman ultimately proved to be too much for even Bresnahan to handle, and on August 14, in a 12–2 loss in St. Louis—during which Bresnahan was ejected—Zimmerman got into a fight in the dugout with pitcher George Pierce. According to one account, after Zimmerman committed two errors in the fifth inning and "Pierce, sore over Zim's woozy fielding, dropped a remark which roiled the temperamental Heinie. Wheeling from the bat rack, where he was selecting his favorite mace, the German swung from the ground, aiming flush for Filbert's jaw, but the punch missed Pierce and lodged on the lip of Hippo Vaughn who, scenting trouble, arose in the role of peacemaker." The police had to move in to break up the fight.[16] By the end of August, the Cubs were under .500 and eight games out of first; the White Sox were in third place, seven-and-a-half games out.

But the Whales weren't through. With the Terrapins struggling through an abominable season in Baltimore (they would wind up 47–107) and the team rumored to be for sale, Weeghman was able to pluck two reinforcements to help the North Siders through what would be a grind that would include eight doubleheaders in the final thirty-three days of the season. On September 2, the Whales acquired former Phillies shortstop Mickey Doolin, and eleven days later, they got pitcher Bill Bailey. Doolin was badly needed because young Jimmy Smith had not worked out at shortstop, batting only .217 on the year with 476 errors in 932 games so he was shipped to Baltimore along with cash for Doolan, who was thirty-five but his experience was valuable and he hit .267 down the stretch for the Whales. Bailey was needed too because with Ad Brennan struggling again in 1915, the Whales had no lefthanders. Bailey had been 6–19 in Baltimore but was strong down the stretch for Chicago, going 3–1 with a 2.16 ERA in five starts.

Bailey's performance gave Tinker a reliable option behind Slats McConnell, who finished the season strong thanks in part to a new "freak" pitch developed in the wake of the banning of the emery ball: the mud ball. The Whales got their first look at the mud ball—invented that summer by former Cub Ed Reulbach (now with the Newark Feds)—when former emery ball master Cy Falkenberg used it to pitch Newark past Chicago on August 1. Tinker had protested to the umpire about the pitch, but there was nothing in the rules against using the mud ball. Thereafter, Tinker ordered his pitchers to learn it, and, McConnell became a master. To throw the pitch, "the idea is to first drop some tobacco juice in the glove, pick up some dirt around the pitcher's slab and squeeze it on the sphere. This has a tendency to make the ball do a regular 'hoochie-coochie' and the batter cannot land on it with any degree of success."[17] McConnell was 13–8 before he began using the mud ball and hoochie-coochied his way to an impressive 12–2 record thereafter.

The influx of talent in places the Whales were sorely lacking paid immediate dividends. Chicago closed with a 17–6 record in September, going into
the final stretch of October games at 83-65, a half-game behind St. Louis
(83–66) and 1.5 games behind Pittsburgh (85–64). Because of a rained out
doubleheader in Pittsburgh on Friday, October 1, the Whales and Rebels
would finish the year with back-to-back doubleheaders, one in Pittsburgh
followed by one that Weeghman suggested be played on the North Side
because Pennsylvania law forbade Sunday baseball. Pittsburgh, naturally,
objected to this scenario, but Gilmore ruled in favor of Weeghman and
the games would have to be played in Chicago. When the Terriers lost on
Saturday while the Whales were sweeping Pittsburgh in the first doubleheader—winning the second game in eleven innings when Les Mann scored
on a hit by Doolin to start a three-run rally—Chicago was bumped up into
first place. That set up a dramatic finish to the 1915 season. The Whales,
playing at Weeghman Park, needed to win only one of its two games against
Pittsburgh to take the Federal League championship.

Ultimately, in return for everything that happened over the course of
two tumultuous Federal League seasons, Charley Weeghman and Joe Tinker
would be rewarded with one perfect day. They would get one brief taste
of what the Federal League could have been, and, more important, of the
promise of baseball on the North Side at Clark and Addison. That perfect
day, that one taste, came on the final day of the season, October 3, 1915.
The weather, for what felt like the first time that season, was ideal. At 10 AM
it was seventy degrees and sunny, and as Weeghman and secretary Charley
Williams prepared for what was expected to be a sold-out park, they had to
get a sense that something bigger was afoot. By 11 AM, hundreds of fans
were crowding around the ticket windows, and by 12:30, the fans buzzed
in the streets as they came off the elevated trains and streetcars, creating a
carnival atmosphere up and down Addison. There were so many fans at the
park that the gates had to be closed early—an estimated 10,000 fans were
denied entry, and 5,000 of them stuck around outside the park just to watch
the scoreboard and follow the proceedings. About 300 fans even crowded
into the press box, and the aisles were so overrun with patrons that when
Mayor Thompson and his wife showed up, Williams had some difficulty
cutting a swath through the crowd to get Thompson to his box.

As was customary for oversold crowds, fans who couldn't get seats lined up along the outfield, "extending from the Whales bench clear around the park and back to the bench occupied by the Rebels, there was stretched one gigantic horseshoe of yelling fans of both sexes. At its thinnest point the horseshoe was six and seven deep, while in the more favored spots there were fifteen lined in each row. ... Underneath the stand, at the little portholes, there were three and four faces showing where not even one person could sit without bending into a knot."[18] The official count given out by Williams was stunning: 34,212 fans were in attendance.

They did not go home disappointed—though they came close. In the first game, McConnell was brilliant, despite having injured his arm the previous Wednesday. On Thursday, he went from Pittsburgh to Youngstown, Ohio, to visit famed trainer Bonesetter Reese, who told him he would have trouble throwing curves if he pitched on Sunday. But McConnell took the mound in the first game anyway, and struck out nine, taking a 4–1 lead into the final inning. The championship could have been decided there, but, in the ninth, Les Mann ran into Dutch Zwilling on a fly ball that would have been the final out, causing Zwilling to drop the ball and opening the way to a three-run rally that sent the game into extra innings. The Rebels won in the eleventh, and the crowd was so distraught "a meat ax was needed to cut the gloom."[19]

After the first game, umpire Bill Brennan approached the writers in the press box to ask what time sundown was expected. When he was told it was 5:24, he told both managers that he would call the game after the last inning that started before that time. That put the Whales in a perilous spot—if the second game ended in a tie because of darkness, St. Louis would win the pennant. For five innings, that possibility grew more real as sidearmer Bill Bailey battled Elmer Knetzer and his sweeping curveball, neither team able to get a runner past second base. In the sixth, the Whales had their breakthrough, though. Doolin started the inning with a single through the third base hole, and was moved to second on a sacrifice from Bailey. Rollie Zeider pushed Doolin to third with an infield out, bringing Max Flack to the plate. Flack worked the count to two balls, two strikes when he connected with a pitch from Knetzer. As he did, "the roars from the stand bleachers and field died down to a whisper as a blurred, round object started on a journey for the fence in right center. Max had collided with the ball and the noise of the blow carried around the Federal League circuit as the wallop put Pittsburgh and St. Louis out of the pennant race."[20] Flack's double was followed by hits from Zwilling and Art Wilson, staking Bailey to a 3–0 lead. He set down the Rebels in the seventh inning and, with Brennan's watch showing 5:25 PM, the game was over. At 86–66, by a margin of .000854 over the 87–67 St. Louis Terriers, the Whales were Federal League champions.

Fans on the field stormed to the dugout. The grandstand dwellers hurled their seat cushions into the air and on to the field, and when Weeghman got to his office, he was mobbed. He hugged his mother, who told him, "I knew you would win the pennant, Charley."[21] The thrill of the win carried Weeghman clear through to the next day, when he reported to his office in the Loop and was greeted by Tinker, Doolin, and Three Finger Brown, and "put out a spread for scribes and intimate friends. There was food and there were libations in abundance. Every few minutes, President Chas. went around the room shaking hands with all the folks to celebrate his good luck."[22] He did take a moment to write a letter to Garry Herrmann of the National Commission, challenging the winner of the Red Sox-Phillies World Series to a series against the Whales. Two days earlier, the Whales had entered a petition (signed by 45,000 fans) with Mayor Thompson, hoping to get him to intervene to have the Whales included in Chicago's City Series. Weeghman was turned down on both counts.

Knowing that O. B. teams would not deign to play the Whales, Gilmore sent a message declaring, "Chicago is not only champion of the Federal League, but also baseball champion of the world."[23] No matter how dubious that claim might have been, it would be the only time in history that there would be legitimate cause to declare the occupant of the North Side baseball park "champion of the world."

While the Whales were playing to an overflow crowd on the North Side, on the West Side, the Cubs sputtered to a close with a 7–2 win over the Cardinals in front of 2,800 fans. It would be the last major league game played on the West Side of Chicago.

# CHAPTER TWENTY-TWO

# The Cubs Head North

The grand finale on the North Side was the highlight of the year for the Feds but there wasn't much time to spend celebrating. The World Series between the Phillies and Red Sox got underway on October 8, and representatives from the Federal League made their way to Philadelphia for Game 1 with more than baseball in mind—the monied magnates of the league badly wanted a settlement to the baseball war. Late on the night after the series opener, in a meeting arranged by Jim Gaffney, owner of the Braves, Jim Gilmore, Harry Sinclair, Phil Ball, Edward Gwinner, and other Federal League representatives got together with N. L. president John Tener and Garry Herrmann at the Bellevue-Stratford Hotel in Philadelphia, prepared to make an offer for peace. The Feds wanted Ban Johnson included in the conference, bringing together the whole of the National Commission, and Johnson was reached while eating dinner in the hotel restaurant. Told there would be little harm in at least hearing out the Federal Leaguers, Johnson consented to join the conference, but only if Gilmore left the room. Johnson might not have countenanced the Federal League as much of a threat, but his personal enmity toward Gilmore had not dissipated. Gilmore may have been president of the league, but he didn't have much real money invested. Thus, when Sinclair, Ball, and Gwinner told him to leave, he left.

Under the plan presented to the commissioners in Philadelphia, both the American and National leagues would be expanded to ten teams, with the Federal League franchises in Brooklyn and Pittsburgh going to the A. L. and two out of the trio of Baltimore, Buffalo, and Kansas City going to the N. L. Weeghman would buy the Cubs, Ball would buy one of the two St. Louis teams, and Sinclair would be allowed to buy into a major league club too. The idea didn't gain much traction—the National League wouldn't do well by adding two minor league cities, and owners Charles Ebbets of Brooklyn and Barney Dreyfuss of Pittsburgh wouldn't want A. L. competition in their towns. Besides, ten-team circuits would be difficult and expensive to arrange from a travel standpoint. In the aftermath, there was the usual war rhetoric, with Johnson asserting that the A. L. was strongly against a compromise with the Federal Leagues and Dreyfuss the lone hold-out in the N. L. against peace.[1]

Getting all the important players into a room, though, represented progress, and negotiations would continue, with Sinclair doing most of the talking for his league while William Baker of the Phillies and Jim Gaffney of the Braves represented O. B., maintaining contact with American Leaguers Johnson and Comiskey in Chicago.[2] The Federal League did have some leverage—namely, the bankrolls of their richest owners, which could keep the league afloat for another year if necessary. Publicly, that was always Gilmore's top bargaining chip, and he continued to try to sell the press on the fact that the Federal League would be moving to a spot in Manhattan in 1916, going so far as to have a rendering of the park drawn up. (Gilmore would claim, in later legal proceedings, that the New York plans were all a bluff and that the Federal League never had a real intention to enter the city.) But the moves for peace made it even more apparent that Ward and Ball, having discussed the baseball situation with Johnson personally the previous spring, were more certain that they wanted out of the Federal League and that even the brash and super-wealthy Sinclair could see that it was time to quit.

Hopes for a favorable settlement for the Federal League, though, took a tough blow on October 18, when Ward died suddenly at his estate in New Rochelle at age sixty-three. If the Federal League hoped to at least use the threat of playing another season in 1916, with a team in Manhattan, to spook O. B. into a peace that was somehow satisfactory to all eight Fed teams, they needed Ward, his bankroll, and his enthusiasm for the venture. His brother, George, was equally invested in the Federals, but George did not have Robert's passion for baseball, especially in the face of the significant losses the venture had caused the family. When, two years after his death, Ward's estate was appraised, it was estimated that he had lost between $1 million and $1.5 million on the Federal League—$220,800 worth of promissory notes on the league and the Tip-Tops, with 1,347 shares of preferred stock in the league and 2,373 shares of common stock purchased at about $373,000. He had also advanced $59,000 to the league, and those figures do not include the cost of rebuilding Washington Park and other loans made to the Federals that went unrecorded.[3] Ban Johnson, rather callously, said, "I think it was the Federal League that put him under the sod as he could not stand the strain of worries and losses."[4]

On November 9, the Federal League held a meeting in Indianapolis, and even without Ward, kept up the preparations for 1916. Gilmore announced that Kansas City and Buffalo were forfeited to the league—it was rumored that Buffalo had lost $50,000 in 1915 and borrowed $40,000 from Ward[5] and that Kansas City lost $85,000[6]—and that, while Buffalo would be reorganized and stay in the circuit, the Packers would be moved into a 55,000-seat stadium in Manhattan. The following day, the Federal Leaguers moved over to French Lick, Indiana, where they thought they would find Charles Comiskey, Barney Dreyfuss of the Pirates, and Col. Jacob Ruppert, new owner of the Yankees, and could engage in peace talks. Instead, "Colonel Ruppert was the only one they saw. He had little interest in the outlaw league's plans for peace or war."[7] The Feds moved the meeting to Chicago the following day and broke up having made no progress on coming to a settlement with O. B.

Just a few days later, Weeghman was struck with a tragedy of his own. At his apartment on Argyle Street, near Weeghman's home on Sheridan Avenue, August Weeghman—Lucky Charley's father, who just six weeks earlier had been celebrating the Whales' championship at his son's North Side park—slit his throat with a razor, at age sixty-five. Five years earlier,

Charley Weeghman had implored his parents to leave Richmond, Indiana, and come live in Chicago. But city life and retirement after years of hard work, did not agree with his father. "To my father time was a burden," Charley said. "He was a blacksmith and he had worked hard for many years. Since his retirement he had nothing to do. Time was really a burden on his hands. He had plenty of money—everything he wished. I believe that inactivity deranged his mind. I saw him less than a week ago and apparently he was happy then. I never heard him mention a thought of suicide. Often he had complained because he had nothing to do after having a busy life. He said it got on his nerves, but his health was such that he should not have returned to active life."[8]

With Ward gone and Weeghman now coping with the loss of his father, it was time for the Federal League to call it quits.

‡

Around the time of the death of his father, Weeghman made a trip with Harry Sinclair to Cincinnati to meet with Charles Taft about purchasing the Cubs, much as he had done one year earlier. This time around, though, there was no fanfare, the conference was held in secret, and there would be no Federal League peace settlement strings attached to their negotiation. Taft had reason to be a more eager seller in these meetings. The Cubs' attendance had shown slight improvement, but going from 202,000 to 217,000, hardly represented a return to the good old days of six-figure annual profits. It was obvious that, as Chicago writers had been stating all year, the only way for the Cubs to compete on the West Side would be to build a new park, and that would require an outlay of money Taft wasn't interested in spending. He was interested in the Cubs as long as they were a paying proposition. They no longer were paying enough to keep his interest, however. The negotiation between Taft and Weeghman had ended in acrimony in 1914, in part because of claims that Weeghman couldn't come up with a significant enough payment to cover the purchase price of the team. Sinclair, though, could offer some backing, and Taft was now willing to make a deal for the Cubs at the relatively inexpensive price of $500,000.

There was still the same impediment in the way of the deal, though—
Charles W. Murphy, who, though he wasn't solely responsible, had effectively quashed the sale of the Cubs to Weeghman in 1914. Murphy still
controlled a considerable number of shares of Cubs stock for which he
had not been paid and had half the lease on the West Side grounds.
Sometime in early December, Taft summoned Murphy to Cincinnati to
talk over the situation.[9] Two conditions of the sale imposed by Taft probably emanated from Murphy: If the Cubs were to leave the West Side
Grounds, they would be responsible for the remaining years on the lease
of the land, and, any deal would have to be in cash. In the last negotiation for the Cubs, Weeghman had tried to include his ballpark as part of
the deal. That wasn't going to fly this time. The deal would have to be
$500,000 in real dollars.

While the Cubs deal was being arranged, Phil Ball was meeting with
Helene and Schuyler Britton in regards to the Cardinals and the sides had
reportedly come to terms on a price for the team.[10] Sinclair, who was also
delegated to represent the Wards' baseball interests, was in talks to purchase
the Giants, though whether those talks ever came close to yielding a deal
was a matter of dispute. Sinclair insisted a deal that would pay $1 million for
controlling interest of the Giants was close while owner Harry Hempstead
said that Sinclair had only spoken to Garry Hermmann and that no firm
offer was discussed.[11] With or without the Giants' involvement, the path
was clear for a settlement—at least, on the National League side. The
N. L. was slated to meet in New York beginning on December 14 and
suggested to Ban Johnson that the American League meeting, scheduled for
December 15, be moved from Chicago to New York in order to facilitate a
peace negotiation. Showing he was still firmly against the Federals, though,
Johnson declined to move the A. L. confab. On Monday afternoon, the
thirteenth, the National League board of directors held a preliminary meeting to discuss how best to achieve peace, and when the group broke up
the meeting, John Tener invited the N. L. magnates to dinner at the Elks
Club (it was also reported that the dinner was at the Republican Club.)
After further discussion there, the group agreed to invite representatives
of the Federal League too. Gilmore, Harry Sinclair, and Pat Powers were

agreeable, and for six hours, the two sides ate, drank, and whittled down the framework of a baseball settlement.

The group was adamant about keeping the details of the meeting and what was in the framework of the settlement out of the press, and all involved took a secrecy pledge. Still, Joe Vila got wind of the meeting and reported it in the *Evening Sun* the following afternoon. The basis of the settlement would encompass sales talks that were already ongoing—Ball and the Cardinals, plus Weeghman and the Cubs, and whatever team Sinclair or Ward would be able to purchase. The hope was that the National League could provide the Federal League with enough satisfaction to bring the war to an end and all that would be required of the American League would be a rubber-stamp approval. With Johnson at the head of the A. L., though, approval was no cinch. Tener, in a statement, said, "Certain club owners of the National League met representatives of the Federal League, but no readjustment of baseball conditions can be made without an agreement of major leagues and pending the decision of Judge Landis in Chicago." Commenting on the statement, reporter Hal Richards wrote, "In other words, peace is now up to the American League."[12]

When the N. L. formally met the following day, the magnates gave their approval to the plan discussed at dinner. With the A. L. meeting taking place 1,500 miles away and with an ill-timed snowstorm blanketing New York, lines of communication to Chicago were hard to come by, and the proposal would have to be made in person. The National League chose Pittsburgh head Barney Dreyfuss, whose anti-Federal credentials were as staunch as Johnson's over the duration of the war. In a dispatch from Pittsburgh the day before the Elks club dinner, Dreyfuss was asked about the possibilities of peace discussions and said, "As far as I am concerned, there is nothing to discuss. I don't know anything about the Feds. I am satisfied, as I have said repeatedly, to go along as we have been going. We'll fight our battle and let the Feds fight theirs. I am satisfied to let things go as they have been going. I am not squealing, and I guess I've been as hard hit by this war as any other big league club owner."[13]

Now, with Dreyfuss going to Chicago, the N. L. knew that the peace plan would be given more gravity in Johnson's eyes. Dreyfuss arrived at the

Congress Hotel slightly ahead of schedule, at just after 2 PM on the fifteenth, and once there. he found a surprisingly receptive audience among his A. L. colleagues. It took him just an hour to explain the plan, after which he left the room and headed to the hotel lobby, mingling with the managers and officials gathered there, uncertain as to how the Americans had taken his proposal. It didn't take long for the A. L. to give its preliminary consent. At about 6 PM, Johnson opened the door to the A. L. meeting room, smiling and ready to meet with reporters. Declining to give specifics, he said that a committee of Federal Leaguers would meet with representatives of the A. L. and N. L. and that, "The proposition offered was quite complete and I think there will be no trouble in straightening out the tangle." More important, Johnson said this: "I can say that the outlook for peace in baseball is good."[14]

‡

Over the days and weeks that followed, the final negotiations for peace in baseball met with considerable obstacles, the sides first meeting in New York before setting up a final conference to take place at the Sinton Hotel in Cincinnati. Ball, prepared to get the Cardinals, was jilted and frustrated when Helene Britton decided, again, that she was taking the team off the market, putting the entire peace agreement in peril. Johnson rescued the deal, though, by offering Ball the opportunity to buy the St. Louis Browns from Robert Hedges instead, at a price of $525,000. Hedges was easily talked into the deal. Besides franchises for Ball and Weeghman, the deal would provide $400,000 to be paid to the Wards. That sum would offset some of the family's losses on the Federal League, but according to the agreement, the payments would be made over twenty years, each league putting up $10,000 per year. That meant, to buy out Ward, the sixteen major-leagues teams would pay just $1,250 per year, a virtually painless amount. It was eventually decided that to recoup losses from the $385,000 worth of player contracts, Sinclair would be given charge of conducting an auction, selling as many of the seventy-two players (those players who jumped to the Feds, as part of the settlement, were not to be blacklisted) at his disposal to major league teams, from which he hoped to stockpile $100,000.[15] He did better:

Sinclair eventually sold off seventeen players for a total of $129,000, includ-ing a hefty $30,000 purchase price for outfielder Benny Kauff, arguably the biggest star in the Federal League.

In Pittsburgh, Ed Gwinner got very little to show for his troubles. While there was some suggestion that Gwinner might purchase the Indians, he could not come to terms on a price for the team and Dreyfuss was not inclined to take him on as a partner in the Pirates. He claimed he wasn't that interested, anyway. For all his trouble with the Federal League, Gwinner was given $50,000 to offset improvements he had made to his ballpark. His personal loss, he figured, ran to $100,000. He was happy to be done with baseball. "Whenever I get kicked out of an organization it is time for me to quit, and that is what I am going to do as regards the Federal League," Gwinner said. "I was willing to string along until the league became a paying proposition, but when my associates saw fit to feather their own nests and drop me overboard I decided in my own mind that baseball politics was too much for me, and I am out. I do not want any franchise of any kind."[16]

The spurned investors in Baltimore, who had made the arrival of the Federal League such a point of pride, reaffirming the town's big league status, did not go away as quietly as Gwinner. Having been frozen out of the peace negotiations and left with nothing but a $50,000 buyout when the agree-ment was made, Baltimore's investors demanded the right to purchase a major league team and move it to the city. Denied that, they then demanded an International League team. Again, they got nowhere. It wasn't until the Federal League and Organized Baseball were scheduled to appear before Judge Landis to confirm the dismissal of the Feds' lawsuit in February 1916, that Baltimore finally withdrew its objection to the buyout, having been made promises of future concessions. Those concessions never materialized, and Baltimore's owners later reinstated a suit against the Federal League and Organized Baseball, one that went all the way to the Supreme Court in 1922. Once Baltimore's objection was removed from the Federal League case against O. B., though, Landis was free to dismiss the lawsuit, which he did without objection on February 7, 1916.

Of all the repercussions from the peace deal, none was as significant as Weeghman's purchase of the Cubs, then and now. With Taft away in Texas on a three-week hunting trip, Weeghman would have to wait until after the new year to complete the deal, but by January 5, he was on a train to Cincinnati, arriving at Taft's office at the Times-Star building at noon, with Sinclair present. For ninety minutes, the three men discussed the sale and once Sinclair was satisfied that the deal for the Cubs would be completed, he left the meeting. Taft and Weeghman spent another hour ironing out the future of the West Side Grounds, finally settling on a compromise that would have the Cubs take over the eighty-year lease, but that required the current owners to look for a buyer within two years. With that, it was agreed that Weeghman would deposit $500,000 in the bank by noon on January 20, and the team would be his. Weeghman offered Taft a certified check for $100,000 as a deposit on the club but Taft waved him off, telling Weeghman he would take him at his word that the money would be in place at the appointed time.[17] Emerging from the meeting, Weeghman found his partner, William Walker, waiting for him at the Sinton, killing time with a marathon pool match against fellow Whales investor Adolph Schuettler. The Cubs were theirs, Weeghman informed them. Also present was Mike Cantillon, visionary of baseball on Chicago's North Side. He was "one of the happiest men in the lobby of the Hotel Sinton when he heard that the Cub deal had been closed. 'Now I am sure to get my rent for some years to come,' he said." Weeghman then met with the press to discuss the deal. Answering questions, Weeghman slyly stated, "I might add that the name of C.W. Murphy was not mentioned once during the discussion of the deal."[18]

Ten days later, at a dinner for former White Sox manager Jimmy Callahan (recently hired to take over the Pirates), Weeghman let out part of the impressive list of Chicago investors he had lined up to back the Cubs—in the Chicago papers, this was taken as a sign of the strength of the club, but in reality, it was an indication of how financially weakened Weeghman had been by the Federal League war, and how little of his own money he actually had left to put in the club. He would later say, "I was young—and cocky—and I thought I could afford to sink a half million in the Cubs,"[19] though not much of it was his actual money. Among his top investors were some of the wealthiest men in the city, including meatpacking magnate J. Ogden Armour and chewing gum king William Wrigley.

Julius Rosenwald of Sears and Roebuck was to be added to list too, and it was later revealed that Weeghman's rival, John R. Thompson, was an investor as well, as was advertising executive Albert Lasker and former Cubs bidder Charles McCullough. In all, it was estimated that the Cubs backers were worth $100,000,000.[20]

Weeghman was prepared to hand over the check to Taft on January 19, but because John Tener could not be present to sign over Cubs to Weeghman, the sides would have to go through with the deal on the twentieth as planned. First, Weeghman would have to get $500,000 into the bank by noon, and he encountered trouble at the last moment, he would later recall, when he found that two checks that were supposed to have come in from the Federal League failed to reach the bank. Weeghman said he had to call a friend at a nearby bank, and with not much time to spare, Weeghman was handed an envelope containing $78,000 in cash. It was a very nervous walk through the Loop back to the Corn Exchange bank, where the transaction with Taft was set to take place. Just minutes before his noon deadline, Weeghman made the final deposit and, at 2:31 PM, a crowd witnessed Weeghman pass an oversized check for $500,000 to Taft. Just like that, "the deal which transferred Chicago's historic ball club from the West to the North side was complete."[21]

Said Weeghman: "This is the biggest day of my life and I'm happy that it is all completed. Mr. Walker and myself were rabid Cubs fans in the good old days. We talked even then of buying the club at some future date. Now we have it and we have a great bunch of Chicago men in with us. I hope we can restore the Cubs to the place they once held in the hearts of Chicago fans."[22]

# Epilogue

In light of the two seasons of double-crossing and underhanded tactics, the public vitriol and dragged-out legal proceedings, and the cost to both organizations in terms both of public good will and expenses, it was a wonder that the principals of the Federal League and Organized Baseball could ever have worked out a solution to their rift. Even more of a wonder is how quickly it all was forgotten. Charley Weeghman took control of the Cubs in January of 1916, and just three months later, he was parading over downtown streets in Cincinnati, leading his team and a pack of loyal fans in a triumphant march to celebrate Opening Day. Once in the city, Charles Taft and Charles W. Murphy, such antagonists in the story of the past two-and-a-half years of Weeghman's life (remember Weeghman, half-jokingly, said things had deteriorated between him and Murphy to the point that he feared Murphy might poison his bulldog) were there to greet him and offer their huzzahs and waves, smiling down from a balcony like reformed villains in a Dickens novel. Weeghman had emerged from the Federal League fight the clear winner, and, in general, the baseball situation was looking up for the North Siders.

As part of the Federal League settlement, Weeghman was allowed to combine the rosters of the Whales and the Cubs, without being subject to the N. L.'s twenty-one-player limit. (The Browns, who were to be combined with the Terriers in St. Louis under new owner Phil Ball, would also have their roster limit waived.) That, though, also left the Cubs with two managers—Joe Tinker and Roger Bresnahan. Weeghman obviously wanted to keep Tinker on in the job, but Bresnahan threatened to sue. Eventually,

Bresnahan was placated when he was granted Charley Somers's American Association team in Toledo, Bresnahan's hometown. Once Tinker was solidified as the Cubs' manager, he had an army of National Leaguers and Federal Leaguers on hand, so that the Cubs appeared poised to dominate the N. L. in their initial season on the North Side. Unfortunately, quantity didn't mean quality. Further calling into question the Feds' claims of major league status, most of Tinker's Federal League stars were exposed once they had to face major league talent on a daily basis. Slats McConnell, who had been 25-10 with the Whales in 1915 and was Tinker's Opening Day starter, went 4–12 in 1916 and was out of the major leagues the following year. Claude Hendrix, the Federal League's best pitcher in 1914, went 8–16. Dutch Zwilling, who clubbed 29 home runs in two Fed seasons and led the league in runs batted in with 94 in 1915, hit .113 in the 1916 season, his last in the big leagues. Mickey Doolin, at age thirty-six, hit only .214 before he was traded, and played only one more subsequent season.

The sheer lack of chemistry was a bigger issue, though. Even before the season started, there were complaints that in choosing players and roster roles, Tinker was too generous toward his ex–Federal League charges, favoring them over the incumbent Cubs (his choice of McConnell as his ace being a good example). Heinie Zimmerman didn't help much. He had been a headache for Bresnahan and every other manager he'd had with the Cubs, but he pushed Tinker to the limit. At last, the Cubs gave up on their enigmatic slugger, despite his .291 batting average and six home runs. In late August, while Zimmerman was serving a ten-game suspension for "lying down," the Cubs finally washed their hands of him, trading Zimmerman with Doolin to the Giants in a deal that brought back infielder Larry Doyle and two bit players.

A month earlier, on July 29, Weeghman and Tinker had to OK a trade that would carry some sorrow for diehard fans of the former West Siders—they traded Frank "Wildfire" Schulte, 1911 Chalmers Award winner, to Pittsburgh, bringing back former Whales catcher Art Wilson in the deal. It was significant because, though Tinker and Mordecai Brown were on hand, Schulte was the only remaining player to have played consecutively (for over twelve seasons) with the Cubs going to back to the days

of Tinker-to-Evers-to-Chance. The Cubs were leaving the dynasty behind
for good. "Schulte was practically the last of the 'old guard' that made up
Frank Chance's famous pennant machine," Weeghman said in announcing
the trade. "I hated to let him go."

In all, there would be a mind-boggling forty-five players coming through
the North Side in 1916, and between the disappointments of some of
Tinker's Federal Leaguers and the lack of chemistry that attends so much
roster turnover, the Cubs hit just .239 as a team, seventh in the eight team
National League, and posted a 2.65 ERA, which ranked fifth. At 67–86,
they were fifth in the league, a major disappointment, and that flop, as
well as the taint of having favored his Fed players, cost Tinker his job after
1916. The Cubs would hire Fred Mitchell for the following season, the
team's sixth manager in as many years. Tinker would never manage or play
in the big leagues again, though his players would not have been surprised
to have learned that being released from baseball allowed Tinker to spend
more time with one of his passions—real estate. During one of the Chifeds'
Spring Training trips in Louisiana, Tinker actually gave a day off training
to take his team men to inspect a piece of land that potentially contained a
valuable amount of oil, suggesting to the players that they invest. After his
release from the Cubs, Tinker took his own advice, and went on to build
a fortune in Florida real estate—though when the stock market crash that
initiated the Great Depression hit, Tinker lost everything.

After the Federal League endeavor, things did not go so well for Weeghman
either. He had been borrowing heavily to keep the Whales afloat and hoped
that a Cubs pennant winner on the North Side in 1916 would turn around
his flagging financial fortunes in baseball. But that season fell flat, and even
with a respectable 453,000 fans coming to the North Side in the Cubs' first
year at Weeghman Park, the profits were not close to what the Cubs had
earned in their dynasty heyday on the West Side, when they twice surpassed
650,000 in attendance. And 1917 was no better in the standings, where the
Cubs went 74–80 and again finished fifth. By then, the U.S. had entered
World War I and attendance shrank to 360,000. Weeghman was suffering a
double blow—the war caused prices of food and supplies to skyrocket, and
with rationing and general austerity, his restaurant business was collapsing.

Weeghman and the Cubs did make one last stand, though, in 1918. The team's wealthy backers ordered him to spend at all costs in order to build a pennant winner, and with the war in Europe deepening, many teams were all too willing to sell off players and prepare for economic hard times. Weeghman made a splash by acquiring star pitcher Grover Cleveland Alexander from the Phillies, along with catcher Bill Killefer—the same Killefer who signed with the Chifeds in January 1914 only to hand the Federal League a huge blow by returning to O. B. days later. Alexander only pitched three games before he was drafted into the war, but the Cubs still did win the N. L. pennant. It was to no avail. With war raging, players dodging the draft, and the country unsure whether baseball should be played at all, interest in the game hit an all-time low.

Weeghman never seemed able to get his timing just right, was never able to turn his passion for baseball into profits the way that Charles W. Murphy had done when he was running the Cubs. After the 1918 season, Weeghman had simply borrowed too much and the revenues from his entities—the Cubs, the restaurants, the theaters, and pool halls—weren't covering his bills. In 1919, Weeghman's wife, Bessie, divorced him on the grounds of infidelity. She was awarded $400 per month in the settlement. The following year, Weeghman's business interests were placed in receivership. After that embarrassment, he moved east and attempted to open restaurants in Manhattan three different times, but each failed. He died in 1938, working as the manager at the Riviera Club in the Palisades in New Jersey at the time.

But Weeghman's misfortunes turned out to be a boon for his friend, William Wrigley, and for the Cubs. It wasn't so much that Wrigley, one of the shrewdest and wealthiest businessmen in the city, wanted to be a baseball magnate, he just felt that the Cubs should be a point of pride for Chicago and that the city's leading men had a duty to invest in the team. By the end of 1916, with Weeghman desperate for cash—Wrigley would later say that Weeghman had, "buttered his bread too thin"—Wrigley already had $180,000 worth of Cubs stock. After the grind of the war-torn 1918 season, Wrigley had bought out all of Weeghman's stock, would soon be the Cubs' majority shareholder, and was beginning to like his status as baseball magnate. He made a crucial decision after the 1918 season too, having been impressed with the work of Bill Bailey of the *Chicago American* in writing about the team, both positive and negative. Bailey's real last name was Veeck, and rather than rail against the young journalist when he was critical of the team, Wrigley wanted to get him a spot in the organization. Fred Mitchell was made president, but Veeck became the team's vice president, essentially replacing Weeghman's Federal League partner, William Walker.

Wrigley and Veeck helped to take the stadium that Weeghman built on the North Side and transform it into what it is known as today: a unique park in which to celebrate baseball and Chicago. By 1920, the Weeghman name was taken off the park altogether, and for seven seasons, it was known simply as Cubs Park. In 1927, it was officially renamed Wrigley Field and the first part of the second deck that Weeghman had originally imagined was finally added, boosting the seating capacity to 38,400. That year, the Cubs became the first N. L. team in history to top one million in attendance. The rest of the second deck came along in 1928, and in 1929, the Cubs hosted 1.485 million fans.

In true Cubs fashion, though, winning proved less easy for Veeck and Wrigley than drumming up interest in the team. After the miserable 1918 World Series, the Cubs went through a rough decade, finishing no higher than third in the National League from 1919–28. They finally had a break-through in 1929, though, when a promising offensive bunch was joined by reigning batting champ Rogers Hornsby (who, oddly enough, had been one of Weeghman's targets for the Cubs as far back as 1917). That team easily won the National League pennant by scoring 982 runs, 78 more than the next best team. But they couldn't outslug the Philadelphia Athletics in the World Series and lost in five games. That would be the only Cubs World Series that Wrigley would witness. He died in January 1932, and though the Cubs earned a spot in that year's World Series, they were outclassed and swept by the Yankees.

As legend has it, as Wrigley lay on his deathbed, he implored his son, P. K. Wrigley, not to sell the Cubs. Alas, P. K. Wrigley was not the Chicago booster nor the baseball fan that his father was, and though he would always honor that deathbed wish—he held onto the Cubs until his death in 1977—the younger Wrigley ran the team with the bottom line in mind, refusing to go after high-priced stars, declining to install lights at the park, and coming in as one of the last teams to set up a minor league farm system. After reaching the '32 World Series, that core of Cubs also won pennants in 1935 and 1938, but lost the championship both times. They reached the World Series in 1945, the first postwar season but lost in seven games to the Tigers. Under the halfhearted leadership of P. K. Wrigley for thirty-two years after that, the Cubs did not win another pennant. The last Cubs World Series victory, of course, remains the 1908 championship, when Frank Chance was at first base, Johnny Evers was at second, Joe Tinker was at shortstop, and Charles W. Murphy was collecting the profits. The 1915 Federal League championship won by the Whales—declared a World Championship by Jim Gilmore, since the World Series champs would not engage in a series—is the closest thing to a world title that the park has ever known.

In Glenn Stout's thorough and entertaining historical book, *The Cubs*, the writer William Nack summed up Wrigley Field's importance in Chicago and nationally (bear in mind that the original Yankee Stadium has since been torn down): "Wrigley Field has a place in our cultural history unmatched by any other sporting edifice west of Yankee Stadium. In Chicago it is viewed as a Midwestern shrine, especially since they tore down old Comiskey Park after the 1990 season and replaced it with that soulless monstrosity known as whatever. Not even Soldier Field, the site of the famous Dempsey-Tunney heavyweight championship fight in 1927— the combat known in boxing lore as 'the infamous Long Count'—can match Wrigley in its long, often bittersweet drumroll of timeless moments. Indeed, Wrigley Field has been the spiritual center of Chicago sports for most of the last one hundred years … and today it stands as a kind of municipal reliquary for that city's sporting life, an aging chamber of memories."

The chamber of memories at Clark, Sheffield, and Addison is deep. Baseball has become synonymous with the North Side park, and rightfully so. But there is more to the story than Wrigley, more than the Cubs. It is a story that includes Charley Weeghman and his Whales, Walter Johnson and the near-misses of the Federal League, the Cantillon brothers and their visionary purchase of a plot of seminary land, Charles Taft and the number of potential Cub owners who never would have left the West Side had he just been willing to sell. All of the history that we associate with Wrigley Field and the identity it gives to the North Side didn't necessarily have to come about the way it did. Fortune, treachery, and foresight were all factors, all emanating from the fascinating characters and tumultuous events that came before Wrigley.

# NOTES

(One of the most useful set of documents in researching the events surrounding Weeghman Park and, in a wider scope, the Federal League, is housed on the South Side of Chicago, where the records from the league's lawsuit against Organized Baseball, over which Judge Kenesaw Mountain Landis presided, are in the National Archives and Records Administration. Affadavits from the trial are listed by the affiant in question, followed by, "Landis case, NARA file.")

**Chapter 1: The Cubs and the North Side, Day One**
1. *Chicago Daily News*, April 13, 1916.
2. *Chicago Tribune*, April 20, 1916.
3. *Chicago Daily News* and *Chicago Herald*, April 19, 1916.
4. *Chicago Daily News*, April 20, 1916.
5. *Chicago Herald*, April 21, 1916.
6. *Chicago Herald*, April 21, 1916.
7. *Chicago Herald*, April 21, 1916.
8. *Chicago Tribune*, April 21, 1916.
9. *Chicago Tribune*, April 18, 1916.
10. Associated Press, July 15, 1999.

**Chapter 2: The Chicago Theologic Lutheran Seminary Lot**
1. *Chicago Tribune*, June 21, 1909.
2. *Chicago Tribune*, February 22, 1907.
3. *Chicago Tribune*, February 19, 1907.
4. *Chicago Tribune*, February 29, 1907.
5. *Chicago Tribune*, February 22, 1907.

6. *Chicago Tribune*, February 19, 1907.

7. *Chicago Tribune*, June 20, 1909.

8. *Chicago Tribune*, June 21, 1909.

9. *Chicago Tribune*, June 20, 1909.

10. *The Sporting News*, February 6, 1930.

11. *Chicago Tribune*, February 22, 1907.

12. *Chicago Tribune*, February 29, 1910.

## Chapter 3: Lucky Charley Weeghman

1. *Chicago Tribune*, March 30, 1911.

2. *Sporting Life*, April 8, 1911.

3. *Chicago Tribune*, March 31, 1911.

4. *Chicago Tribune*, April 6, 1911.

5. *Chicago Tribune*, April 8, 1911.

6. Weeghman investments from *Chicago Tribune*, real estate pages, 1910, 1913.

7. Jan Whitaker, Restaurant-ing Through History, Early Chains: John R. Thompson. http://restaurant-ingthroughhistory.com/2010/06/10/early-chains-john-r-thompson

8. *Chicago Tribune*, April 26, 1914.

9. Duis, p. 210.

10. *Baseball Magazine*, September 1915.

11. *Chicago Tribune*, April 26, 1914.

12. Interview with Rev. Sonny Smith, Weeghman's nephew, September 2008.

13. *Chicago Tribune*, April 26, 1914.

14. *Chicago Tribune*, January 7, 1903.

15. *Baseball Magazine*, September 1915.

16. *Chicago Tribune*, April 24, 1909.

## Chapter 4: Charles Webb Murphy

1. *Chicago Tribune*, February 29, 1912.

2. Mordecai Brown deposition, Landis case, NARA file; *Chicago Tribune*, October 13, 1912.

3. *Chicago Daily News*, October 17, 1912.

4. *The Sporting News*, October 17, 1912.

5. *Sporting Life*, November 2, 1912.

6. *Sport*, November 1953.

7. *Chicago Herald*, October 3, 1915.

8. *The Sporting News*, October 17, 1912.

9. *Chicago Daily News*, October 14, 1912.

10. Lenny Jacobsen, "Charles Murphy," SABR Baseball Biography Project. http://sabr.org/bioproj/person/e707728f

11. *Sporting Life*, November 2, 1912.

12. Lenny Jacobsen, "Charles Murphy," SABR Baseball Biography Project. http://sabr.org/bioproj/person/e707728f

13. *Chicago Tribune*, February 22, 1908.

14. *The Sporting News*, October 3, 1912.

15. *Chicago Tribune*, September 29, 1912.

16. *Chicago Tribune*, September 24, 1912; *Chicago Tribune*, September 26, 1912.

17. *Chicago Tribune*, September 11, 1912.

18. *Chicago Tribune*, September 18, 1912; *Sporting Life*, September 21, 1912.

19. *Sporting Life*, September 28, 1912.

20. *Chicago Tribune*, September 27, 1912.

21. *The Sporting News*, October 3, 1912.

22. *Chicago Daily News*, October 19, 1912; *Chicago Tribune*, October 19, 1912.

23. *Chicago Daily News*, October 21, 1912.

24. *Chicago Tribune*, October 23, 1912

25. *The Sporting News*, October 3, 1912.

26. *The Sporting News*, January 25, 1912.

27. *Chicago Tribune*, September 30, 1912; *Sporting Life*, November 16, 1912.

## Chapter 5: Joe Tinker and the Federal League

1. *Chicago Tribune*, January 27, 1913.

2. *Chicago Daily News*, December 13, 1913.

3. *Chicago Daily News*, December 11, 1913.

4. Joe Tinker deposition, Landis case, NARA file.

5. Cook, p. 176.

6. *Chicago Daily News*, December 16, 1913.

7. *Chicago Daily News*, December 15, 1913.

8. Joe Tinker deposition, Landis case, NARA file.

9. Joe Tinker deposition, Landis case, NARA file.

10. *Chicago Daily News*, December 30, 1913.

11. *Chicago Daily News*, December 24, 1913.

12. *The Sporting News*, January 25, 1912.

13. *The Sporting News*, November 6, 1913.

14. *Baseball Magazine*, September 1915.

15. *Sporting Life*, December 17, 1913.

16. *Chicago Tribune*, December 24, 1913.

17. *Baseball Magazine*, September 1915.

18. *Chicago Daily News*, December 29, 1913.

19. *Chicago Tribune*, December 31, 1913.

20. *Chicago Tribune*, January 25, 1914.

## Chapter 6: Weeghman and the War

1. *Sporting Life*, January 24, 1914.

2. *Sporting Life*, January 24, 1914.

3. *Chicago Tribune*, January 17, 1914.

4. *New York Times*, January 17, 1914.

5. *Sporting Life*, April 5, 1915.

6. *Sporting Life*, February 7, 1914.

7. *Sporting Life*, January 24, 1914.

8. *Chicago Tribune*, January 18, 1914.

9. *The Sporting News*, January 8, 1914.

10. *Chicago Daily News*, January 17, 1914.

11. *Chicago Daily News*, January 17, 1914.

12. *Chicago Daily News*, January 17, 1914.

13. *Chicago Tribune*, January 18, 1914.

14. *Chicago Tribune*, January 18, 1914.

15. *Sporting Life*, January 24, 1914.

16. *The Sporting News*, January 29, 1914.

17. *The Sporting News*, January 22, 1914.

18. *The Sporting News*, February 5, 1914.

19. *Chicago Tribune*, January 18, 1914.

## Chapter 7: Crisis Management

1. *The Sporting News*, December 20, 1915.

2. *The Sporting News*, January 29, 1914.

3. *Baseball Magazine*, February 1914.

4. *Sporting Life*, March 13, 1915.

5. *Chicago Tribune*, January 26, 1914

6. *Chicago Tribune*, February 1, 1914.
7. *The Sporting News*, February 5, 1914.
8. *Chicago Tribune*, March 13, 1912.
9. *Chicago Tribune*, December 31, 1913.
10. *Chicago Tribune*, January 22, 1914.
11. *Sporting Life*, April 25, 1914.
12. *The Sporting News*, February 5, 1914.
13. Joe Tinker deposition, Landis case, NARA file.
14. *The Sporting News*, February 5, 1914.
15. *Chicago Tribune*, January 19, 1914.
16. *Chicago Tribune*, January 21, 1914.

**Chapter 8: Murphy and Evers**
1. *Sporting Life*, January 24, 1914.
2. *The Sporting News*, February 12, 1914.
3. *Chicago Tribune*, February 12, 1914.
4. *The Sporting News*, February 19, 1914.
5. *Baseball Magazine*, August, 1914.
6. *Sporting Life*, November 28, 1914.
7. *Chicago Tribune*, February 12, 1914.
8. *Chicago Tribune*, February 13, 1914.
9. *Chicago Daily News*, February 7, 1914.
10. *Chicago Tribune*, February 15, 1914.
11. *Chicago Tribune*, February 14, 1914.
12. *Sporting Life*, February 28, 1914.
13. *Chicago Tribune*, February 21, 1914.
14. *Chicago Daily News*, February 11, 1914.

**Chapter 9: Groundbreaking on the North Side**
1. *Chicago Daily News*, March 4, 1914; *Chicago Tribune*, March 5, 1914.
2. *Chicago Daily News*, March 4, 1914.
3. *Chicago Daily News*, February 21, 1914.
4. Raymond D. Kush, "Building of Wrigley Field," Research.sabr.org.
5. *Chicago Daily News*, March 4, 1914.
6. Mayer and Wade, p. 262.
7. Mayer and Wade, p. 212.
8. *Chicago Daily News*, March 4, 1914.

9. *The Sporting News*, January 20, 1916.

10. *The Sporting News*, March 5, 1914.

11. *Chicago Daily News*, February 23, 1914.

12. *Chicago Daily News*, February 24, 1914.

13. *Chicago Tribune*, February 26, 1914.

14. *Chicago Tribune*, February 26, 1914.

15. *The Sporting News*, March 26, 1914.

16. *The Sporting News*, March 5, 1914.

17. *New York Times*, March 3, 1914.

18. *Chicago Herald*, October 22, 1914.

19. *Sporting Life*, March 21, 1914.

20. *Sporting Life*, March 28, 1914.

21. *Chicago Tribune*, March 19, 1914.

**Chapter 10: The Battle of the Dock**

1. *New York Times*, March 7, 1914.

2. *Sporting Life*, March 14, 1914.

3. *New York Times*, March 6, 1914.

4. *The Day*, New London, Conn., March 7, 1914.

5. *Chicago Daily News*, March 6, 1914.

6. William Baker deposition, Landis case, NARA file.

7. *The Sporting News*, March 12, 1914.

8. *The Day*, March 7, 1914.

9. *The Sporting News*, March 5, 1914.

10. *Boston Globe*, March 7, 1914.

11. *Boston Globe*, March 7, 1914.

12. Lee Magee deposition, Landis case, NARA file.

13. *Sporting Life*, March 14, 1914.

14. *The Sporting News*, March 19, 1914.

15. From Baseball-almanac.com, at http://www.baseball-almanac.com/yearly/yr1914f.shtml

16. *Sporting Life*, March 21, 1914.

17. *Chicago Daily News*, March 9, 1914.

18. *Boston Globe*, March 6, 1914.

19. *Sporting Life*, March 14, 1914.

20. *Sporting Life*, March 14, 1914.

21. *Chicago Tribune*, March 9, 1914.

**Chapter 11: "The Fellows from the North Side Were Actuated with Pride"**
1. *Chicago Daily News*, March 10, 1914.
2. *Chicago Tribune*, April 4, 1914.
3. *Chicago Tribune*, March 21, 1914.
4. *Chicago Tribune*, April 9, 1914.
5. *Chicago Tribune*, April 11, 1914.
6. *Chicago Tribune*, April 11, 1914.
7. *Chicago Tribune*, April 14, 1914.
8. *Chicago Tribune*, April 14, 1914.
9. *Baltimore Sun*, April 13, 1914.
10. *Chicago Tribune*, April 17, 1914.
11. *Sporting Life*, April 25, 1914.
12. *Sporting Life*, April 5, 1914.
13. *Chicago Herald*, April 23, 1914.
14. *Chicago American*, April 23, 1914.
15. *Chicago Tribune*, April 24, 1914.
16. *Chicago American*, April 23, 1914.
17. *Chicago Tribune*, April 24, 1914.
18. *Chicago Tribune*, April 24, 1914.
19. *Chicago Daily News*, April 23, 1914.
20. *Chicago American*, April 23, 1914.

**Chapter 12: A Promising Start for the New League**
1. *Chicago Tribune*, April 24, 1914.
2. *Chicago Post*, April 24, 1914.
3. *Chicago Tribune*, April 25, 1914.
4. *Chicago Tribune*, April 26, 1914.
5. *Sporting Life*, May 23, 1914.
6. *Chicago Daily News*, April 24, 1914.
7. *Chicago American*, April 25, 1914.
8. *Chicago Tribune*, April 28, 1914.
9. *Chicago Tribune*, April 28, 1914.
10. *Sporting News*, April 23, 1914.
11. *Chicago Tribune*, April 22, 1914.

12. *Chicago Tribune*, April 22, 1914.
13. *Sporting Life*, May 2, 1914.
14. *Chicago American*, April 22, 1914.
15. *Chicago American*, April 23, 1914.
16. *Sporting Life*, May 30, 1914.
17. *Chicago American*, April 23, 1914.
18. *The Sporting News*, April 23, 1914.
19. *Sporting Life*, May 2, 1914.
20. *Sporting Life*, May 2, 1914.

## Chapter 13: War and Strategy

1. *Chicago Tribune*, May 8, 1914.
2. *Sporting Life*, May 9, 1914.
3. *Sporting Life*, May 16, 1914.
4. *Chicago Tribune*, May 13, 1914.
5. *Chicago Tribune*, May 25, 1914.
6. *Washington Post*, June 5, 1914.
7. *Washington Post*, May 25, 1914.
8. *Washington Post*, May 28, 1914.
9. *Sporting Life*, June 6, 1914.
10. *Chicago Tribune*, June 1, 1914.
11. *Sporting Life*, May 30, 1914.
12. *Sporting Life*, May 30, 1914.
13. *Chicago Tribune*, May 30, 1914.
14. *Sporting Life*, June 13, 1914.
15. *Chicago Tribune*, June 4, 1914.
16. *Washington Post*, June 5, 1914.
17. *Sporting Life*, June 13, 1914.
18. *Chicago Daily Journal*, June 16, 1914.
19. *Washington Post*, June 5, 1914.
20. *Chicago Daily News*, June 17, 1914.
21. *Chicago Daily Journal*, June 16, 1914.
22. *Chicago Tribune*, March 5, 1914.
23. *Chicago Daily Journal*, June 15, 1914.
24. *Sporting Life*, June 11, 1914.
25. *Chicago Daily News*, June 18, 1914.

**Chapter 14: Lazy Days**

1. *Chicago Tribune*, June 22, 1914.
2. *Sporting Life*, July 4, 1914.
3. *Sporting Life*, June 27, 1914.
4. Charles Comiskey deposition, Landis case, NARA file.
5. *Sporting Life*, July 25, 1914.
6. *The Sporting News*, July 2, 1914.
7. *Sporting Life*, July 4, 1914.
8. *Chicago Tribune*, July 1, 1914.
9. *Sporting Life*, October 3, 1914.
10. *Sporting Life*, August 22, 1914.
11. *Sporting Life*, July 4, 1914.
12. *The Sporting News*, June 11, 1914.
13. *Sporting Life*, July 18, 1914.
14. *The Sporting News*, July 2, 1914.
15. *Sporting Life*, July 18, 1914.
16. *Chicago Tribune*, July 6, 1914.
17. *The Sporting News*, July 9, 1914.
18. Levitt, 124.
19. *The Sporting News*, July 16, 1914.
20. *The Sporting News*, May 14, 1914.
21. *The Sporting News*, May 14, 1914.
22. *Chicago Daily Journal*, June 29, 1914.
23. *The Sporting News*, June 25, 1914.
24. *The Sporting News*, June 11, 1914.
25. *Sporting Life*, May 23, 1914.

**Chapter 15: Stretch Run, 1914**

1. *Sporting Life*, March 28, 1914.
2. *Sporting Life*, April 18, 1914.
3. *Chicago Tribune*, August 10, 1914.
4. *The Sporting News*, September 17, 1914.
5. *Boston Globe*, August 9, 1914.
6. *Chicago Herald*, August 18, 1914.
7. *Chicago Tribune*, September 30, 1914.
8. *Chicago Tribune*, September 12, 1914.

9.  *Chicago Herald*, October 6, 1914.

10.  *Chicago Tribune*, October 7, 1914.

11.  *Chicago Tribune*, September 20, 1914.

12.  *Chicago Tribune*, October 9, 1914.

**Chapter 16: Peace Foiled**

1.  *Sporting Life*, July 18, 1914.

2.  *The Sporting News*, December 3, 1914.

3.  *Sporting Life*, July 18, 1914.

4.  Details of the amalgamation plan from the depositions of Mike Cantillon and Garry Hermann, Landis case, NARA file.

5.  Herrmann deposition, Landis case, NARA file.

6.  *Chicago Herald*, October 23, 1914.

7.  *New York Times*, October 24, 1914.

8.  *Baseball Magazine*, September 1915.

9.  *The Sporting News*, October 29, 1914.

10.  *Sporting Life*, October 31, 1914.

11.  *New York Times*, October 27, 1914.

12.  *The Sporting News*, November 12, 1914.

13.  *Chicago Herald*, November 2, 1914.

14.  Herrmann deposition, Landis case, NARA file.

15.  *Sporting Life*, November 7, 1914.

16.  *Chicago Tribune*, September 1, 1914.

17.  *Chicago Herald*, November 6, 1914.

18.  *Sporting Life*, October 3, 1914.

19.  Charles Somers deposition, Landis case, NARA file.

20.  *Sporting Life*, October 31, 1914.

21.  *Chicago Herald*, November 13, 1914.

22.  *Chicago Daily News*, November 14, 1914.

23.  *Chicago Herald*, November 13, 1914.

24.  Charles Thomas deposition, Landis case, NARA file.

25.  *Chicago Herald*, November 13, 1914.

26.  *The Sporting News*, November 12, 1914.

27.  *Sporting Life*, November 28, 1914.

28.  *Chicago Herald*, November 19, 1914.

29.  *The Sporting News*, November 26, 1914.

30.  *Chicago Herald*, November 22, 1914.

31.  *Chicago Daily News*, November 18, 1914.

32.  *Chicago Herald*, November 19, 1914.

**Chapter 17: "I Have Just Signed Walter"**

1.  *Chicago Herald* and *Chicago Daily News*, December 4, 1914.

2.  *Baseball Magazine*, April 1915.

3.  *Baseball Magazine*, April 1915.

4.  *Sporting Life*, November 14, 1914.

5.  *Washington Post*, September 9, 1914.

6.  *Sporting Life*, December 12, 1914.

7.  *Sporting Life*, December 12, 1914.

8.  *Chicago Daily News*, December 6, 1914.

9.  *Washington Post*, December 15, 1914.

10.  *Washington Post*, December 4, 1914.

11.  *Chicago Herald*, December 4 and 6, 1914.

12.  *New York Times*, January 31, 1915.

13.  *Sporting Life*, October 10, 1914.

14.  *New York Times*, January 31, 1915.

15.  *The Sporting News*, December 3, 1914.

16.  *Sporting Life*, November 28, 1914.

17.  *New York Times*, January 31, 1915.

18.  Attendance figures from Baseball-reference.com.

19.  Unemployment rates from http://www.nber.org/chapters/c2644.pdf

20.  *Chicago Daily News*, December 4, 1914.

21.  *Chicago Tribune*, December 28, 1914.

**Chapter 18: Showdown in Judge Landis's court**

1.  *The Sporting News*, December 17, 1914.

2.  *Chicago Daily News*, December 8, 1914.

3.  *Baseball Magazine*, April 1915

4.  *Baseball Magazine*, April 1915

5.  *Chicago Tribune*, December 24, 1914.

6.  *Washington Post*, February 5, 1938.

7.  *Chicago Tribune*, December 20, 1914.

8.  *Sporting Life*, January 2, 1915.

9. Harry Hempstead deposition, Landis case, NARA file.

10. *Sporting Life*, January 2, 1915.

11. Sigman, p. 283.

12. *Washington Post*, January 6, 1915.

13. *Chicago Tribune*, January 8, 1915.

14. Mordecai Brown deposition, Landis case, NARA file.

15. *The Sporting News*, January 14, 1915.

16. *The Sporting News*, January 14, 1915.

17. *Chicago Tribune*, January 21, 1915.

18. *New York Times*, January 21, 1915.

19. *Chicago Tribune* and *New York Times*, January 22, 1915.

20. *Chicago Tribune*, January 23, 1915.

21. *Chicago Tribune*, January 24, 1915; Seymour, p. 220; Pietruzsa p. 157.

22. *Chicago Tribune*, January 24, 1915.

23. *Chicago Tribune*, January 24, 1915.

**Chapter 19: The 1915 season begins**

1. *Chicago Tribune*, February 5, 1915.

2. *Chicago Herald*, March 5, 1915.

3. *Chicago Tribune*, March 5, 1915.

4. *The Sporting News*, February 25, 1915.

5. *The Sporting News*, March 11, 1915.

6. *Chicago Tribune*, March 16, 1915.

7. *Chicago Tribune*, February 13, 1915.

8. *Sporting Life*, March 20, 1915.

9. *Chicago Tribune*, February 13, 1915.

10. *Chicago Tribune*, August 22, 1914.

11. *Sporting Life*, March 13, 1915.

12. *Sporting Life*, April 24, 1915

13. *The Sporting News*, February 11, 1915.

14. *Sporting Life*, April 1, 1915.

15. Seymour, 230.

16. *The Sporting News*, April 29, 1915; *Sporting Life*, May 1, 1915

17. *Chicago Herald*, March 6, 1915.

18. *Chicago Tribune*, March 8, 1915

19. *Sporting Life*, March 20, 1915

20. *Chicago Tribune*, April 3, 1915.
21. *Chicago American*, April 10, 1915; *Chicago Tribune*, February 13, 1915.
22. *Chicago Daily News*, April 9, 1915
23. *Chicago American*, April 10, 1915.
24. *Chicago Herald*, April 10, 1915.
25. *Chicago Herald*, April 9, 1915.
26. *Chicago Herald*, April 11, 1915.
27. *Chicago Tribune*, April 11, 1915.

**Chapter 20: The Cubs, the Whales, and the Future of Chicago baseball**
1. *Sporting Life*, June 5, 1915.
2. *The Sporting News*, April 22, 1915.
3. *Chicago Herald*, September 21, 1915.
4. *The Sporting News*, July 15, 1915.
5. *The Sporting News*, May 20, 1915.
6. *Chicago Tribune*, May 26, 1915.
7. *Chicago Herald*, April 14, 1915.
8. Roger Bresnahan deposition, Landis case, NARA file.
9. Roger Bresnahan, Robert Ward depositions, Landis case, NARA file.
10. *Sporting Life*, February 13, 1915.
11. *Chicago Herald*, April 10, 1915.
12. *The Sporting News*, July 1, 1915.
13. *Chicago Herald*, May 29, 1915.
14. *The Sporting News*, May 13, 1915.
15. *The Sporting News*, June 5, 1915.
16. *Chicago Tribune*, May 31, 1915.
17. *Chicago Herald*, June 29, 1915.
18. *The Sporting News*, July 8, 1915.
19. *Chicago Herald*, June 27, 1915.
20. *Chicago Herald*, August 10, 1915.

**Chapter 21: A Champion on the North Side**
1. *Chicago Tribune*, July 17, 1915.
2. *The Sporting News*, May 20, 1915.
3. *The Sporting News*, February 10, 1916.
4. *Chicago Herald*, May 25, 1915.

5. *Chicago Herald*, May 27, 1915.

6. *Chicago Herald*, June 22, 1915.

7. *Chicago Tribune* July 16, 1915; *New York Times*, May 6, 1917.

8. *The Sporting News*, August 5, 1915.

9. *Sporting Life*, April 17, 1915.

10. *The Sporting News*, July 15, 1915.

11. *Sporting Life*, September 4, 1914.

12. *Chicago Herald*, August 16, 1915.

13. *Sporting Life*, August 28, 1915; *The Sporting News*, September 2, 1915.

14. *The Sporting News*, August 28, 1915; *Chicago Herald*, August 22, 1915.

15. *The Sporting News*, September 2, 1915.

16. *Chicago Herald*, August 15, 1915.

17. *Chicago Herald*, August 5, 1915.

18. *Chicago Tribune*, October 4, 1915.

19. *Chicago Herald*, October 4, 1915.

20. *Chicago Herald*, October 4, 1915.

21. *Chicago Herald*, October 4, 1915.

22. *Chicago Tribune*, October 5, 1915.

23. *Chicago Tribune*, October 5, 1915.

## Chapter 22: The Cubs Head North

1. *The Sporting News*, October 14, 1915.

2. *The Sporting News*, December 23, 1915.

3. *New York Times*, May 6, 1917.

4. *Sporting Life*, October 30, 1915.

5. *The Sporting News*, October 28, 1915.

6. *The Sporting News*, November 4, 1915.

7. *New York Times*, November 11, 1915.

8. *Sporting Life*, November 27, 1915.

9. *Chicago Tribune*, December 17, 1915.

10. *Chicago Herald*, December 15, 1915.

11. *The Sporting News*, November 11, 1915.

12. *Chicago Herald*, December 15, 1915.

13. *The Sporting News*, December 16, 1915.

14. *Chicago Herald*, December 16, 1915.

15. *Chicago Herald*, December 22, 1915.

16. *Chicago Herald*, December 24, 1915.
17. *Chicago Tribune*, January 21, 1916.
18. *Chicago Herald*, January 6, 1916.
19. *Chicago Tribune*, January 4, 1916
20. *Chicago Tribune*, January 23, 1916.
21. *Chicago Tribune*, January 21, 1916.
22. *Chicago Tribune*, January 21, 1916.

# BIBLIOGRAPHY

**Newspapers**

*Boston Globe*
*Chicago Tribune*
*Chicago Herald*
*Chicago Daily News*
*Chicago American*
*Chicago Post*
*Chicago Daily Journal*
*New York Times*
*The Day, New London, Conn.*
*Baltimore Sun*
*Washington Post*
*Boston Herald*

**Websites**

Baseball-almanac.com
Baseballhalloffame.org
Baseballlibrary.com
Baseball-reference.com
Minorleaguebaseball.com
Nber.org/chapters/c2644.pdf
Newspaperarchive.com
Sabr.org/bioproj/

**Magazines**

*The Sporting News*

*Sporting Life*
*Baseball Magazine*
*Sport*

## Legal Documents

*The Federal League of Baseball Clubs v. The National League, the American League, et al.* National Archives and Records Administration—Great Lakes Region, Chicago.

*The Federal Baseball Club of Baltimore, Inc., v. National League of Professional Clubs, et al.*

## Books

Ahrens, Art, and Gold, Eddie. *Day by Day in Chicago Cubs History.* West Point, NY: Leisure Press, 1982.

Alexander, Charles C. *Ty Cobb.* New York: Oxford University Press, 1984.

Allen, Lee. *The National League Story.* New York: Hill and Wang, 1961.

Allen, Lee. *The Cincinnati Reds.* New York: Putnam, 1948.

Asbury, Herbert. *The Gangs of Chicago.* New York: Basic Books, 1940.

Asinof, Eliot. *Eight Men Out: The Black Sox and the 1919 World Series.* New York: Henry Holt and Company, LLC, 1966.

Bonasinga, Jay. *The Sinking of the Eastland.* New York: Citadel, 2004.

Bukowski, Douglas. *Big Bill Thompson, Chicago, and the Politics of Image.* Champaign, Ill.: University of Illinois Press, 1997.

Cook, William A. *August 'Garry' Herrmann: A Baseball Biography.* Jefferson, N.C.: McFarland, 2008.

Deveney, Sean. *The Original Curse.* New York: McGraw-Hill, 2010.

Dewey, Donald, and Acocella, Nicholas. *The Black Prince of Baseball: Hal Chase and the Mythology of Baseball.* Wilmington, Del: Sport Media Publishing Inc., 2004.

Duis, Perry R. *Challenging Chicago: Coping with Everyday Life, 1837-1920.* Urbana, Ill.: The University of Illinois Press, 1998.

Ellis, Edward Robb. *Echoes of Distant Thunder: Life in the United States, 1914-1918.* New York: Kodansha, 1996.

Elfers, James E. *The Tour to End All Tours: The Story of Major League Baseball's 1913-1914 World Tour.* Lincoln: University of Nebraska Press, 2003.

Evers, John J., and Fullerton, Hugh. *Touching Second.* Chicago: Reilly and Britton, 1910.

Gershman, Michael. *Diamonds: The Evolution of the Ballpark.* Boston: Houghton Mifflin, 1993.

Ginsberg, Daniel. *The Fix Is In: A History of Baseball Gambling and Game Fixing Scandals.* Jefferson, N.C.: McFarland, 1995.

Holli, Melvin G, and Jones, Peter. *Ethnic Chicago: A Multicultural Portrait.* Grand Rapids, Mich: Wm. B. Eerdmans Publishing Company, 1977.

Huhn, Rick. *Eddie Collins: A Baseball Biography.* Jefferson, N.C.: McFarland, 2008.

James, Bill. *The New Bill James Historical Baseball Abstract.* New York: The Free Press, 2001.

Jones, David. *Deadball Stars of the American League.* Dulles, Va.: Potomac Books, 2006.

Kohout, Martin Donnell. *Hal Chase: The Defiant Life and Turbulent Times of Baseball's Biggest Crook.* Jefferson, N.C.: McFarland & Company, Inc., 2001.

Levitt, Daniel R. *The Battle that Forged Modern Baseball.* Lanham, Md.: Ivan R. Dee, 2012.

Lieb, Fred. *Baseball as I have Known It.* Lincoln, Neb.: University of Nebraska Press, 1977.

Mayer, Harold M., and Wade, Richard C. *Chicago: Growth of a Metropolis.* Chicago: University of Chicago Press, 1969.

Murdock, Eugene. *Ban Johnson: Czar of Baseball.* Westport, Ct.: Greenwood Press, 1982.

Murphy, Cait. *Crazy '08.* New York: HarperCollins, 2007.

Okkonen, Marc. *The Federal League of 1914-1915: Baseball's Third Major League.* Garret Park, Md.: Society for American Baseball Research, 1989.

Pietrusza, David. *Judge and Jury: The Life and Times of Judge Kenesaw Mountain Landis.* South Bend, Ind.: Diamond Communications, Inc., 1998.

Povich, Shirley. *The Washington Senators: An Informal History.* New York: Putnam, 1954.

Ritter, Lawrence S. *The Glory of their Times: The Story of the Early Days of Baseball Told by the Men who Played It.* New York: Macmillan and Company, 1966.

Seymour, Harold. *Baseball: The Golden Age.* New York: Oxford University Press, 1971.

Seymour, Harold. *The Early Years. New York*: Oxford University Press, 1960.

Shea, Stuart. *Wrigley Field, The Unauthorized Biography*. Washington, D.C.: Potomac Books, 2004.

Sheard, Bradley. *Lost Voyages: Two Centuries of Shipwrecks in the Approaches to New York*. New York: Aqua Quest Publications, Inc., 1998.

Sigman, Shayna M. *The Jurisprudence of Judge Kenesaw Mountain Landis*. Milwaukee: Marquette Sports Law Review, 2005.

Simon, Tom. *Deadball Stars of the National League*. Dulles, Va.: Brassey's, Inc, 2004.

Spink, J. G. Taylor. *Judge Landis and Twenty-Five Years of Baseball*. New York: Thomas Y. Crowell, 1947.

Stout, Glenn, and Johnson, Richard A. *The Cubs*. New York: Houghton Mifflin Company, 2007.

Stump, Al. *Cobb: A Biography*. Chapel Hill, N.C.: Algonquin Books, 1994.

Sullivan, Dean A. *Middle Innings: A Documentary of Baseball, 1900 – 1948*. Lincoln, Neb.: University of Nebraska Press, 1998.

Thomas, Henry W. *Walter Johnson: Baseball's Big Train*. Washington, D.C.: Phenom Press, 1995.

Toot, Peter T. *Armando Marsans: A Cuban Pioneer in the Major Leagues*. Jefferson, N.C.: McFarland, 2004.

Wiggins, Robert Peyton. *The Federal League of Baseball Clubs*. Jefferson, N.C.: McFarland, 2009.

# Index